"Paul Andersen tells the story, as a passionate front-line participant, of how a townspeople challenged a global mining corporation, fought it off for four decades, and were finally victorious.

—GEORGE SIBLEY | writer, educator and long-time Crested Butte/Gunnison citizen

"Paul Andersen fought in this unlikely eco-battle as well as reporting on it, so beyond facts, he gives us fully fleshed characters, a rich sense of place and lively storytelling.
Like Crested Butte in the '70s, his writing is astute, heartfelt, good-natured and, as needed, irreverent."

—SANDY FAILS | Editor, *Crested Butte Magazine*

"In an astounding contribution to the historical cannon of the west, Paul Andersen lays it all out: the coal miners, the hippies, the industrialists—and the town that made it go right.
...'Hell, No!' is an honest, warm book, written with love, melding the story of one man's life with that of Crested Butte's battle for the survival of it soul...all from a diehard conservationist's point of view."

—LOUIS DAWSON | Legendary Ski Mountaineer and creator of WildSnow.com

"In this story rooted in a time and place, Paul Andersen uses a classic environmental conflict as a mirror to reflect back not just how a community saw itself, but to flash images of where it might see itself headed."

–IAN BILLICK | Mayor of Crested Butte, Colorado
Executive Director fo the Rocky Mountain Biological Lab

BOOKS BY PAUL ANDERSEN

The Town that Said 'Hell, No!'

The Friends' Hut

High Road to Aspen

The Story of Snowmass

Moonlight Over Pearl

Aspen | Rocky Mountain Paradise

Aspen's Rugged Splendor

Power in the Mountains

East of Aspen

Aspen | Body, Mind, & Spirit

Elk Mountains Odyssey

The Preacher and the Pilot

Aspen | Portrait of a Rocky Mountain Town

Aspen in Color

THE TOWN THAT SAID 'HELL, NO!'

The Town that Said 'Hell, No!'

Crested Butte Fights a Mine
to Save its Soul

PAUL ANDERSEN

ROARING FORK PRESS • BASALT, COLORADO

The Town that Said 'Hell, No!'
Copyright © 2022 by Paul Andersen

ISBN | 978-1-7376436-2-3

DESIGN | Curt Carpenter

TITLE PAGE PHOTO: **A peak experience took place at the summit of Mt. Emmons when local celebrants cheered the departure of AMAX and demonstrated the deep spirit of community that had buoyed the town during the protracted battle.** CRESTED BUTTE CHRONICLE ARCHIVES

All rights reserved. No part of this book may be reproduced or transmitted in any form or by any means, electronic or mechanical, including photocopying, recording, or by any information storage and retrieval system, without permission in writing from the publisher.

PRINTED IN THE UNITED STATES

ROARING FORK PRESS
Post Office Box 2047 | Basalt, Colorado 81621
andersen@rof.net

TABLE OF CONTENTS

	Acknowledgements	xii
	Introduction	xiv
PART 1	**The Uninvited Guest**	1
1	Getting There	2
2	Falling in Love, Crested Butte-style	7
3	Beginnings	13
4	Heaven Can Wait, This is Paradise	19
5	A Mountain Full of Dark Gray Stuff	27
6	Hello, Moly!	32
7	The Coming Out Party	39
8	Mitchell	48
9	The Shotgun at our Heads	55
10	Stewards of Paradise	61
11	You Wanna do What?!	69
12	Resistance from the Grassroots	75
13	War of Words	79
14	Water Fight	87
15	The Right-to-Mine	97
16	"The Best Mine in the World"	106
17	The Belly of the Beast	117
18	Save the Lady!	124
19	Celebrity Reinforcements	138
PART II	**A Pyrrhic Victory**	147
20	The Crash	148
21	Dancing in the Streets	151
22	In Retrospect	157
23	The Damage Done	162
24	Post Mortem	168

PART III	**An Onslaught of Suitors**	175
25	Phelps-Dodge Devours AMAX	177
26	'Lucky Jack' Strikes Out and so does Thompson Creek Metals	182
27	The Rogue Returns with a Vengeance	187
28	Fighting a Mine is Hardwired	194
29	Saving the Red Lady–Forever	199
30	Disappearing Act on Mt. Emmons	205
PART IV	**The Thrall of Tourism**	211
31	'Small is Beautiful'	213
32	Pave it and They Will Come	217
33	The Budweiser Blues	223
34	'Love is Slipping Away'	230
35	The Vail-ization of Crested Butte	234
EPILOGUE	The Soul of "The Little Town that Could"	239
TIMELINE	A Brief History of the Mt. Emmons/ Red Lady Mining Issue	249
ADDENDUM	Song Medley from the Red Lady Salvation Ball	250
	Index	258
	About the Author	266

ACKNOWLEDGEMENTS

GRATITUDE goes to the late Joanne Williams, a former editor of the *Gunnison Country Times*, who hired me in the fall of 1977 for my first reporting job in what became a 45-year journalistic career. While reporting from Bohemian Crested Butte, I became the *Times* first "foreign correspondent."

Thanks to Gil and Marion Hersch of the *Crested Butte Chronicle*, who hired me after my departure from the *Times* in 1979. Gil and I became friends as we covered the Gunnison Valley and editorialized on the plight of Crested Butte under AMAX and encroaching commercialization.

Thanks to *Chronicle* owner Myles Arber, who stalked into my house and shook me awake in my bed at 2 a.m. to insist that I step in as editor of the *Chronicle* after he had dismissed Gil and Marion because of differences in management style. Myles was desperate enough to thrust me into the editor role, and I was naïve enough to do it.

Life experiences were payment enough, but I could not have coped as editor without a supportive team at the *Chronicle*—Christy Best, Joyce Lamb, Nathan Bilow, Sandy Cortner, Eduard Oliemans, Sandy Fails and others who made the newspaper a fun and gratifying place to work. Respect is due to our competition at the time, the *Crested Butte Pilot*, whose owners, Lee and Jane Ervin, plus a great staff of writers, gave the *Pilot* a smart and irreverent voice.

Thanks to Crested Butte's civic leaders who taught me the value of small-town autonomy and demonstrated leadership qualities from the grassroots. Governance of the town was a circus at times, wild and entertaining, and it was the highly charged atmosphere of orchestrated chaos that so artfully confused AMAX and bemused the rest of us.

High fives go to those brave and spirited mountaineers who skied into Red Lady Bowl with 300 road flares and, in the dark of night, emblazoned upon the Lady's breast a poignant message that illuminated the mood of Crested Butte at the height of the AMAX battle. You guys set a high tone!

Thanks to the characters of Crested Butte, those authentic human beings who shared their colorful personas with laughter, frivolity and authentic spirit. May the spouses, offspring and therapists of these free spirits be kind and understanding.

Special thanks to Sue Navy, who painstakingly proof-read two versions of this book and helped me tweak many seemingly small, but significant, details. Sue has displayed her good nature on the front lines defending Crested Butte for over four decades.

Gratitude to Charla Brown, Rob Burnett and Cherry Jensen for proofing this manuscript and encouraging its publication. Awe and respect are due Curt Carpenter, who designed this book with his artist's eye, cultural context and acute sense of place. Curt has designed half a dozen of the fifteen books I've written. He is a friend and trusted collaborator.

Lastly, to my enduring and endearing wife, Lu, and our son, Tait, for their tolerance and sense of humor as I have recounted many of the episodes that follow here during family dinners around the kitchen table and over crackling campfires. Thank you for your love, patience and understanding.

—P.A. | January 2022

DEDICATION

*This book is dedicated to those who discover a deep
and enduring love for place and community,
who appreciate the delicate balance
between environment and economy,
who discover the good, the true and the beautiful in life,
and who find themselves in unique places
and are willing to defend these places with the full measure
of their courage, integrity, creativity and spirit.*

AUTHOR'S NOTE

The issues, events and personalities in this story
are drawn primarily from my reporting in the
Gunnison Country Times (1977-1981) and
the *Crested Butte Chronicle* (1981-1984).
Other sources include interviews
and various book projects I authored.
This book is deeply influenced by personal observations
and emotional connections.
While pure objectivity is impossible for any writer,
I have maintained a striving for balance, fairness, accountability
and honesty.

INTRODUCTION

A Phoenix Rises

LIGHT DRIZZLE FALLS from a dim morning sky. Blankets of mist settle in cotton candy clouds over green-clad mountains. A wet, bedraggled troop cloaked in hooded jackets and woolen sweaters gathers on a mountaintop that scrapes the heavens. A great, protracted battle has ended in our favor, so we make a pilgrimage to the mountain and rejoice.

Treading on the grave of the vanquished puts us in a celebratory mood, even though we know that what lies beneath us, inside this mountain, can never be buried deeply enough. The ranks of the adversary will fill with fresh recruits, and the fighting will resume. The celebration on the mountaintop marks only a brief respite in a struggle against the material appetites of the Industrial Age.

From a rock-strewn ridge budding with delicate tundra flowers, we survey a deep valley where a river meanders between glacially-carved ridges. Below is a patchwork of emerald green hay meadows, lush conifer forests, and bright green aspen groves. A seemingly endless expanse of mountain peaks stretches across the horizon. How, we ask, could anyone defame such immortal beauty? What but a demon could denigrate such a paradise for a profit?

This obscure mountaintop in the Central Rockies of Colorado is coveted, not only by summit seekers on this day, but by corporate shareholders who have never seen it and probably never will. On the summit ridge at over 11,000 feet we celebrants tread lightly upon the object of an industrial treasure hunt. A crusade-like euphoria makes us proud, self-satisfied, and yet plagued by uncertainty. We have met the enemy face-to-face and recognize a shadow of ourselves.

When our leader appears, born from the heavens like a phoenix, he raises a gloved hand that's missing its fingers. That misshapen fist, bound in a leather mitten, is a symbol of defiance, of personal trials and tragedies, of a crucible beyond words. Cheers rise from the crowd on the mountaintop. Grins spread across jubilant faces. Tears moisten eyes as a fine mist filters from sodden clouds. The very heavens seem to weep in sympathy for this man and for this small "guerrilla band" that has waged an inspired insurgency with the equivalent of slings and stones.

We stand diminutive against the enormity of the landscape before our inspirational leader. Cheers are shouted into the cool, moist air. The mountain is saved, even though it is mapped, explored, tested and tunneled, even though a precious porphyritic dome of metals, a bank of raw materials, is enfolded in its depths. This mountain is sacred, though it has already been reduced to numbers on ledgers representing latent wealth to those who conspire, plan and scheme to seize it.

The revelers at the summit turn a blind eye to that eventuality. Instead, we look down from the mountain at something small and seemingly insignificant, a human artifact dwarfed by the immensity of nature's grand design. Nestled between the high ridges and the sheltering mountains lies a grid of streets etched on the valley floor. This is our Thermopylae. It is to this town, this mountain community, that our allegiance is most strongly tied. This place and the communal strength it represents is what we have fought for. It is the reason we will fight again.

Mt. Emmons (12,392 feet) and beloved "Red Lady Bowl."
In the core of this mountain, standing tall just west of Crested Butte,
lies a porphyritic dome of low grade molybdenum ore
estimated at 300 million tons.
This is the prize sought after by a succession of mining companies,
none of which has succeeded in industrializing the town.

CRESTED BUTTE CHRONICLE ARCHIVES

PART I

The Uninvited Guest

"I couldn't choose where I was born, but I chose Crested Butte as my spiritual home."

—PAUL ANDERSEN

1
Getting There

IN JUNE 1969, this Chicago-born suburban child of the Sixties stepped off a Frontier Airlines DC3 and had my first look at Gunnison. I was 18 years old, and all I could do was shrug. I had traveled from Chicago to take an entrance exam at Western State College (today's Western Colorado University) and quickly realized that Gunnison, despite its proximity to a nearby ski resort, was not the Swiss Alps I had envisioned. Rather, it appeared as a somewhat drab, rural ranching community set within austere hills of high desert sagebrush, the sere beauty of which took me decades to fully appreciate.

As a hippie who protested the Vietnam War, I didn't fit well into the conservative culture I immediately confronted in Gunnison. However, any misgivings were soon assuaged. The rudimentary exam took place in a classroom at the quiet college campus. This test not only gauged the academic potential of us borderline aspirants to higher education, it gave the admissions folks the opportunity to survey the dimmest of collegiate candidates (but who could still pay tuition).

The test ended, and two hippies from Denver invited me for a drive to Crested Butte. Like me, they had come to Western with poor high school grades, few college prospects, and the Selective Service breathing down their necks. Like me, they had long hair, which linked us to the hippie brotherhood, a distinct minority in Gunnison, and that made us instant friends. While we were anxious about qualifying for the freshman class of 1969, I later learned that Western was as desperate to have us as we were desperate to be accepted there.

The Lovejoy College Catalogue had described a ski area twenty-eight miles up the road from Gunnison, which is what had cinched my application to Western in the first place. Beyond skiing, I had no idea how Crested Butte would shape my life. These friendly hippies gave me my first view of Crested Butte, of which I had only the vaguest picture in my mind.

Driving up the East River Valley on that beautiful June afternoon was an awakening. By the time we reached Almont, the guy in the passenger seat lit a joint and passed it back to me. Unlike Bill Clinton, I inhaled, and I inhaled deeply, inviting the pungent smoke to fill my lungs and infiltrate my blood with tetra hydra cannabinol (THC). From then on the journey became truly transformative. Watching jagged mountain peaks emerge beyond Round Mountain, my heart beat faster. When Teocalli Mountain came into view, I was ecstatic. As Whetstone, Paradise Divide, Crested Butte Mountain and the rest of the Elk Range rose up through the windshield, my eyes widened, along with my grin. I was experiencing what longtime airport shuttle driver and former Crested Butte Mayor Jim "Deli" Schmidt has referred to as the "Oh, My God! Corner."

When we topped the hill overlooking town, with its plain dirt streets laid out like an artist's conception of a fairytale fantasy, I felt something I had never felt before. My eyes became misted. I laughed with a giddy sense of euphoria, and it wasn't just the THC that enlivened my ebullience. I can only describe it as a spiritual connection to a place that would, over many years, remain the place I loved most of all. In what sounds like a John Denver cliché, I had come home to a place I had never been before.

I was accepted in the freshman class of '69 and returned in September as a wide-eyed innocent, rooming in the dorm at Chipeta Hall. Residence halls were segregated by gender, so the women's dorms at Escalante Terrace were at the top of the campus, bordering the wide sage hills of this high desert landscape that stood like a rolling sea beneath an expansive blue sky. If you kissed a girl in the Escalante lobby, both of you could be issued a PDA—Public Display of Affection—which was mailed home as a warning to your parents. This happened to me on one of my first dates. Anything more than a kiss, and you could be expelled. Escaping from dorm life had a strong urgency that accelerated the desire for me to tune in and drop out.

Prominent among those early memories of Gunnison that first winter was the shock of seeing the Gunnison National Bank thermometer registering 50-below zero. On some Arctic days, the high for the day was well below zero. The icy, dry cold was intensified on those completely still mornings by frozen, airborne crystals sparkling like diamond dust as ambient moisture was fast frozen in suspension. On those mornings, Gunnison appeared as a scene from a glimmering snow globe, well shaken. My journalism teacher, J. D. Campbell, handed out to his students an essay he had written for the Denver Post about Gunnison's bitter cold: "Caution Directs My Feet to the Sunny Side of the Street."

I had grown up ice skating a frozen pond at the end of my street in suburban Chicago. When I discovered the ice on Blue Mesa Reservoir, ten miles west of Gunnison, the pleasures of sub-zero winters grew on me. Friends and I would bundle up in everything we had for night skating under glittering stars or in the brilliant silver glow of a full moon. The thermometer often stood around 20-below zero as we skimmed across a foot or two of ice, clambering over pressure ridges that formed where ice plates pushed up against each other in tectonic fashion. Ice fishing became another frosty pastime when we augured a large hand drill through two feet of ice, dropped in a hook baited with salmon eggs, and stood around waiting for a bite. Meanwhile, the ice seemed alive as it boomed and groaned and made strange pinging sounds from pressure faulting. One day, standing at my fishing hole, rod in hand, I felt something warm on the back of my leg. I quickly swiveled around. A dog that had wandered over looking for a place to relieve himself had evidently decided my leg was the only marker worth peeing on.

Though I eventually became endeared to some aspects of Gunnison, college life became abysmal. I was openly persecuted by several of my professors and college administrators for refusing to cut my hair, so my enthusiasm for higher education waned. Disenchantment was reflected in my grades, which went from bad to worse. Smoking weed and sampling psychedelics soon defined my "higher education," and that didn't help my GPA.

Alma Mater: Looking across the Tomichi River Valley at W Mountain from the campus of what was fondly referred to as "Wasted State."
WESTERN COLORADO UNIVERSITY

Such was the climate in which my friends and I were slowly and reluctantly coming of age. Our greatest pleasure was getting stoned and listening to the latest rock and roll vinyl LPs. Trying to stay musically current in Gunnison was a challenge, but we were inspired by the famous rock bands of the day. Music was the message to our "je-je-generation," as The Who stuttered. The overwhelming message of the era was that we should each march to our own drummer. I did so without informing the college, and simply stopped going to classes. My academic standings hit a low the winter quarter of 1970 with a grade point average of 0.9: three Ds and two Fs. It took some doing, but I flunked out of Western and, at 19, was suddenly adrift in a war-torn and socially conflicted America to which rural Colorado was not immune.

Through that trying time in my life, a barrage of hostile judgments and the very real threat of violence against my hippie lifestyle weighed heavily in Gunnison. I refused any compromise that would ease my condition because nonconformity was my determined stance. My hip couture was defined by leather moccasins, bellbottom jeans studded with silver conchos down the outside seams, and a leather belt I had made for myself from which hung a fringed leather dope pouch where I carried my pack of Camel straights. This ensemble was topped by a Chairman Mao denim jacket that hung to my knees. I flew my freak flag down past my shoulders despite fears of violent retribution from the jocks at the college and the cowboys in town. I did so with flamboyant loyalty to my peacenik sensibilities and counter culture identity—and also because there were some really cute and willing hippie chicks who dug my scene.

A deep internal conflict tore at me as I failed to match the expectations of my parents and the strictures of the education morass at which I had long been at odds. It all culminated one day during a college business course I was failing. Toward the end of one particularly dreary session, I was afflicted by a rising internal panic that manifested as a crescendo of chaotic noise akin to the tuning of an orchestra. It felt like the cacophonic ending of the Beatles song, *A Day in the Life*, was blasting stereo within the echo chamber of my troubled brain. The sensation grew in volume and intensity until I was about to scream. I sucked in deep breaths and clenched my fists until the bell rang and class was dismissed. I grabbed my books and sprinted out the door, my brow covered with sweat, my pulse racing. I rushed out onto the wide lawn of the commons and inhaled deep draughts of cool mountain air under a serene blue sky.

The turmoil in my head calmed, and the crisis was over. Something had snapped. At that instant I determined to live my life on my own terms and on no one else's. My vow was to be true to my inner self, which seemed to have suddenly awakened like a butterfly escaping a claustrophobic chrysalis. The new, self-actualized me quit school and walked away from all those troubles. I was free and felt the stresses and strains quickly evaporate.

2
Falling in Love, Crested Butte-Style

OTHER HIPPIE COLLEGE FRIENDS at Western had rented an old miner's home on Second and Maroon in Crested Butte from where they commuted to school. They had an extra bedroom that I could rent for $30 a month. I moved out of the dorm and, in a borrowed car, moved my travel trunk to Crested Butte. The Holmes House, owned by Dr. Hubert W. Smith, had character and a warmth I found deeply gratifying. This despite shacking up in an unheated, upstairs bedroom where every night the mercury plunged below zero.

Dr. Smith, an MD and lawyer from Texas, had founded in 1958 his Law Science Academy in Crested Butte, where Smith officiated over seminars for scientific and cultural exchanges. Invited participants enjoyed quasi vacations during which to polish their credentials with intellectual pursuits complemented by fishing and hiking. That big, clapboard house where my friends and I spent the winter of 1969-'70, would be rented to Smith's acolytes during the summers. The wooden floors were crooked, primitive plumbing often froze, and an ancient, out-of-tune piano was there to plink away on. The Holmes House bore a palpable feel of history, and I loved every minute in what felt like living in a club house.

As cold as it was in my unheated room, my memories conjure the first warmth of community I had felt in Crested Butte, thanks to my old friends, for whom I still feel a heart tug from our many escapades.

That was when Crested Butte was smaller, simpler and more humble and lovable than it is today. Donning a huge down parka to climb the creaking stairs to my walk-in-cooler bedroom and hibernating beneath a thick pile of quilts and blankets was the first nurturing of soul I had discovered on my own. And when I fell in love with Sandy, one of my half dozen roommates, my heart opened for the first time to a romantic passion I had seen only in the movies.

Sandy had come into my life in fall 1969, when we were both freshmen at Western. Sandy and her friend, Linda, had snipped locks of their hair and pasted them over their lips as mustaches. Wearing the hippie costume of the day—faded jeans and flannel shirts—Sandy and Linda cavorted around the Western State campus looking like the hippest hippies of us all. I noticed these two "brothers" and was drawn to them for friendship and mutual support. But as I approached, they made a fast retreat into the girls' dorm, leaving me mystified.

Sandy was a beautiful girl in the classic sense of a mountain woman, the first I had known. Her hair was golden and streaked naturally with highlights of blonde, and it fell around her shoulders in gentle waves. She had a small, freckled nose and sparkling blue eyes. Her front teeth were beaver-like and endearing when she revealed them in a smile. She wore the same clothes the rest of us guys wore, and they completely hid her womanly figure. This lent credibility to the saying: "Crested Butte, where the men are men—and so are the women." Sandy was so much one of the guys that I forgot altogether that she bore feminine attributes until the normal circumstances of living together revealed her charms. When I recognized Sandy's unadorned, natural beauty, it hit me like a two-by-four, and I was forever smitten. Such was my growing up in Crested Butte where life was new, romantic and utterly enchanting.

Winters were a dream come true for this snow-deprived Midwestern skier. There was romance in swishing through the lightest fluff in the world on skis and childlike glee from walking through town among towering snowbanks pushed up by huge front-end loaders. There was a ritual my friends and I loved in those halcyon days of the early 1970s. We would venture over to Elk Avenue by walking the foot-packed snow trails through Crested Butte's back alleys. These merry journeys brought us to pinball tournaments at Tony's Tavern over pitchers of 3.2

Coors and on shopping jaunts for comics and Big Hunks at Stefanic's grocery store. If you stepped off the narrow footpaths, you plunged in up to your hip. This occurrence was far more common on our way home after a few pitchers when pratfalls elicited guffaws. Hilarity was just one step off the trodden path.

Tony's Tavern was a sanctuary for us long-hairs under the proprietorship of good-natured Don Bachman, who accepted all kinds with equanimity and happily drew foamy beers from the taps. His dog, Sam, was legendary as a mythological canine who battled coyotes when they strayed into town at night. There was a night I'll never forget when I was coldcocked by a swaggering cowboy who didn't like my long hair. One minute I was standing there innocently conversing with another hippie, the next minute I was spun around by a roundhouse punch to the jaw that flung me up against the pinball machine. The machine went tilt! In an instant the bar erupted into a full-on brawl in true Wild West fashion.

There were summer nights when a band of adventuresome hippies would imbibe whatever psychedelics were available and explore old mine tunnels. On powder days, the same suspects would hotbox the old lozenge-shaped, three-person gondola which dangled precariously over International ski run like a pear on a shaky branch.

There were winter movies at the Princess Theater when the stove pipe of the coal-burning potbelly glowed deep red, and you wore a parka to stay warm while quaffing a cold brew. There was the acrid smell of coal smoke on the frosty night air when the snow squeaked loudly underfoot. That crunch of snow was the only sound other than coyotes yipping from Gibson's Ridge or an owl hooting from the bare branch of a cottonwood.

There were wet t-shirt contests at a bar whose name I no longer remember, packs of loose-running dogs on the empty streets late at night. There were lessons in finesse on the pool table from Pauly Panian, neighborly love from gracious Annie Perko, shared cigarettes with Tommy Sneller, and glowering glances from warm-hearted curmudgeon Tony Verzuh. There was a feeling of veneration from running my hand over the porcelain finish of the most beautiful enamel cook stove I had ever seen in the impeccable Victorian home of

Author Paul Andersen throws an organic turn on wooden skis with cable bindings, bamboo poles and wool apparel.
PAUL ANDERSEN COLLECTION

Frances "Granny" Yaklich, who was my landlady for the several years I lived in the "AIR CONDITIONED" house on First Street.

There was the pleasure of learning social graces from Tony Mihelich at Tony's Conoco and lessons in humility and pride by visiting the beautifully kept home of Johnny and Frances Somrak. There were the ever-pleasant countenances of Mary and Frank Yelenick and Tony and Eleanor Stefanic when one desired "fine wine" to complement a blood-fresh beefsteak butchered by Tony on his thick, wooden butcher block. And there were quick friendships and kindly smiles from Teeny Tezak, Frank Orazem and other hospitable old-timers who took us young hippies in stride and watched over us like foster parents. These home folks with Eastern European surnames represented the old world in the new world of a western frontier that allowed them, and now me, to recreate ourselves within the community in which we satisfied our mutual homing instinct.

There was a feeling of athletic grace from successfully executing my first telemark turn up the Slate River in the mid-'70s on wooden Bonna 2400 skis with leather boots, cable bindings, bamboo poles, wool pants, and "feeling it." Ski tours were sublime gliding expeditions over a deep snowpack, my wood skis corked with green kicker wax over pine tar, perfectly suited to the cold, dry snow. Tracking quietly through the woods and across mountain meadows was a purely organic immersion during subzero winters.

Friends and I would find just the right slope to build ski jumps and then take turns soaring over glittering crystals shining in the sun. We camped in snow caves like hibernating bears and learned to appreciate the exuberance we adapted from living and playing in intense cold. As the telemark turn was being reinvented in Crested Butte, equipment improved to where we took our skinny skis on the lift-served runs for the first time at any ski resort in the U.S., testing the flimsy gear and our supple, young knees on the Glades and the North Face, and laughing with pleasure at every face plant.

There were pioneering rides on first generation mountain bikes on every trail we could find, from Hartman's Rocks to Reno Divide, and from West Maroon Pass to Fossil Ridge, cow trails that had never seen a snake belly tire track. There were lunch rides to the town of Marble over Schofield Pass for a beaver burger at the Beaver Lodge with Carol "Bowzer" Bauer, Kay Peterson, Don and Steve Cook, Dave Lindsey, Steve Curray, Mitch Hoffman, Gail Burford, Roxie Lypps and other loving friends. There were Pearl Pass tours on the newest designs in bike frames with California mountain bike innovators Joe Breeze, Charlie Kelly, Charlie Cunningham, Jacque "Alice B. Toeclips" Phelan, Tom Ritchie, Gary Fisher and Victor Vincente of America. I will never forget Victor riding my wheel on Trail 401 moaning with orgasmic ecstasy as we cruised dreamlike over one of the finest singletracks in the world. Or riding back seat behind Mike Rust on a tandem mountain bike bounding down the rock-strewn Farris Creek descent, a pioneering first.

I was invited to perform at the Mountain Bike Hall of Fame under the stage name, "Shifty Freewheel." Costumed in Tony Lama boots, a huge Stetson, a cycling jersey and fringed Lycra shorts, "Shifty" played guitar and sang my trademark song *Ghost Bikers in the Sky*, followed by an encore, *Squished Upon the Road*. There was incredible exuberance in that room as everyone realized that we were on the verge of a major new trend in cycling, which was quickly proven true with the explosive popularity of mountain biking worldwide. We were among the first to feel the magic of it.

There were backpacking trips to the high basins, high lakes and high peaks where I first sensed the purity of wilderness and learned essential lessons in self-reliance and trust in the natural world in which I was so blessedly enfolded. One backpack sojourn from Gothic over Triangle Pass to Conundrum Hot Springs stands out because we all hiked naked—except for the heavy leather Dachstein boots that were then in fashion—while tripping lightly along on purple acid.

There were winters when I was cozily shacked up in what most would consider a hovel on First Street when the snow was piled above the eaves and I had to shovel the back yard to make room for more snow from the sagging roof. The front window of that tiny home perfectly framed Crested Butte Mountain. From there, I would watch for comely Tracey Wickland, Crested Butte's beloved nightingale folksinger, to walk by, heading for a soak at Sunshine's Paradise Bathhouse. I would quickly pack my birthday suit and discreetly follow a few steps behind. "Oh, Tracey, what a pleasant surprise to see you here!"

There were those early Thursday mornings when I delivered the weekly *Crested Butte Chronicle* page negatives to the printer in Gunnison. On one memorable, 30-below zero morning, the *Chronicle* Subaru wouldn't start, so I rode my bicycle all over town to find someone else up at 6 a.m. whose car started and would give me a jump.

And then there was the magic of just being here in an idyllic, picturesque outpost, of living with the seasonal rhythms of this small, intimate town, of feeling the warmth of the summer sun in July and the frosty chill of winters in January. There was the blissed out magic of watching the snow fall . . . and fall . . . and fall . . . and never tiring of it . . . ever. . . !

Now, looking back fifty years, the Crested Butte I once knew and still love plays on my mind with recurring dreams of dirt streets and weathered wooden buildings. Crested Butte was the first real home of my adult life, the first home of my choosing, the first home that soothed my soul with its intimate social warmth, unique ethnic flavors, and sublime natural beauty.

I couldn't choose where I was born, but I chose Crested Butte as my spiritual home, and that's a connection I will always honor and appreciate as a defining influence on the rest of my life.

3
Beginnings

FERDINAND VANDEVEER HAYDEN (1828-1887), noted surveyor, skilled map maker, expert geologist and renowned explorer, also had an esthetic appreciation for the Elk Range. He noted the "eruptive" formations and the deep faulting of a "geologic jumble" that produced a unique chain of mountains rich in geological and biological diversity.

Hayden was most notable for having surveyed Yellowstone in the mid-1850s, long before it became a national park. He had witnessed natural wonders few had seen or imagined. Assigned to further the documenting of landforms for the U.S. Geological and Geographical Survey of the Territories in the early 1870s, Hayden walked the valleys and trod the peaks of the Elks. This earned him his namesake Mt. Hayden, a dramatic peak that stands at 13,561 feet near the headwaters of Castle Creek, between Crested Butte and Aspen.

Exhilarated by a rigorous mountain climb, perhaps a first ascent, he gained the summit of 13,000-foot Teocalli Mountain at the head of Middle Brush Creek. Gazing to the west at nearby twin, rocky summits, he proclaimed them the "Crested Buttes." One of those peaks, Crested Butte Mountain, retained that euphemistic name; the other came to be known as Gothic Peak.

The Hayden party issued names to the landmark peaks they saw, but they weren't the first to gaze at this rugged topography. Roaming bands of indigenous Mountain Utes hunted and gathered in what they called "the shining mountains" long before Hayden's brief visit. Their prehistoric visitations are not documented and hardly recognizable;

neither were the possible habitations of Early Man, remote ancestors who may have preceded the Utes by millennia.

Hayden's job was to explore, file reports on geology and resources, document his findings with photographs and drawings, triangulate peaks, and map this little-known region. This versatile scientist had served as a field surgeon with the Union Army during the Civil War. Like many Civil War veterans, he came west to distance himself from battlefields and the industrializing of the East. Perhaps, like many, he came to reinvent himself far from the killing fields and exorcize his post-traumatic stress in the wilds of what was about to become, in 1876, the "Centennial State," Colorado.

Among Hayden's "Rover Boys" charting the earth's resources in the Elk Range was Samuel Franklin Emmons (1841-1911), an American geologist for whom Mount Emmons is named. It was Emmons who won fame as head of the Colorado division of the United States Geological Survey and whose namesake mountain stands over the town of Crested Butte, just to the west. Unknown then, Mt. Emmons holds deep within its breast a potential treasure that would lay dormant for the next century.

The hard work that followed Hayden's discoveries was left to hardy prospectors who were guided by Hayden's maps. These enduring, hard-bitten, savvy, practical-minded geologists were, as one historian called them, "the greatest opportunists of all." With hobnail boots, homespun clothes, and strings of pack animals, they explored the rugged Elk Mountains bearing picks, shovels, dynamite, bold determination, and quicksilver mobility.

Once the rich veins of metal were found and depleted, they moved on to the next "excitement." Their first loyalty was not to a particular place, but to the elusive riches that forever carried them off on the whisper of a rumor, the promise of a strike, the fulfillment of a dream, and the prayer that they would survive the raw elements of the American wilderness. In the Elk Range, their leavings are seen as scattered diggings on mountainsides, in crude tunnels blasted into escarpments, in collapsed log cabins, and in ruins at the old town sites of Ruby, Gothic, Crystal, Schofield, Ashcroft, Pieplant, Dorchester, Independence and many other prospects that have decayed into obscurity. These faceless, nameless men are long gone, but they left indelible traces on the landscape and a romantic mythos.

In the gritty streets of frontier mining towns, natural law often ruled in a Hobbesian world where life was "solitary, poor, nasty, brutish and short." Men were hanged for petty offenses, gunned down for dislikes, whims, greed, racism, drunkenness. Desperate women plied the trade of the brothels. Certain ethnic groups were blatantly exploited for their labor, foremost the Chinese. The rules of civilization were subjective and spontaneous and distant, if they were thought of at all. Mineral wealth was the lure. Civilization would follow when there was valuable property to give it meaning. Until then, civil authority was vague, random, self-serving and often fleeting.

On the alluvial fan of Coal Creek, near where it spills into the Slate River, a town grew. Crested Butte was founded under Colorado law in 1880, beginning as a tent city, then growing into rows of wood frame buildings along streets of dirt and mud. Except for its stone-built jail and the old rock schoolhouse, Crested Butte was built quickly and expediently of wood milled from the nearest forests. Streets were laid out with utility on a basic grid aligned with true north. The Denver & Rio Grande Western Railroad made the town viable in 1881, coming up the East River Valley from Gunnison bringing commerce to outlying mining districts and shipping out their riches.

Victorian architecture, the look of the day, was often shipped in

Coal mining was the foundation of Crested Butte, and it sanctified the sacrificial toil of heroic miners earning meager livelihoods by risking life and limb deep underground. LIBRARY OF CONGRESS

by rail from mail-order houses like the Sears Catalogue. These modest dwellings were embellished with peaked roofs and gingerbread filigree. The shops, storefronts and cottages, ornate and fanciful with their false fronts, dressed up the simple values and humble ambitions of hard-working miners. Gaily painted façades were erected on rough-cut timbers that had only recently been trees rooted in a wilderness.

When the silver and gold played out in the mines surrounding Crested Butte by the late 1800s, the people dug deeper into the earth, reaching thick seams of anthracite coal. They tunneled into the mountains like trolls. The acrid smoke from their coke ovens tainted blue skies with dusky shade and soiled the wash on their clotheslines. The railroad carted away the livelihood of cramped and coughing miners to the far-off steel mills of Colorado Fuel & Iron (CF&I) in Pueblo.

These human moles in their catacombs, the feckless pawns of industry, Crested Butte miners slaved for poor wages in dust bins far from the sun. They suffered mine cave-ins and deadly blasts that left scores buried. When they weren't digging coal, they were digging snow nine months a year. They dug out from avalanches and shoveled coal into their potbellied stoves to fend off the bitter cold of long winters. Many were Slavs, Croats, Italians, Irish—hopeful immigrants who had flocked to the shining shores of America and brought with them foreign tongues and a rich blend of cultures. Their lives colored Crested Butte for half a century as they carved away at the black anthracite guts of the mountains.

Coal mining, too, had a bitter end. By the early 1900s, industrial steel processes favored oil and gas over coal as fuel for the blast furnaces, so the mines of Crested Butte were shut down. In 1952, the famed "Big Mine," the last mining employer in Crested Butte, closed its portal. The payroll disappeared. The company store drew its shutters. When the railroad pulled up its tracks in 1954 and hauled them away over the mountains, there was widespread mourning. Crested Butte was cut off from the world, a spurned stepchild with no value except to the hangers-on who steadfastly refused to leave their homes, their families, their traditions, their memories, and their mountains. The dearly departed rested in humble graves at the town cemetery on a bend of the Slate River, and the town itself seemed to be breathing its last.

The great, manmade caverns that resulted from their labors would be forever silent. Small pensions meant the difference between hanging on and leaving. Much of the town fled to payrolls elsewhere, many to follow the fortunes of CF&I in Pueblo. Those who stayed made a separate peace with a faraway world that rarely troubled them. Still, they answered the call of service from the greater society and sent their young men to fight the nation's wars. But over time, the outside world became foreign, and they had little contact with it. Those who stayed were sheltered within a sublime and towering barrier of rugged mountain topography, and there was some security in this redoubt.

Within this cloister of mountain peaks where roof-high snowdrifts lasted until June, in a town isolated by flooding rivers and blinding blizzards, the survivors couched their pride, traditions, heirlooms and surnames in their tidy homes, shops, churches, and fraternal orders. While the rest of the world awoke to the Information Age, Crested Butte hibernated, languishing in a dim industrial past in which its loyal citizens continued to take pride for the hard work they had done, the industrious lives they had led.

The majority of those who stayed were Slavic. They nourished a sense of the past by making spicy "kielbasa" sausage and distilling "slivovitz," a native spirit originating from plums. The merry music of accordions and fiddles recalled the good old days and echoed the tunes of the old country for pioneers haunted by nostalgia, melancholy and interrupted dreams. They held their chins high no matter how cash-poor they might be. Their poverty of riches was embellished by their cherished community and in the shared honor of surviving here. Their legacy of hard, dangerous work was their common bond, a blood bond that few outsiders could ever understand.

The peace and quiet of this small, ethnic community was broken only when the noon siren wailed or when the plank floors at Frank & Gal's bar and restaurant resounded with rhythmic polka stomps. The chimneys of humble homes trailed black coal smoke. The Post Office, Tony's Conoco, Stefanic's Grocery, Tony's Tavern, the Way Station, the community churches, the Rock Schoolhouse, the Croatian Hall, and the liquor store were the mainstays of town, the focal points of civic connectivity. Town government was minimalized as a bare necessity for keeping the streets navigable, the waterworks flowing, and the lights on.

Credit was given to those who could not pay their modest expenses in cash. The sick were cared for. Children were educated. People helped one another. The fraternal brotherhood of the miners was stronger than the ups and down of economics and industry, stronger even than ethnic diversity. Poverty was not in the people's lexicon; it was simply called frugality. Making do with grace on a small stipend became an achievement worthy of respect. Humility translated as an ethic, cleanliness as dignity, civility as a requirement.

Beyond the town grid lay a wilderness where black bears rambled, coyotes howled, and herds of elk and deer ranged. Fiercely independent ranchers grew hay crops in the wide, glacially carved valleys and pastured their livestock on the verdant mountainsides. Streams of ice water frothed down from mountain snowmelt and coursed through the lush valleys in creeks and rivers where trout and salmon spawned. Hand-dug irrigation ditches brought life to hay meadows laboriously cleared of rocks and sagebrush. Yeomen ranchers with callused hands, weathered faces, and wide-brimmed felt hats were driven by their labors and steadfast in their traditions. There were no challenges to that authority.

While the ranchers and the idled miners made do in their rugged isolation, a new generation of mountain immigrants was born and raised in places the people of Crested Butte had never heard of. These new immigrants represented the post-World War II Baby Boom. By the 1960s, a smattering of us newcomers began to arrive on the narrow, two-lane highway, peering from car windows, wide-eyed with discovery, hearts quickened by grand mountain vistas. Like the old-timers of Crested Butte, we young nomads were touched by a romantic, utopian vision born of this place, inspired by landscapes that Bierstadt had painted in oil, by a glamorized notion of the West as a place of new beginnings.

We neo-pioneers, costumed in jeans, flannel shirts and leather hiking boots, revered the storied people we found in the town and the outlying ranches, granting them avuncular status and commensurate respect as vaunted elders. The pastoral valley worked a spell on our generation of new immigrants, too, and we soon valued it more than the fast-paced world, the teeming and polluted cities, the conforming and homogenous suburbs from which many of us had come. We had found our Eden and irrefutably laid claim to it.

4
Heaven Can Wait, This is Paradise

WANDERING THE QUAINT STREETS of Crested Butte in the summer of 1969 was like stepping into a museum diorama. The town's unpaved rusticity was characterized by dirt streets and weed-grown alleys among small frame houses and weathered clapboard buildings adorned with Victorian flare. A recent transplant from the homogenous suburbs of Chicago, I felt an immediate sense of history in the town's atmosphere, and I loved every breath of the old world that had taken root in the new world.

On some quiet moonlit nights coyotes could be heard yipping from the timbered heights of Gibson's Ridge, sounding like revelers at a wild party. In the shops and bars I listened quizzically to the tongue-tying Serbo-Croatian spoken by "old-timers," many of whom were veterans of the long-silent coal mines. These salts of the earth viewed us new urban refugees quizzically. What did we children of privilege know of the lives, struggles, roots and values of Crested Butte? How could we free-living, fun-seeking, long-haired youths appreciate the town's traditional work ethic, diverse cultures and mining history?

Some "old-timers" (that's what everybody called them) were more generously available than others. They welcomed us newcomers with smiles across backyard fences and with backslapping over shots and beers in barrooms that served as melting pots: "You buyin,' Captain?" was a familiar proposition from Botsie Spritzer. Over time, as the long, cold winters passed, the old-timers gave us newcomers grudging respect for the stoicism required in 40-below-zero mornings and hip-deep snow. Others resented us transplants. They cringed at what our generation represented—the grinding wheel of change—and they viewed the intrusion we made on their little cloister as they would a contagion—"Filthy long-hairs!"

For most of us newcomers, an immediate affection for Crested Butte came from novelty. We had never seen or known a place like Crested Butte, where we divined a sense of innate purity, a welcoming value of trust. For me, Crested Butte was an antidote to the civilized world of my upbringing where trust was bred out of me and replaced with suspicion. In Crested Butte, doors were never locked. Keys were left in cars. Townspeople said hello to strangers. The intimacy of the community broadcast a sense of frontier humility that made even the most dissolute transplant feel comfortable, even welcome. Fugitives could hide here—and did. Renegades could fictionalize their pasts and conjure new identities. Youth could be prolonged in the absence of social stresses and career expectations. Crested Butte was a place where getting old meant staying young, with a sparkle in your eye.

The town became a haven to us disenfranchised Baby Boomers where contentment was found nestling into the warm bosom of paradise far from the madding crowd. My peers and I were on the move to discover America, and we eddied out in a cul-de-sac on the road less traveled, at the end of a blue highway, at the foot of the unknown mountains, in a town where there was only one stop sign. We sought freedom, ease, and disconnection from the machinations of a world that seemed to perpetuate war, conformity, and gross materialism—the tired, old values of our parents' generation, from which we had fled.

George Sibley, founding publisher of the *Crested Butte Chronicle* and author of a memoir, *Part of a Winter*, captured the mood in "Fifty years of Flauschink," an essay he wrote in 2018 as a personal retrospective. Sibley was a founding member of the Flauschink committee, which came together as a mix of friends from Gunnison and Crested Butte who contrived a folklore celebration with a fantastical name and outlandish ceremonies that would break up Crested Butte's mid-winter lull. Sibley, who went on to teach writing at Western Colorado University, reflected on how the Selective Service draft during the war in Viet-

The author, perched on his VW in front of the Old Town Hall, Crested Butte, 1971, with a "townie dog." PAUL ANDERSEN COLLECTION

nam had turned thousands of young Americans into refugees headed for Canada or remote places like Crested Butte.

Crested Butte already had a history of refugees, people cast out of their ancestral lives by war, enclosure and other dislocations of the Industrial Revolution. The old-timers still here in the 1960s had little patience for the new refugees' drugs of choice, uniforms and casual cohabitations, but many of the older ones had been through the labor wars, Prohibition, and other hot and cold running wars with the mainstream culture, and so had some empathy with the new refugees.

Crested Butte then also seemed to be 'out of this world' economically. With nothing but a marginal hard rock mine on one mountain and a recently bankrupt ski resort on another. Naïfs like me could believe that the Industrial Revolution colonizing the rest of the world had left us behind. Wiser heads among us knew that the money would be back to mine whatever resources, even beauty, lay unexploited; but even they felt like we were at an 'open moment' in history where we could imagine and even begin something different, which might give a different shape to the ultimate homogenizing formulas of 20th century civilization. Most of us were broke, but felt unbroken; it was the 'New World' again.

That sense of being a refugee colony, so far outside the war-making, urban-industrial mainstream as to be free of it, unleashed a decade or so of 'creative community' that is still very much part of what makes Crested Butte something other than just another mountain real estate development peddling amenities to the wealthy.

In the Sixties, Crested Butte was on the fringe. The town was a five-hour drive from Denver in good weather on twisting mountain roads. In bad winter weather, you could double that time or not get there until the next day. In the various VW bugs I drove, the vent heaters never even dented the frost layer, so I drove with my head out the window like an exuberant dog or with an ice scraper in one hand the steering wheel in the other and the shifter nudged by my knee. The only air service was through Gunnison, 28 miles away, on a narrow, two-lane highway where flights were sporadic at best. Winter whiteouts were common on Highway 135 where it threaded along the banks of the Gunnison and East Rivers. In frigid winter weather, the rivers blossomed with thick, heavy clouds of steam.

In the late Sixties, only one television channel reached the town through rabbit ear antennas, a static-filled commercial station from Grand Junction. Radio reception was sketchy. There was one newspaper, one grocery store, one hardware supply, one liquor store, one school, several bars and churches, and a stone jailhouse with bars on

The original three-person gondola on Crested Butte Mountain was imported from Italy and gave the ski resort an elevated stature as the first gondola in Colorado. CRESTED BUTTE CHRONICLE ARCHIVES

the windows, mostly leftovers from the previous century. New construction was minimal, and the old miners' homes revealed gradual add-ons that extended in long sheds to the back alleys. Most of these traditional homes were equipped with coal-burning stoves, coal sheds and coal bins. On winter nights, coal was in the air, a quaint, odor that defied power outages and kept the people warm. Firewood was an even more ubiquitous commodity, which I cut and sold during a few autumn seasons at $50 a cord for prime spruce rounds.

The population of Crested Butte was just a few hundred, far less than most of us new urban transplants had in our high school graduating classes. My graduating class at New Trier in suburban Chicago was double the town's population. Phone numbers required only four turns on the rotary dial. There were no traffic jams and no pileups, and I hardly ever heard the honk of a horn, except in greeting. Life was simple and uncluttered, inviting a slow, measured, deliberate pace that, by contrast, made the mad cadence of contemporary American life seem all the more frenetic and dissonant. Crested Butte provided a soothing contrast to the outside world in a relaxing mood that had a mellowing effect.

British transplant Roy Smith mythologized Crested Butte in his memories of arriving here while leading an Outward Bound trip from the Marble Base Camp over Schofield Pass in the mid-1960s.

> The sun had set over the West Elk Mountains. Hours earlier I had placed all ten of my Outward Bound students in isolated, safe areas to begin their three-day solo with just minimum food and shelter. To relax after several days of trekking through the mountains, always above tree-line, I took a walk by the light of stars along a ridgeline that looked down the Slate River Valley. To my great surprise I saw a cluster of lights set in a sea of complete darkness.
>
> Like a moth to the light, and along with two other instructors, we headed down the Slate River Valley to investigate this unusual phenomenon of lights in the wilderness. What a surprise! The sound of music broke the silence of the still, starlit night; an unfamiliar music.
>
> We walked into Frank and Gal's—now long gone from Elk Avenue—into a world of yesterday and an unfamiliar lively accordion music that energized a coterie of older though lively dancers. It was the Polka. I had seen nothing like it. I was reminded of the scene

from the musical Brigadoon, where a young American stumbles on a surreal, Scottish highland village that appears only once every hundred years.

We wandered back to our camp that night with memories of a place we doubted we'd ever see again. It seemed almost surreal. What was this place and who were these people?

But those lights in the wilderness and the sounds of the Polka still resonated loudly in my consciousness. A search on the map, and I found Crested Butte, which seemed to lie at the end of a road at the head of the Gunnison Valley. Surreal as it seemed at the time, Crested Butte apparently really did exist, nestled in the heart of Elk Mountains like a precious stone whose shine was now somewhat dull but still unblemished from years of coal mining.

In the winter of 1969, I bought my home in Crested Butte for twelve thousand dollars. The mortgage was $128 a month, but possible even on a monthly salary at that time of $600 a month. The snow lay just under the eaves. Undeterred as a new man of property, I dug my way down to a window, pulled off some shuttering, and slid into a cold, un-insulated bleak interior. But it was a home and had been from the late 1800s.

Back then the roads through town were unpaved, uneven, potholed, dusty in summer and muddy or frozen for the rest of the year, and most of the town liked it that way. I can remember in the late Sixties when it wasn't uncommon to see just a couple of cars parked on Elk Ave., and a dog snoozing next to a pothole opposite the Company Store.

It seemed impossible that the civilized world could invade and compromise what economics, humility and geographic isolation had accidentally preserved. But it came in increments, starting with a dramatic shift in 1961, when a pair of Kansas City businessmen—Fred Rice and Dick Eflin—purchased the Malensek Ranch at the foot of Crested Butte Mountain, just three miles from Crested Butte. By 1963, they were operating the Crested Butte ski area with a bottom-to-top three-person gondola imported from Italy, the first gondola to operate in Colorado. A decade later, in 1973, the nascent resort town of Mt. Crested Butte was incorporated to serve the ski area's civic needs.

Before skiing took hold, housing had been easily and cheaply available in the absence of jobs. Now, housing was scarce as a budding econ-

The author pushing the pace (for once) in an early mountain bike criterium, with Jack Panek on his wheel. No helmet, no hat, no brains.
PAUL ANDERSEN COLLECTION

omy began to provide paychecks to anyone who could swing a hammer or wash dishes at a lodge. Development began to dot the hillsides with small homes and occasional condos and lodges. With Western State College 28 miles down the road, students began flocking to ski Crested Butte Mountain. A handful of dropouts, among whose ranks I joined, decided to quit our studies and take up residence in this seductively attractive backwater.

Momentum was building in population and economy, but there were bumps in the road. Delivering tourists to this isolated valley, with scant air service, sparse amenities and a harsh winter climate, was problematic. Despite plentiful snowfall, a grandly scenic mountain backdrop, and the rising popularity of skiing, the Crested Butte ski area failed in the late 1960s. The resort was declared bankrupt and was taken over by a Kansas bank.

Crested Butte remained off the map, and its future looked dim until 1970, when Howard "Bo" Callaway, a landed gentry from Georgia with political aspirations, and his brother-in-law, Ralph Walton, a

Georgia farmer, pulled the ski area out of bankruptcy. Callaway, who would later serve as Secretary of the Army under presidents Nixon and Ford, founded, with Walton, the Crested Butte Development Corporation and infused the resort with $20 million. Despite Callaway's largesse, Crested Butte Mountain Resort for years appeared to be on the verge of financial failure. The old town in the valley and the new town on the hill were totally reliant on a one-season economy based on a trickle of tourists, mostly from Texas and Oklahoma, who braved the long drive into a small resort scattered around the base of the mountain where the infrastructure included rustic log cabins harking back to the early ranching era.

Meanwhile, on the valley floor, Crested Butte was undergoing a political and cultural revolution. In the late-Sixties, a coup occurred when political power was wrested from the "old-timers" by the transplanted youth who had gradually become the majority of the town's voting population. This new leadership was inclined towards a liberal ideology, environmentalism and a policy of controlled growth, which gradually distanced the old town from the wannabe ski resort where growth was a priority. A new tension was defined by the line drawn between community and commodity that separated these namesake towns as they co-existed in strained mutuality. Crested Butte benefitted from the ski economy and skier lifestyle. Mt. Crested Butte benefitted from the charm and character of the old town.

Crested Butte's new mayor and city council hoped to preserve Shangri-La by keeping it removed from the American mainstream. They preached that growth and development, carefully regulated against residential and commercial sprawl, would preserve the town's rural ambiance and allow subsistence living for a small population of roughly 1,000. Maintaining this idyllic balance would later prove impossible as the resort economy grew and spread its influence. This burgeoning conflict brought on a collision of values and a divisive cultural clash in the upper East River Valley. The prosperity of the resort would eventually prevail and gradually tear away at Crested Butte's homespun social fabric, eroding cherished community bonds that had made the old mining town unique, celebrated, loved and hotly defended.

But first, a more pressing matter arose.

5
A Mountain Full of Dark, Gray Stuff

THE CRESTED BUTTE BUBBLE seemed impenetrable from the taint of outside influences. For most of us living there in the 1960s and '70s, the "real world" felt far removed and somehow incapable of disrupting the deep peace and comfort the town and surroundings afforded. Like most Crested Butteicians at the time, I was naïvely caught up in the town's Shangri-la mythos and thought of nothing else.

At the same time the resort economy was gaining traction in the mid-1970s, Crested Butte was becoming known by people who had no interest in tourism, skiing or the town's funky community spirit. These people learned about Crested Butte in a boardroom in Greenwich, Connecticut. They were men in suits and ties who evaluated charts, maps and a prospectus filled with columns of figures. Projections and production schedules culminated into a development plan for a place these men had never been, had never heard of, and knew of only from coordinates on topographical maps, from glossy color photographs, and from reports of ore samples. A vote of the board affirmed a time frame and a preliminary budget for staff, equipment, construction, permits, and legal preparation—all the requisite pieces of an enormous corporate puzzle that would set into motion an ambitious industrial enterprise of calculated risk, careful speculation, and ultimate profitability. So they thought, and so they acted.

The first rumblings of this Olympian directive was felt in Crested

Butte in 1974 when the international mining conglomerate AMAX (American Metals at Climax) leased an interest in the historic Keystone Mine on the southern flank of Mt. Emmons, a bookend mountain that defines the town's western edge with a high, curved basin locals knew as "Red Lady Bowl." According to an avuncular old-timer named Frank Orazem, the basin derived its nickname from a geologic anomaly.

> The sun was shining a certain way and I saw the red ore glowing in what we called Mt. Emmons' basin. Then I saw her, shaped by the ore or shadows or a trick of the light. She was like an Oriental empress with one of those fancy high hairdos and headdresses. And her kimono was bright red and flowed down the sides of the mountain, all the way to her feet. I called her the Red Lady because that's what the basin looked like to me.

"Red Lady," as the mountain was nicknamed, has a way of drawing the eye. It certainly drew the eyes of mining geologists who recognized that the coloration of the Red Lady indicated the underlying geology of a potentially profitable ore deposit. Known as a romantic piece of mountain lore, the Red Lady now became for AMAX a wanton siren who attracted and seduced suitors who peeked underneath her skirt. AMAX knew what charms the Red Lady might bestow, but hardly anybody living then in Crested Butte knew or cared what lay below. They would learn, and quickly, that the courtship of the Red Lady would start with flirtatious overtures followed by a bold proposition. The Red Lady would become a damsel in distress heralding a chivalric defense.

For anyone who took note of Mt. Emmons and Red Lady in the mid-Seventies, there was evidence of activity. One day, I glanced up and saw where a road had been bulldozed across its snowy face, an inexplicable gash that defaced the "Lady." That road provided drill access to the rim of a vast geologic dome formed of low-grade ore. Sure enough, on one auspicious night, the tiny glint of a light appeared in the center of Red Lady Bowl, as if she had been emblazoned by a sparkling diamond. That light came from an exploratory AMAX drill rig. The new road and the twinkling light were harbingers of big things to come.

AMAX represented old school, traditional, entrepreneurial, polished corporate mining. The company dated to 1886, just six years after Crested Butte had been incorporated. Formed from an international consortium of partner companies from the U.S., England and Germany, AMAX was first known as the American Metal Company (AMCO). The English investors soon divested their interests to their American and German partners, at which time AMCO was owned by the German company Metallgesellschaft and the U.S. firm Ladenberg, Thalman & Co.

AMCO smelted and refined lead and copper at multiple mines and mills internationally, selling its products mostly in Europe. During World War I, the U.S. government seized Metallgesellschaft's share of domestic US properties and sold them off to investors, mostly American-owned companies. Midway through the war, a metallurgical breakthrough occurred when a lightweight, durable steel alloy resulted from adding molybdenum to the steel process. This led AMCO to focus on producing molybdenum as a strategic metal for the war effort against Germany, which led the company to Colorado.

In 1916, AMCO bought up molybdenum claims in Bartlett Mountain, near Leadville, an historic Colorado silver mining city and

As modern mechanization dwarfs human scale, modern mining is a far cry from the traditional coal mining that gave Crested Butte its origins.
ARIZONA GEOLOGICAL SURVEY

the highest incorporated city in North America at 10,200 feet. During the silver rush of the 1880s, Leadville grew to become the second largest city in Colorado and was once in the running for state capital. With its new acquisition, AMCO formed a subsidiary known as Climax Molybdenum, Climax being the name of the mine. Opened in 1918, Climax became one of the richest molybdenum finds in the world, holding over 600 million tons of low-grade moly ore. After World War I, AMCO expanded its holdings to Africa and diversified with a focus on copper, which it developed through the end of World War II. With the defeat of Germany a second time in 1945, AMCO expropriated former German mining properties in Africa and boosted production to match the demands of the post-war economic boom.

In 1957, AMCO merged with its now thriving subsidiary, Climax Molybdenum, to form American Metals at Climax, or AMAX. The company expanded rapidly during the 1960s, with acquisitions of smaller, mineral-related companies. By the mid-1970s, the company held diverse mining interests around the world, producing tungsten, oil, copper, manufactured aluminum, and coal. In May 1975, Forbes reported that AMAX ranked 70th among American corporations, had the 97th highest cash flow ($193,950,000.00), and employed more than 12,000 workers.

Like most large, acquisitive corporations, AMAX had links to a number of America's most powerful financial institutions, including Morgan Guarantee and Lehman Bros. AMAX directors personally cultivated numerous advantageous corporate, government, and social connections. These potent relationships enhanced the corporation's position and influence in the global economy. At the peak of its upward swing, AMAX was poised for yet another acquisition and venture, this one in an unknown glacial valley on the Western Slope of the Rocky Mountains of Colorado.

The Keystone Mine, several miles west of Crested Butte and just north of Kebler Pass Road, had been an active mining site since 1881, the year after the town was incorporated. The Keystone Mine remained operational during the 1950s and '60s, when American Smelting and Refinery Corporation (ASARCO) extracted heavy metals: lead, silver and zinc.

While pushing a drift into Mt. Emmons, ASARCO miners had begun encountering a gray material that became an annoyance because it got in the way of the heavy metals they were trying to extract. Not knowing what it was, they dumped the material into tailings piles and called it waste. That gray material turned out to be high-grade molybdenum ore. ASARCO miners had unknowingly nicked a corner of the third largest known molybdenum deposit in the world at the time.

In the late 1960s, the Keystone Mine was acquired by Crested Butte Corporation, a subsidiary of U.S. Energy, a speculative mining venture based in Riverton, Wyoming. U.S. Energy was on a fishing trip for undervalued mining properties, and the mysterious gray material in the tailings dumps of the Keystone Mine became an apparent windfall to which U.S. Energy later directed AMAX.

The aged tunnels of the Keystone Mine became the portals through which AMAX probed Mt. Emmons with core drills. AMAX geologists first estimated an ore pocket of 155 million tons. The more core samples were drilled, the more the figure was revised upwards. By the mid-1970s, AMAX estimated that Mt. Emmons, in the heart of its porphyritic core, held nearly 300 million tons of moly ore. Now lead, zinc, and silver became subsidiary metals. Molybdenum was the prize.

Much of the Mt. Emmons orebody was low-grade, but a sizable portion was high-grade, with enough quantity to make a ripple in the international metals market. As the price of moly went up, Mt. Emmons gained prominence on the global resource map and on the AMAX books. While this underground treasure hunt was enlivening the interests of the AMAX board in Greenwich, the discovery went largely unknown in Crested Butte.

6
Hello, Moly!

TERRY HAMLIN knew early on what Mt. Emmons held. He had a rare vantage point as one of the few insiders who watched the Mt. Emmons Project unfold years before most Crested Butte residents got wind of a sea change in their community. In the early 1970s, Hamlin was hired on an exploration crew, drilling holes into Mt. Emmons to produce core samples rich with the gray material AMAX coveted.

As a long-time Crested Butte local, lifetime Coloradan, and descendant of pioneering families of Western Colorado, Hamlin viewed mining as an appropriate economic foundation for Crested Butte. Hamlin grew up in a traditional ranching and farming family in Grand Junction. One of Hamlin's grandfathers had built the first road between Craig and Meeker, using 20-mule teams. As a boy, Hamlin had witnessed the uranium boom of the 1950s, and he described his father and grandfather as advocates for developing natural resources.

"The Colorado Mining Association is the oldest trade association west of the Mississippi," said Hamlin, who would later become Vice President of Public Affairs for AMAX, "and my upbringing said that mining was always part of the economy of Colorado."

Hamlin first saw Crested Butte as a 10-year-old when he traveled over Kebler Pass in 1957 on a fishing trip with his father. That was long before recreation and tourism contributed much to the local economy. Still, the area attracted him to something new. "I grew up on a small farm and knew I didn't want to be a farmer. The closest thing that had a cosmopolitan feel to it was skiing."

Out of high school, Hamlin got a job in Vail during its early development years in the mid-'60s. "I had a passion for skiing," he recalled, "for being in the mountains, for the beauty of the mountains." When it came time for college, he chose Western State College in Gunnison. "WSC had a great geographic location; it was the closest four-year college to skiing." Hamlin graduated from WSC in 1969. That summer, he went to Alaska and fought fires on a Helitack crew. He later found teaching jobs in psychology and sociology at Grand Junction High School. Still, his mind lingered on skiing—and Crested Butte—where he decided to move in 1970.

"Crested Butte in those days was a dilapidated mining town," Hamlin recalled. "The ski area had a gondola, a poma and a T-bar—not even a chairlift." To stay on the forefront of skiing and to keep his passion affordable, Hamlin joined the all-volunteer National Ski Patrol, which became an integral part of Crested Butte in its early ski days because the ski area had no payroll for its own patrol. When the resort could finally afford to finance its own patrol in 1970, Hamlin and his friend Dick Sweitzer, of Gunnison, hired on the newly formed Crested Butte Ski Patrol, which started with just seven patrollers and Mike Burns as patrol leader.

Jobs were scarce in Crested Butte, so Hamlin made ends meet by doing odd jobs at the Way Station restaurant (later Donita's Cantina). "I was cleaning johns, waiting tables, cooking and bartending. I lived in a little house on Sopris with three ladies, Casey Hearn, Linette Ritchie, and Karen Olick. The arrangement was that I would keep the plumbing thawed out and shovel the snow while they cleaned house and cooked."

When Hamlin mentioned his roommates in a later interview, it took me back to freshman year in 1969 at Western State in Gunnison where Casey and Linette were also freshmen and with whom I became fast friends and fellow conspirators in on-campus shenanigans. I fell in love with both of these adorable "hippie chicks," who were among the first students to befriend me in a culture that was otherwise hostile to hippies.

One day a customer came into the Way Station during one of Hamlin's shifts and ordered a cup of coffee. He told the attentive waiter

Terry Hamlin, as a core driller, was among the first to understand the significance of modern mining in Crested Butte. CRESTED BUTTE CHRONICLE ARCHIVES

that his company—the Houston-based Geo-Chemical Survey—would be conducting exploratory drilling in Redwell Basin on the backside of Mt. Emmons. This was in response to an earlier visit to Crested Butte by one of the geologists who had helped develop the AMAX Henderson Mine. That geologist had come to look over Mt. Emmons, having recognized telltale volcanic formations similar to those at Henderson. The geologist had staked out some claims, and Geo-Chemical Survey won the bid to drill the first core samples.

"I was desperate to make some money for the summer," recalled Hamlin, "so I talked to the guy having coffee and I hustled him for the job. I worked the rig on Redwell, pulling core samples, doing 12-hour shifts. We took that first hole over a mile deep. I worked three or four summers until I worked my way up to being a driller. In 1973, AMAX Exploration got involved. There was avalanche terrain near the rigs, and since I had been to National Avalanche School, I did avi-control on Redwell, using the Avalauncher for the first time ever. The inventor taught me how to use it, which led to replacing the howitzer they had been using at the ski area. That job provided me and my wife, Becky, with a down payment for our house on the mountain."

Since he was on the ground floor with AMAX, Hamlin was a prime candidate for the role of local liaison once planning got underway for the Mt. Emmons Project. "They asked me if I would work for them, because they wanted someone with background in the community." Hamlin had been instrumental in forming the Town of Mt. Crested Butte as a member of the charter committee, and he later served as mayor. Hamlin worked for AMAX from February 1978 through February 1981. "I had no problem with mining because of my background, so I took the job."

Despite the enormity of the orebody, Mt. Emmons was, geologically speaking, a "needle in a haystack" within the vastness of the Colorado Mineral Belt, a highly mineralized swath of the Rockies that runs from Durango to Boulder, and includes Crested Butte, Aspen, Leadville, Blackhawk, and other historically rich mining districts. The Mt. Emmons discovery had, for AMAX, all the excitement of a treasure hunter who stumbles upon a rare gem. It just so happened that the gem was in Crested Butte's backyard.

Excited by what was found in the core samples Hamlin and his team had produced, which revealed high concentrations of molybdenum, AMAX was tantalized by the prospect on Mt. Emmons. At its headquarters in Greenwich, Connecticut, the mining division assembled an A-team of mining professionals to bring the Mt. Emmons Project to fruition, a team that would bring keen skills to Crested Butte and pioneer what it envisioned as a mutually beneficial partnership with the communities of Crested Butte, Mt. Crested Butte and Gunnison. AMAX assumed that the locals would accept modern mining the way Terry Hamlin had, as an appropriate industry with a positive economic outcome for all. The assumption was dead wrong, but that would take nearly five years and a hundred million dollars to find out.

Stan Dempsey, Senior Vice President of Climax Molybdenum and Vice President of Environmental Affairs, would head the AMAX team. Dempsey had a strong track record in mining development. Throughout his decades-long career with AMAX, he would be involved with thirty mining and industrial development projects around the world.

"At that time," said Dempsey, reflecting on the initial phases of Mt. Emmons, "AMAX was the largest producer of moly in the world.

We also did product development, so we knew what the needs would be for moly and that we needed more molybdenum than the mines at Climax and Henderson were producing. The decision for the Mt. Emmons Project was made by the board of directors acting on a 'board note' from the people who ran the exploration part of the company."

Dempsey first learned of the Mt. Emmons Project in the mid-70s, just as he was trying to move his family from Lakewood, Colorado to AMAX corporate headquarters in Greenwich. "I knew we had made a discovery," he said, knowing that AMAX Exploration and Climax Exploration had looked up and down the Colorado Mineral Belt for ore bodies. "What they look for," he said, "are ancient volcanoes that didn't vent; basically, frozen volcanoes. The orebody in Mt. Emmons was first recognized by the iron stains on the surface rocks—on what they call 'The Red Lady.'"

Dempsey was selected to head the Mt. Emmons team because he had diplomatically forged relationships with environmental groups during development of the Henderson Mine in the early 1970s. He had earned personal access to the Chairman of the Board, Pierre Gousseland, and to AMAX President Jack Goff, on all environmental matters that affected the company. Dempsey was also familiar with Crested Butte. In the 1960s, he had looked over an historic silver mine near Gothic. On that trip, he had been more of a tourist and historian than a mine developer, but he had formed impressions of the region and had a strong appreciation for the Elk Mountain Range.

Dempsey was a mining attorney, but he was also a mountaineer. He had climbed peaks in Colorado for many years and was intrigued by the history of mountain towns. He had a particular fascination with ghost towns like Gothic. Dempsey was a member of the American Alpine Club. He was one of the first mining executives to advocate environmental balance within the mining industry, a balance he would attempt to achieve in Crested Butte.

"We knew there were interesting people in Crested Butte who could provide leadership in the environmental area," allowed Dempsey, "and I was thrilled by the opportunity to work with the community and build a mine."

Art Biddle was another mining attorney on the AMAX team. By

Public hearings on the AMAX mining proposal drew attentive local audiences as Crested Butte citizens rose to the challenge before them.
CRESTED BUTTE CHRONICLE ARCHIVES

the time the Mt. Emmons Project came on line, he had been with AMAX for seven years. Biddle would serve the Mt. Emmons Project, under Dempsey, as Project Manager for External Affairs, where he would administer the day-to-day responsibilities for legal, environmental, and governmental affairs. Biddle would also oversee public relations with Terry Hamlin. Biddle had just overseen a successful mining venture—the MinnAmax Project in Minnesota—a formidable copper/nickel strip mine near the Boundary Waters Wilderness Area. At MinnAmax, Biddle had paved the way for AMAX to drive a shaft into a potential orebody by addressing acute environmental concerns like those AMAX anticipated in Crested Butte. Biddle and Dempsey were seasoned mining veterans, and confident.

The AMAX corporate side was rounded out by two outstanding mining engineers, Max Gelwix and Ralph Barnett. Gelwix was reserved and businesslike, steeped in procedures and technology. Barnett was equally the technician, but he brought with him an irrepressibly gregarious and outspoken nature. The convivial Barnett became a locals' favorite as he shared many a drink in Crested Butte watering holes, often imbibing with avowed opponents to the mine. As the local community got to know him, "Barney" nurtured stronger community

PART I • THE UNINVITED GUEST • 37

relations for AMAX than the rest of the team, albeit in an unofficial and informal capacity. Barnett hoisted beers at the Wooden Nickel and the Grubstake, and he seemed to fit in naturally with Crested Butte as a peer with the town's old-timers.

With the A-team in place, AMAX approached the Mt. Emmons Project with the affirmation that good will and reason would prevail with the local populace. The community would be educated to the practical need for the mine, and the people would be enlightened enough to accept the environmental approach AMAX would introduce, with the celebrated Henderson Mine as its model. The AMAX team saw Mt. Emmons as a worthy challenge and a rare opportunity.

The first community relations challenge was introducing the mine to Crested Butte with diplomatic aplomb and bold assurance. The AMAX strategy was to be openhanded, casual, friendly, inviting and firm in its determination. The team members would ingratiate themselves to the townsfolk with an overture based on providence, necessity, and mutual benefits. Once the overview of the project was delineated to the satisfaction of the community, the many and problematic details would follow with a carefully orchestrated mitigation strategy.

An allegory to the relationship between AMAX and Crested Butte comes to mind in the 1966 film, *King of Hearts*, where a Scottish bomb expert is sent on a mission at the end of World War II to a village in the French countryside to disarm a bomb set by the retreating German army. The Scot enters the town only to discover that it is occupied by the inmates of the local psychiatric hospital who had escaped after all the other villagers had fled. The remaining misanthropes assume various roles, all of them eccentric, and the ensuing relationships make for satire and tragicomedy.

Such was the nature of a most unlikely liaison between AMAX and Crested Butte. The invaders encountered the inpatients, and a spontaneous script developed over a plotline that only French director Philippe de Broca could have contrived. That it played out in Crested Butte is a testament to the power of serendipity in the most bizarre of human relations. The irony is that craziness, when properly viewed, can accommodate genius.

7
The Coming Out Party

O N A COOL AUTUMN EVENING in 1977, AMAX headlined a town meeting in Crested Butte to share the news of the Mt. Emmons Project, an announcement that would jolt Crested Butte with seismic force. This was one of my first assignments for the *Gunnison Country Times*, so I arrived early and got a front row seat. I had moved back to town the week before after a several year hiatus while finishing my undergraduate degree in English in Gunnison and had secured a beautiful little apartment above the atrium in Penelope's, a popular restaurant owned by Eric Roemer and Lynn Heutchy.

I watched with curiosity as Crested Butte citizens arrived, seemingly reluctant to gather for something other than a potluck dinner. Gradually they packed the school gymnasium. All were in a cautious mood. AMAX was a mysterious acronym that somehow had a bearing on their lives, but few had any idea what it meant. The rumor mill, which had considerable authority in town, had churned out an ominous portent, which meant that a wide assortment of mountain folk, starved for entertainment, had gathered simply out of curiosity to find out how an acronym might figure in their lives.

Crested Butte was more comfortable with informality than with corporate confabulations, so AMAX officials attempted to discreetly blend in. They donned "Get High On Mountains" t-shirts, which they stretched over their starched collars and conspicuous paunches, their hair sporting recent quaffs. The t-shirt, with its catchy slogan, was an early marketing tool for furthering Crested Butte's economic development. T-shirt marketing was about as sophisticated as Crested Butte

Meet the AMAX team: Ralph Barnett, Stan Dempsey, Art Biddle, and Max Gelwix wearing "Get High on Mountains" Crested Butte t-shirts in 1977. CRESTED BUTTE CHRONICLE ARCHIVES

was at that point in promoting itself to the world.

Art Biddle, cordial, soft-spoken and wearing what he considered casual attire, modeled a rather absurd fashion ensemble. He stretched on the Crested Butte t-shirt over his long-sleeved, button-down, dress shirt and tugged it over his plaid slacks. Biddle's slacks were more suited to a country club than to a mountain town at 9,000 feet in the Central Rockies of Colorado where plaid was banned by an unspoken dress code that mandated jeans and flannels. As one observer remarked, Biddle's plaid slacks became the first eyesore perpetrated by AMAX.

Most of the rest of us were clothed in a ragtag assortment of haphazard, hippie/mountain fashion. Our apparel wasn't Vogue—it was Vague—being authentic Crested Butte chic. The meeting was called to order and the crowd hushed as AMAX representatives introduced themselves to the wide-eyed assemblage. One of them announced, with complete assurance, that AMAX would mine Mt. Emmons and produce molybdenum for the needs of the civilized world. Period.

The message was conveyed that Crested Butte would once again become a mining town and that AMAX would provide for the town's new and prosperous industrial future and identity. Mt. Emmons would be added to the AMAX portfolio, and the townsfolk would enjoy steady jobs and a dependable payroll. We would thrive together with newfound respectability as we worked, shoulder-to-shoulder, producing real material goods for the American and global economies. The AMAX team was on the brink of sanctimony, effusing over the mining of molybdenum as if it were an act of altruism. The response from the audience was the utter silence of shocked disbelief. You could have heard a snowflake drop.

During this scripted, rehearsed and choreographed presentation, Dempsey, Biddle, Hamlin, Gelwix and Barnett prattled contrapuntally while the people of Crested Butte simply gaped. The attentive observers could hardly pronounce "molybdenum," let alone comprehend its importance to the "civilized world." One woman, observing from the back of the room, quietly remarked, "If you can't dazzle them with brilliance, baffle them with bullshit." Seemingly unaware of their disconnection with the stunned audience, the AMAX team was all smiles while unveiling the alchemical properties of the tongue-tying metal that AMAX so desired for its portfolio.

Biddle explained that "moly" is a steel-strengthening alloy used for everything from antiballistic missile nose cones to the very automotive parts that made our cars run. Moly, he said, with a swell of pride, was on the nation's strategic metals list because of its value in a wide array of weaponry and defense technologies. For that reason alone, Mt. Emmons took on major significance as an underpinning for U.S. security. Cloaked in that remark was a patriotic undertone that did not slip by unnoticed. Moly, said Biddle, was even in the bicycles we rode, a statement that had far more meaning and impact to this audience, many of whom had commuted to this auspicious event on townies, then known as "klunkers," some of which, we learned later, were of such ancient vintage as to be moly-free.

The AMAX team was positive, beneficent and effusive over the promise for great prosperity ahead. Soon the town would become the recipient of glowing opportunities for good, deserving, hard-working people who showed the kind of enterprise, pluck and grit that had distinguished Crested Butte's old guard coal miners. AMAX would revive Crested Butte's traditional work ethic. A payroll would set residents free from the financial vagaries of seasonal tourism. Rising personal incomes and the largesse of AMAX property taxes would swell the tax base and provide for future generations with all the amenities a small mountain town could ever desire.

Crested Butte would harken back to its honorable mining traditions, a pledge that resonated with some of the town's old-timers whose wistful memories conjured a time when hard labor underground was the town's sole lifeblood. This ethos of hard labor would draw a clear line between the deserving working people of the town and the itinerant hippies for whom living in Crested Butte was a lark. The wheat would be separated from the chaff and give the town a newfound sense of legitimacy.

These amiable AMAX executives were so certain that the people of Crested Butte would embrace their glowing vision that they promised not to build a mine unless invited to do so by the residents who sat stunned before them. "We're not going to mine if you don't want us to mine," pledged AMAX spokesman Tony Barker with a magnanimous smile. Here the AMAX team dug a hole for itself deeper than the exploratory bores in Redwell Basin.

In an interview 30 years later, Biddle said he wasn't certain who had made that statement, which came back to haunt AMAX like a Dickens specter. "Whoever said that," he reflected, "was thinking deep down in their heart that, with adequate planning, good will would arise, and the policy makers would see this as a good thing."

In a detailed evaluation of the AMAX proposal submitted as a letter-to-the-editor in August 1977, by Don Bachman of Tony's Tavern renown, he pinpointed the source of that statement to Barker and urged the community to hold AMAX to that pledge. Bachman was perhaps the first to categorically denounce the AMAX overture by calling on local elected officials to oppose at all costs any mineral production from the Red Lady orebody.

About a year later, in 1978, the *Gunnison Country Times* ran a front page headline: "We're in elephant country; there will be a mine." That assurance, which the paper tacitly endorsed, was pronounced by AMAX engineer Ralph Barnett, who appealed to the fatalistic logic that because a huge molybdenum orebody—"the elephant"—was trumpeting from Mt. Emmons, a mine would be built to extract it.

"When you're hunting elephants," Barnett was quoted, "you've got to go to elephant country, and Gunnison and Crested Butte are right smack in the middle of it." Elephant country referred to the Colorado Mineral Belt, which was about to put Crested Butte under the thrall of industry.

By openly announcing industrial mining plans for Crested Butte, AMAX took on a confident mien while simultaneously testing the community for a reaction. "We didn't expect anybody to stand up and cheer," explained Biddle years later. "It was a first step in trying to deal directly with a community and gain credibility by having our top people there. It seemed like a common sense sort of thing to do, a reasonable first effort to gain some kind of respect and credibility. Open planning was our goal. We were not going to bulldoze our way in. We wanted to mix it up with the locals to see who was there."

Tony's Tavern as it looked in the late 1960s/early 1970s, with Don Bachman at the bar and a lone patron chatting him up.

CRESTED BUTTE CHRONICLE ARCHIVES

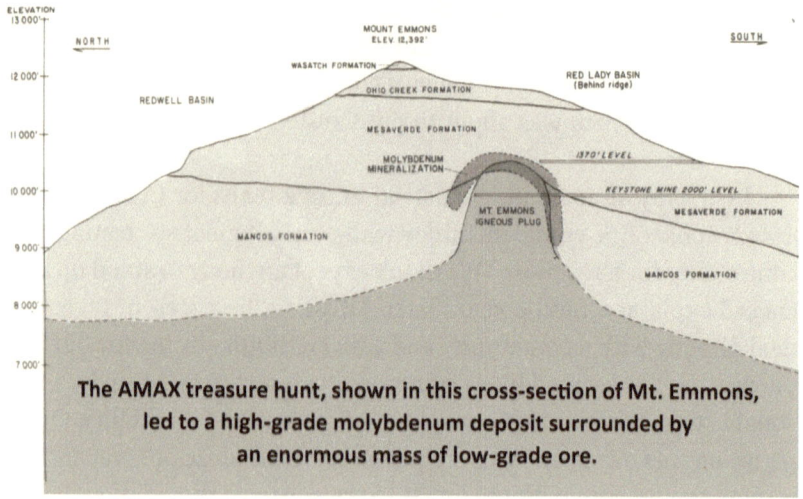

The AMAX treasure hunt, shown in this cross-section of Mt. Emmons, led to a high-grade molybdenum deposit surrounded by an enormous mass of low-grade ore.

All of us paying witness that night to the AMAX song and dance were transfixed, mesmerized and generally flummoxed. Our natural curiosity turned to pained silence. With much head shaking, we peered at poster boards propped up on easels around the room showing industrial schematics and artist renderings. Now that the word had been delivered by the venerable scions of the mining industry, the concept they had so convincingly articulated was laid out in full color, revealing the enormous size and incomparable scale of the proposed AMAX mine.

One glance at renderings of the mine and mill sites made it obvious that AMAX would not manifest a return to the traditional days of coal mining. Instead of pick and shovel, the Mt. Emmons Project was a behemoth that would install miles of ore slurries awash with local stream water, vast tailings impoundments that would fill entire valleys, snaking power lines draped from huge steel towers along clear cut corridors, a pulverizing and sorting mill the size of an urban airport terminal, and a work force that would multiply Crested Butte's population by magnitudes.

Discreetly soft pedaled by AMAX was the likelihood that the excavation of the orebody would cause a collapse of Red Lady Bowl, an occurrence known euphemistically as "subsidence." Red Lady Basin would sink into a vast "glory hole." To most of us locals, this was as unthinkable as it was to don a hard hat, pack a lunch pail and carve out the guts of the mountain ourselves, no matter how grand was the promise of individual prosperity.

The AMAX representatives, with their mountain t-shirts, polished Oxfords, and disarming smiles, assured us that environmental and social issues would be offset by appropriate mitigation and made palatable by the promise of good jobs, steady incomes, and state-of-the-art mining techniques. Crested Butte would discover that the mine was "a good neighbor." We lucky townspeople would share in the glory of productivity by fulfilling an overarching sense of duty in contributing to the Military-Industrial Complex, the GDP, and the advance of human progress. AMAX, we were told, would do the best job possible with the best technology for the best overall results.

The meeting drew to a close with a strange disquiet. We citizens of Crested Butte walked out into the autumn night shell-shocked. Slowly, ponderously, many retreated to cozy hobbit homes, burrowed into threadbare, second-hand couches, warmed away the autumn chill next to cast iron heat stoves, and considered what had just happened. I walked the quiet streets, gazing at the stars, contemplating the tone of the story I had due the next day at the *Gunnison Country Times*, which I would peck out on my manual typewriter. When I got to my tiny apartment, I scrolled a sheet of paper into the carriage and began key stroking the events of the night in a story that would write itself as my feelings poured onto the pages. That draft I submitted was charged with emotional force and tempered with an edge of bias that would be edited into a compliant, acceptable and politically correct version that would serve the *Times* conservative editorial stance. I knew then that I was not long destined for a career at the *Times*, but such was the life of a crusading reporter who placed values before objectivity.

Mining was not a foreign concept for anyone who knew anything about Crested Butte's backstory because there were plenty of remnant mine workings throughout this part of the Elk Range. The closest and most visible was at Peanut Lake where Gronk, a long-abandoned concrete coal tipple, rose up like Stonehenge. There was the Smith Hill mine and abandoned town site. There were workings throughout

Poverty Gulch that had poisoned whole water courses. The lifeless, orange slurry that was Coal Creek was the most prominent visual and olfactory reminder of toxic acid effluent, which came directly from the AMAX mine site and was deadly to the natural world. Coal Creek carried the blood of the Red Lady as it leeched from deep inside Mt. Emmons and flowed through town as a reminder of the mining legacy.

There was a pervasive sense of disbelief in Crested Butte as reactions to the mine proposal gelled over the next few weeks. Crested Butte was being targeted for a molybdenum mine like the one many of us had seen while driving over Fremont Pass. The desecration caused by the Climax mine was breathtaking, a monumental open pit "glory hole" and vast waste dumps that loomed apocalyptically at the headwaters of the Arkansas River.

Mining was known to us locals from half a century ago, but nothing on this scale. We knew intuitively that there was no way it could fit harmoniously within the idealized setting of Crested Butte. And so, in humble little homes, in bars and restaurants, at the post office, in the Bath House—anywhere people met—conversations distilled the meaning of AMAX into only one possible resolve: a vocal and uncompromising rejection of the dictates of Big Business, Big Government and Big Brother. The town would simply answer, "Hell No!"

What we failed to comprehend was that "No!" was not on the check boxes of appropriate responses. AMAX had made a Godfather-like offer that the town could not refuse. The people of Crested Butte had little idea of how one word—"No!"—would translate into five years of contentious battle. Neither did AMAX.

This was not the AMAX Henderson Mine, where there had been no local community to fight it. This was not Climax, where moly production in Leadville had been almost uninterrupted since World War I. This was Crested Butte, a community formed of disparate personalities united by a common sense of place and aligned in a mutual love for mountains, rivers, forests and the whole of the natural world. This was a community uncompromised by the enticements of lucre. This was Crested Butte, a place where wealth was defined not as crass currency, but in sentiments of living well, with purpose, meaning and simplicity, in honoring the sanctity of nature with a spiritual capacity that transcended the AMAX business model.

This was a town that would not sit passively by as it was overrun by the status quo of market capitalism and free enterprise. This community would raise a grassroots insurgency to match the resistance of the French Revolution. Vive la Butte!

Crested Butte would marshal troops. Crested Butte would innovate a battle plan, erect barricades, foment rebellion and, in any way possible, thwart the grinding gears of the industrial machine. AMAX would not march into the East River Valley like a Roman emperor demanding tribute from a subjugated race. If the mine meant "progress" then there would be none in Crested Butte because, in the context of a rapacious mine, progress became a dirty word.

Slowly, irrevocably, irreversibly, the majority of Crested Butte citizens began to steel ourselves for the fight of our lives and the defense of the very soul of our town. All Crested Butte lacked to achieve success was—well, everything!—organization, strategy, know-how, funding, forethought, and a leader who could carry the banner to the very doorstep of AMAX and send a tremor through the boardroom at corporate headquarters in Greenwich.

That leader was waiting in the wings.

Despite the ominous rumblings of the AMAX announcement, life as we knew it went on in Crested Butte. Here Author Paul Andersen gets himself into hot water with Sunshine Williams at her iconic Sunshine's Paradise Bathhouse in the late 1970s. Sunshine's was a place where you could see more of your friends.

CRESTED BUTTE CHRONICLE ARCHIVES

8
Mitchell

CRESTED BUTTE in the late-1970s was imbued with spirited anarchy. The populace was a rabble, not a citizenry. Who wanted a governing force over them when many residents of the town had no governing force over themselves? Sober governance would have been anathema to the irrepressibly free spirit Crested Butte recklessly endowed in its youthful and exuberant population.

With AMAX knocking at the gate, the town needed a leader, a figurehead, a large and galvanizing presence who could focus the town's character into a well-spoken, determined, invincible, impassioned, charming, outrageous and likable guardian of our public lands. A banner-carrier was needed, and a more unlikely one could not have been found.

In November 1977, shortly after the AMAX announcement, Crested Butte elected a new mayor, a remarkable man who defied convention with every element of his being. He was "The Wheelchair Mayor," and he broadcast an irresistible spirit, a scrappy demeanor and an engaging personality. He was familiar to all by his grim disfigurement.

How memorable was my first encounter with this remarkable man. Fresh into a journalism career that would run 45 years, my editor at the *Gunnison Times*, the sweet and affable Joanne Williams, gave me my first assignment: interview the newly elected mayor of Crested Butte. Joanne gave me only a vague heads-up that Mitchell was "different." With a knowing smirk, she sent me on my way.

I arrived at the door of a small, beautiful Victorian on Maroon

Avenue, my notepad in hand. I took a deep breath and knocked. "Alloh!" said a beautiful young woman with a thick French accent who stood with the door open on a cool October evening. "You must be Pohl, yays?" she smiled with disarming friendliness. I was led to a small office off the wood-paneled living room where a large Vermont Castings wood-burning stove emitted a welcome warmth. Mitchell was seated with his back to the door. Adeptly, he spun his wheelchair to face his uncertain visitor.

"Hello!" he boomed, gazing at me and waiting for the reaction he expected. I was stunned by Mitchell's scarred and mottled face. And when his hand shot out as a greeting, or what should have been a hand, I had no time to react other than to reach out my open hand. Mitchell slipped his paw through my fingers so that when I instinctively gripped, it was his wrist I held, and not the distorted hand with no fingers.

"Please, sit down," he said in a voice that was at once commanding and comforting. How many times Mitchell had encountered shocked visitors is anyone's guess, but he was accustomed to looks of surprise, horror and even revulsion. That he was so at ease with his outward appearance evinced a rock solid interior buoyed by unflappable self-esteem.

Mitchell was his own man, and that was made clear as he told me his story, step-by-painful-step, to the point where he was now the mayor with a daunting issue to face—the AMAX mining threat. I felt a growing attraction to Mitchell as he described his messianic mission to save the soul of his town. Simultaneously, I felt deep respect for this man for having overcome crushing adversities that would have destroyed most. We were friends from that moment on, and I determined to write the most glowing interview of my career, which would be easy given that this was the first interview of my journalistic career.

Mitchell, at that time, described his face as "a poorly made leather quilt," more scar tissue than skin. He had no fingers. He could not walk or stand. But the man's spirit could soar. He possessed a strong personal magnetism and a wry, self-deprecating sense of humor that belittled his personal tragedies, which he boldly converted into brilliant opportunities. As an astute politician, an articulate speaker and

The voice of Crested Butte was heard in the deep baritone of Mitchell, a man who was at ease with his outward appearance because of a rock solid interior buoyed by unflappable self-esteem. CRESTED BUTTE CHRONICLE ARCHIVES

a compelling advocate for social justice, Mitchell was unique. That he lived in a remote mountain town at 9,000 feet set him further apart, which is just how Mitchell liked it.

Mitchell, an adopted last name that became his singular appellation, was born in 1943, in Pennsylvania, as William John Schiff III. His parents divorced and his mother remarried Luke Mitchell, who became her young son's role model. Troubles in public school led young Mitchell to military academy, then to a stint in the U.S. Marine Corps, where he was assigned to the infamous "Black Sheep" Squadron. In 1964, Mitchell left the military. A month later, he was marching in demonstrations protesting the Vietnam War.

In the late '60s, Mitchell moved to San Francisco, where he had a dream job as "grip man" on a cable car, a role that suited his swashbuckling, romantic, gregarious nature. He worked part time as a radio announcer, capitalizing on his deep baritone and gift for gab. In 1971, riding home from work on his Honda 750 motorcycle, Mitchell was sideswiped by a truck. The bike went down, the gas cap came loose, and Mitchell was soaked with gasoline. A spark ignited a blazing fireball that engulfed him. He survived, thanks to a man on the street corner, who literally put him out with a fire extinguisher. Mitchell was burned over 65 percent of his body. His fingers were burned off, as were most of his facial features. His recovery was long and terribly painful, as Mitchell wrote in his memoir, *The Man Who Would Not Be Defeated:*

I looked horrific. An appropriate question for a stranger upon seeing me for the first time was not 'Who is it?' but, rather 'What is it?' The burns were bad enough; add to that the fact that my eyelids were sewn shut to keep my eyes moist; I had a tracheotomy tube inserted into my throat to help me breathe; my weight quickly plummeted from 175 to 125; and you have a pretty ghastly specimen. I have heard that visitors, including tough guys with whom I had worked on the cable cars, would faint upon seeing me.

The pain of being burned is so extreme because you will die from fluid loss or infection if you are left alone, so you are never left alone. Something terribly painful is being done to you virtually every hour of the day, day after day. Skin is whirlpooled away, grafted back on, stretched, squeezed, lubricated, bandaged, poked for intravenous feeding. . . I had sixteen skin-graft surgeries in four months. I turned to my nurse and said quietly, 'I've died. I am dead. This is all a fantasy. I didn't survive the accident. I'm actually dead.'

No. Mitchell was very much alive. He pulled through with steely resolve, something innate in his constitution that has surfaced more than once in his eventful life. The lucrative settlement of a lawsuit against Honda because of a faulty gas cap gave Mitchell financial independence. He invested in Vermont Castings, a wood-burning stove company, and in real estate. He built his portfolio into a considerable sum and re-entered life with full enthusiasm as a skier, surfer and world traveler.

Mitchell learned to fly, earned his pilot's license, and bought an airplane. He discovered Crested Butte and bought an historic home on Maroon Avenue. His appearance was startling, but Mitchell had an airplane, mobility, friends, women and money. He was flying high, as if bouncing back on a trampoline. Then he fell again.

On a cold November morning in 1975, Mitchell was taking off in his Cessna 206 from Gunnison Airport. He had filed a flight plan to Reno, Nevada with a few friends to attend the National Avalanche School. Upon liftoff, Mitchell's plane failed to respond appropriately to the controls. After gaining 100 feet of altitude, Mitchell made an instinctive decision and put the plane down on the end of the runway. The plane "pancaked" hard, breaking one of the landing gear, which caused the fuselage to list. Gas spilled from the overflow vents and flooded over the wing. Fire was the first thing on Mitchell's mind.

"Get out!" Mitchell barked to his passengers. While they scrambled to safety, Mitchell realized that he was unable to move. At first he thought his feet were stuck beneath the rudder pedals, then he felt a white hot surge of pain in his back. Mitchell had to be extricated by paramedics. An examination revealed that the crash had broken his back. There had been no fire, but Mitchell was left with no feeling below the waist.

The night of his plane crash, as he lay in a hospital in Denver facing a life sentence in a wheelchair, Mitchell's beautiful Victorian home was gutted by fire. Devastation is the word that comes to mind, that and a bottomless pit of despair and victimhood. Mitchell, however, did not wallow in agony, nor were his friends about to let him. An outpouring from Crested Butte filled his hospital room with brotherhood and good cheer. Friends formed a team of volunteers, and they rebuilt his home. Crested Butte became an indissoluble life link to which Mitchell was deeply bound. In a way, he owed his life to the town.

Mitchell's home had burned and it was rebuilt by his friends. Mitchell's life had collapsed and he rebuilt that himself. Winning the mayoral election in 1977 was a huge personal triumph. He boasted facetiously that he had "won by a landslide of five votes." The coincidence of the AMAX announcement added fuel to Mitchell's campaign and brought to his natural leadership qualities a mission and a need. The threat of AMAX served to call up a personal debt Mitchell owed to the town he loved. He would repay that debt with everything he had.

Mitchell was adamantly opposed to the AMAX assault on his Rocky Mountain paradise. The specter of corporate hegemony riled him as much as the social injustice he had seen in the Vietnam War. Mitchell launched a crusade that would bolster a defense for the town's right to autonomy and self-determination. In this, Mitchell and the town became one, united in an unwavering vow of interdependence. Mitchell took on AMAX with raw passion, becoming the town's foremost spokesman. He was interviewed on the "Today Show," featured in *Newsweek* and *Time*, his picture on the front page of the *Rocky Mountain News*, his name mentioned on most of the Denver TV news programs. Mitchell, and by association Crested Butte, became an irresistible human interest story.

The press loved to characterize Mitchell as an embattled, small town mayor holding off a menacing giant. The stereotype was simplistic, but the national media loves stereotypes, especially when they so perfectly portray underdog heroes. Mitchell played to them all by personifying the vibrant independence of rural America. He was an undaunted cripple raising his fist to the world, a prophet of the oppressed holed up in the heart of the Rocky Mountains, a righteous man taking on the machine with élan, a respected scion of democratic courage. Mitchell was a John Henry of the 20th Century, and he made the cold steel sing as he struck back at AMAX with the hammer of his truth.

Mitchell fought for Crested Butte and he fought for nature. He championed the preservation of wilderness to which he was denied access because wheelchairs, which are defined as mechanized vehicles, are technically not allowed. Being bound to his chair made Mitchell an even more effective defender of wild places. "I could only look at it," he said of wilderness, but that was reason enough to defend the mountains that surrounded Crested Butte. And though it wasn't statutory wilderness, Mitchell's realm included the backdrop mountain to which AMAX had laid claim.

As his persona gained notoriety, Mitchell relished his role as an ultimate politician who desired to move into ever-higher political circles. As the mayor of Crested Butte, he used his office to springboard among

The Crested Butte Town Council, 1981 (top, l. to r.) Mike Verplank and Tommy Drake, (seated, l. to r.) "Sleepy" Jim Adams, Mitchell, Gary Sporcich, Claudia Richards. *CRESTED BUTTE CHRONICLE* ARCHIVES

prominent politicos while building the image of a magnetic populist. Among those he befriended were President Jimmy Carter, Congressman Tip O'Neil, Senator Gary Hart, vice presidential candidate Geraldine Ferraro, Senator Paul Simon, Senator Tim Wirth, Senator Floyd Haskell, and former Speaker of the House Jim Wright.

In 1980, Mitchell was named as a delegate to the Democratic National Convention, where he waded into the deep waters of national partisan politics and swam with the best of them. In 1982, Mitchell was again chosen as a delegate to the Democratic National Convention. Two years later, in 1984, he mounted a campaign for Congress in Colorado's Third District and won the Democratic primary. He ran unsuccessfully in a heated campaign against Aspen rancher and Republican Mike Strang.

On the walls of his town hall office, Mitchell hung a gallery of framed photographs. The Wall of Fame showed him shaking hands with dozens of politicians, dignitaries and celebrities to whom he had gained access and had cultivated lasting friendships. Crested Butte Town Attorney Wes Light routinely joked that in order to equal Mitchell's fame, he need only hang one framed picture on the wall of his office—Wes Light shaking hands with Mitchell.

One role Mitchell never accepted was victimhood. By the sheer ebullience of his disarming personality, he deflected sympathy and sorrow for what had befallen him. Adversity was something to rise above, to conquer. *Semper Fi!* His tragedies were necessary crucibles for his personal growth and inner development. They gave him fearless resolve and unyielding strength. Mitchell later became a motivational speaker and, in 1993, produced a book and video tape, both of which broadcast his mantra: "It's not what happens to you, it's what you do about it."

Mitchell applied that credo to Crested Butte: AMAX is what happened to Crested Butte and it was up to Crested Butte to do something about it. The question was: Could a sometimes fractious, dysfunctional, disparate community pull itself together into a unified front? Could Crested Butte weigh the gravity of AMAX against its frivolous nature and take its future seriously enough to mount an effective defense? Strong glue was needed to cement the pieces into a whole, and the right cohesion was found one formative night in a popular Crested Butte barroom.

9
'The Shotgun at Our Heads'

MYLES RADEMAN came to Crested Butte as a Philadelphia-born, New York University-educated attorney with a master's degree in urban planning and experience as a community organizer. Working as a political activist in Latino neighborhoods in Denver through Head Start, Rademan took part in the socially proactive agenda of the Johnson Administration. Head Start was founded in 1965 and was managed under the United States Department of Health and Human Services. Rademan's role on the streets of Denver was to empower underserved, low-income neighborhoods to provide comprehensive early childhood education, health, nutrition, and parent involvement services.

In the early 1970s, Crested Butte fell under Head Start's parameters as a qualifying community, and Rademan was offered a planning role for the nascent town government. He jumped at the chance and soon joined forces with Town Manager Bruce Baumgartner and his friend, Jim Kuziak. Together, they formed a consulting firm, BKR, an acronym representing their last names, which offered clients engineering, planning and vision, all of which the Town of Crested Butte needed as it faced the growing pressures of tourism. B, K and R had opted out of big city hustle for the supposedly quiet life in a remote mountain town where Rademan's community organizing background would serve him well. His job as Crested Butte town planner, a role he defined as he invented it, was simple: orchestrate willful anarchy into a healthy, functional community.

"In Crested Butte," said Rademan in a 1981 interview, "we tend to

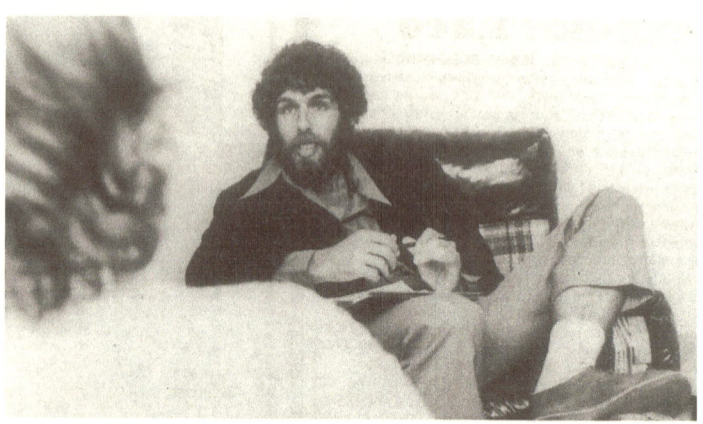

Crested Butte town planner Myles Rademan, a true visionary with the skills of a seasoned community organizer, helped transform the rabble into a unified force. CRESTED BUTTE CHRONICLE ARCHIVES

look out to the wilderness; the frontier is the boundary of the town. We are not surrounded by other communities. It is hard to get here and even harder to stay. Our consciousness is formed by the concept of being on the edge."

Crested Butte, and later to some extent, Gunnison County, were guided by this enlightened triumvirate of Rademan, Kuziak and Baumgartner—all early arrivals in town during the great hippie migration. This trio helped form the foundation of the loosely defined community that was Crested Butte.

"I was in charge of words," Rademan told the *Crested Butte News* in a 2015 interview, "Kuziak was in charge of pictures, and Baumgartner was in charge of numbers." Because of a shared liberalism based on progressive values, their influence and collective vision subtly and presciently spread into Gunnison County where their ideas helped define community values that eventually ruled against industrial mining and called for moderation in resort development.

As town planner, Rademan's ability to forge a coherent vision derived from his reasoned, insightful, and coalescing oratory. Perhaps his most glowing achievement as a community organizer at the onset of the AMAX proposal was artfully portraying a set of communal values that he wove into a community fabric from the colorful threads of a disparate population. That he did so in just one night proved a brilliant stroke of daring. It happened at the Grubstake Saloon, a bar more known for drunken fracases than for community solidarity. The bar served as a gathering place for a cadre of townspeople and was the unofficial headquarters for the Crested Butte Hot Shots, a disreputable group of reputable firefighters with legendary derring-do. The "Trip Wheeler Window," a plate glass storefront at the Grubstake, was part of the town's lore, notorious for the drunken debauchers who threw themselves through it, most of all the free-living, hard-charging Freeman "Trip" Wheeler (1944-2006), whose obit labeled him as builder/developer, teacher, tuna spotter, pilot, surfer, hunter, etc.

That Rademan chose the Grubstake as his community venue acknowledged the importance of a key watering hole in the affairs of Crested Butte. It was at the Grubstake, under Rademan's influence, where Crested Butte discovered an element of brotherhood, a pervasive sense of pride, and a deep emotional identity with the town's heart and soul, something that had hitherto lacked definition. In one auspicious night Rademan helped galvanize a sense of place that was unique and irreplaceable. And he did it with the beer taps flowing.

His strategy relied, in part, on the townspeople's aesthetic appreciation for nature and their widespread fear of losing that which was loved and familiar. Crested Butte's natural protectionism equated with the ecotherapeutic term, "solastalgia": the pain experienced when the place where one lives and which one loves falls under a threat. Add to the equation an innate community sense of biophilia, or love of life, and you have an epoxy-like bond. Biophilia came through the natural world as displayed magnificently in the Elk Range where an unspoken sense of place took on the sacred overtones of an intrinsic, pagan spirit.

To establish a visual context for love of place, Rademan assembled a unique slide show. To do so, he visited photographers in Crested Butte—there were plenty of good ones—asking for their best local scenic landscapes. Next, he added images of the town and its people, forming a homespun pastiche that would have warmed the heart of a latter day Norman Rockwell. He skillfully assembled these images into a photo album depicting what was at stake with AMAX. As for the venue, Rademan gambled on the Grubstake instead of town hall. He knew that attendance was crucial, and he assumed that even the most ambivalent, apolitical and debauched elements of town would convene there for a beer and some homey pictures. And convene they did.

On the appointed night, the Grubstake was packed. I wedged myself into a gap at the bar as the "audience" tipped a few in preparation for the promised show. Rademan had the projector set up with a screen against one wall. He clinked a spoon against a beer mug and the room quieted down. He thanked the audience for attending and said he had some pictures to show, something that might shed light on the proposed mine. He asked for the lights to be turned out. After the room went dark, he switched on the projector.

The first round of images was postcard beautiful—stunning landscapes of high mountain lakes and towering peaks, coursing whitewater streams, scenes of powdery, glistening snow, and wildflower meadows set against impossibly blue skies. The show began to feel like a chamber of commerce promotion, and the audience became restive. Beer glasses clinked and whispered conversations reacted to certain photos. A loud undercurrent of conversation threatened to drown out Rademan's opening narrative in which he described the places in the pictures as part of the town's greater backyard, all of it part of the public trust.

The next bank of images focused on the people of Crested Butte and the commonplace activities of life in town. Laughter erupted at pictures of friends on the town baseball diamond or at a street dance, of people at work and at play. The mood changed as the audience was hit with something it had never considered before. Here, in Kodachrome, emerged a cumulative impression of the town's culture. The scenery was stellar—everyone knew that—but what mattered more were the people who Rademan skillfully wove into familiar landscapes and townscapes.

Gradually, the human element in the photographs blended with mountain scenes, combining into something idyllic and tangible. The framing of nearly every meaningful community aspect of Crested

Butte life was set against a backdrop of mountains and valleys, lakes and streams, which most of the audience recognized and knew intimately. And then came the *coup de grace* with telling portraits of the children of the town, ragamuffins with gap-toothed grins, the gamins of Crested Butte who described a nascent future that suddenly hove into view through the eyes, the laughter and the innocence of the town's children.

That clinched it. Any snickering died away into silence. The bar fell into a deep hush of reverence as the flow of images stitched together the social fabric through generations. Tears were discreetly wiped on sleeves. Emotions peaked. The standing-room-only audience was enraptured by Rademan's easy, yet poignant, story of an enchanted town in a magical valley blessed with natural beauty, an invaluable sense of belonging, and a young and innocent future. The program concluded with a dramatic statement, a call to arms: "AMAX," announced Rademan in theatrical tones, "is geographically situated like a shotgun at our heads." With that, the last image faded.

There was no applause. In place of barroom chatter, there was a breathless knowing that something wonderful had happened. Rademan's message had hit home, straight to the heart, deep in the

The Grubstake Saloon with Red Lady Bowl in the background.
It was here, at the start of the battle with AMAX, that town planner
Myles Rademan helped coalesce a unified front against the mine.
OH BE JOYFUL GALLERY

collective soul. There were no other words, no other speeches. There was simply an unspoken resolve in the ranks and a growing sense of urgency. Born was a dedicated and selfless insurgent army. AMAX was in for the fight of its life, and so was Crested Butte.

Myles Rademan knew Crested Butte perhaps better than anyone. He had studied its foibles and caprices. He knew how its random elements clicked into a unique and savory mosaic. He knew there was strength in the town's spontaneity, a raw, untapped energy built on love and irreverence. With Mitchell as the point man and Rademan as the visionary, citizens enlisted themselves to the fight against AMAX with a bold, rebellious, unified and often hysterical spirit.

"I liken the town to Las Vegas," Rademan remarked years later. "People don't come here to win or lose; rather, they come here to gamble and dream. This is an avoid-reality center, and the country desperately needs places like this. If the town ever becomes too real, it will lose it. My advice, and it is given with love, is never become too real; never take life too seriously. We must care and feel that this place is unique, and that feeling has to be constantly reinforced and perpetuated.

"The more people that believe the dream, the stronger the dream becomes. There is a danger that somebody will come here to rip off the community, to take the dream, package it, and sell it off. But Crested Butte will survive no matter what happens. There is something magical happening here; the amount of energy from such a small town is incredible."

Before Rademan could become too caught up in his own imagery, his own irreverence surfaced as he conjured a new thought. "Crested Butte," he smiled, "is the largest outpatient clinic in Colorado. Sometimes, when I hear that someone is leaving town, I'm afraid for the rest of society. But I am happy and proud to be part of it."

10
Stewards of Paradise

REPORTING ON THE AMAX PROPOSAL gave me a front row seat to an exercise in civics, political science, sociology, land use policy, extractive industries and environmentalism. Here was my master's curriculum for a hands-on graduate program that was far from theoretical. Not surprisingly, Harvard University decided the same. Several years into the Mt. Emmons Project a group of master's students from Harvard came to town and applied the Crested Butte/AMAX conflict to their own graduate program. They used the mine issue as the basis for a real life study of a community in turmoil from the external forces of capitalism and industrialization.

What happened in Crested Butte at that time was certainly educational. It was also incredibly entertaining because of the glaring divergence of values represented by the combatants. Not only was Crested Butte defined by a rigorous testing of municipal autonomy and self-determination, but we who were part of the experience were changed and defined by the issues confronting us. AMAX had no idea of the hornets' nest it was stirring by awakening and radicalizing the town. The community was coming out of hibernation, and it was AMAX that brought it out.

AMAX and Crested Butte were distanced by a huge ideological rift, a cultural, spiritual and values-driven divergence as great as any in America in the 1970s. The town staked claim to the fringe of American culture while AMAX represented the mainstream military-industrial complex and the globalization of the Commons.

Despite AMAX overtures of economic viability for the town, Crested Butte was no unsophisticated Appalachia craving a regular payroll doled out by a glad-handing corporate patron. The town thrived on a diversity fielded serendipitously from creative, thoughtful, intelligent, sensitive, enterprising citizens who had assembled by chance in the cul-de-sac at the end of Highway 135. Most of the young townspeople had readily adapted to a kicked-back, easy-going and, in some ways, indolent lifestyle complemented by an irrepressible penchant for athletic exploits and liberated ways of life. Thanks to AMAX that diversity would coalesce into a dynamic force as the proposed mine became the impetus for a kind of sociological gelling. The populace became activated to the cause the way a yeast culture reacts to sugar. Clearly, AMAX got a rise out of Crested Butte.

Driving this growing passion was Crested Butte's widespread and often vocal disdain for the feckless exploitation of what most residents considered our hallowed ground. Crested Butte, whose identity was humble, organic, and grassroots, seemed determined to hold off the lure of big money in preference for a soulful embrace of the Platonic ideal of the good, the true, and the beautiful. The mien of the town was the antipathy of the Machiavellian triad of money, fame and power. Most residents favored a balance of community and commodity that weighed far more heavily on community, with the emphasis on . . .unity.

AMAX represented a blatant assault on that sense of unity by developing the commodity geologists had identified in Mt. Emmons. Enriching the town materially, as AMAX promised, would follow only as AMAX enriched itself, a point that was not so clearly stated. The hierarchy AMAX was trying to install in Crested Butte put AMAX at the top and left the townsfolk somewhere below. Perhaps the biggest misunderstanding by AMAX was the notion that material wealth could be used as a lever to integrate the townspeople into the company's culture. That was a deeply flawed projection of the corporation's own value structure.

In 1977, Crested Butte's so-called economy was based on nominal income from tourism and recreation. For most residents, subsistence living was fine. Getting rich was not why people moved here. That consensus was stated with a disparaging comparison to "Glitter Gulch" on the other side of the Elk Range: "We don't want to be another Aspen!" The so-called threat of "Aspenization," the commercial sell-out of the town, was the biggest threat Crested Butte had faced until AMAX. A limited tourist trade had replaced coal mining as the town's lifeblood, and that was deemed good because tourism was clean, neat, sustainable, and, best of all, seasonal. "Crested Butte: Love it by Leaving it the Way You Found it," was a town credo printed on posters as a plea for self-restraint from defiling the purity of nature and community. It was also a warning against killing the goose that had laid the golden egg.

At first, AMAX failed to apprehend the town's non-material ethic. The mining company dangled the wrong carrot. Community interests were not about industrial development, strategic metals, patriotic fervor or careers in mining. The town's interests were certainly not about underwriting the consumer-based American Dream. Rather, the town was aligned with modest values as a necessary offset to the flashier, commercial culture of lift-served skiing at Mt. Crested Butte. By cluelessly praising the motives inherent in its bottom line-shareholder-corporate mentality, AMAX threatened Crested Butte's essence. AMAX had artlessly summoned the status quo, from which many had sought to escape by living in Crested Butte in the first place and celebrating the town's independent, laid-back, funky, libertarian, sensual, and occasionally misanthropic lifestyle.

Crested Butte's social contract was based on intimacy, and nothing could be more intimate than nude, co-ed bathing at Sunshine's Paradise Bathhouse. Here was the town's communal baptism—"a place where you could see more of your friends." The Bathhouse offered regular christenings among the unfettered and unclothed populace. Nakedness became rather commonplace and, in a healthy way, removed some of the gender stigma with which American society seems to be so titillated. Curiosity was satisfied, which was usually as far as it went.

Communal spirit was equally nurtured by familiarity in the bars, shops, restaurants, ski runs and at the post office. That spirit was also embodied in the pristine landscapes of the Elk Range where townsfolk practiced the transcendentalist ideal of Emerson and Thoreau. Crested Butte was *Walden* writ large on the western landscape. Like Thoreau, the townspeople often displayed a fierce aversion to the overbearing culture of the outside world, even if, like Thoreau, they ironically depended on it for conveniences and basic necessities.

The East River valley had become a refuge for mostly urban refugees who had broken from the orbit of the post-World War II suburban sprawl of modern industrial life. "Let us be lovers, we'll marry our fortunes together..." sang Simon and Garfunkel, "...we've all gone to look for Amer-i-ca..." As new immigrants who were routinely lumped together as "hippies," we newcomers were intruders ourselves into a traditional social fabric that had existed long before our arrival. The seemingly quaint and contented "Old-Timers" had shaped Crested Butte on completely different terms as coal miners, and yet they were hospitable. For upstart Baby Boomers to now pull up the drawbridge on AMAX and thwart a reversion to the town's mining past violated traditional values some old-timers still held dear. By taking a stand against the mine, the new guard could be seen as selfish, myopic and hypocritical of traditional values. Some of the town's old guard accused us of being disrespectful of the mining way of life made heroic by local coal miners who had endured incommunicable travails underground.

But power was in the politics. By the late 1970s, opponents of the mine comprised the majority of the town's electorate. We outnumbered the old-timers and were fired up with self-righteous fervor. We saw our motivation as pure, especially given the blatantly transparent objectives of AMAX as they appeared to us. We "radicals" sincerely believed that our refutation of AMAX was in the best interests, not only of ourselves and our adopted home, but of the larger American culture that was soon to be knocking at our door. We had assumed the role of self-appointed stewards of a national treasure as defined by a vibrant community set in a landscape of unparalleled natural beauty and ecological purity. The worth of these values was incalculable in economic terms, so preserving them was a service to the greater society, which had no calculus for assessing scenic value, community spirit, or natural capital. We bold, new activists saw

AMAX as an imperial juggernaut looking for one thing only—profits—at the expense of what we called our sense of place.

On a larger stage, the fight against AMAX equated with a plea for the health of the biosphere against the appetites of modern man. By comparison with much of the outside world, Crested Butte was a utopia, an unspoiled haven, where Mother Nature asserted Herself with splendor, grace and compelling spiritual force. Once the values of the town were clearly defined and personally imbued, most of the townspeople vowed not to allow our coveted backyard to become a sacrifice zone. In this, we became unrepentant and unapologetic NIMBYs who would hold back the barbarians at the gates.

Despite the town's backwoods ambiance and quasi-rustic citizens, many of Crested Butte's transplants understood the high stakes game AMAX was playing. The citizenry may have appeared backward, but we were not provincial, many of us having grown up in cities where we had witnessed the potent effects of industrial and commercial influences that had defined American society during the disillusioned post-Vietnam, Cold War and Civil Rights eras. Many who had flocked to Crested Butte had rejected the dictates of oppressive social strictures, seeking instead peace and harmony in the sheltering mountains, or at least to discover if those things were still possible. In Crested Butte, we found solace. We were protected from a world we distrusted and often disdained, a world that AMAX now wanted to lay at our doorstep, purportedly as a gift.

With a martial spirit similar to the farmers at Lexington-Concord two centuries before, the town quickly girded itself for battle. Lines were drawn, alliances formed, commitments made, vows pledged, all with the rapidity of coagulating blood. The issue was painted simplistically in black and white, right and wrong, good and evil, which was necessary for rapid mobilization. The majority of Crested Butte's citizens allied themselves to an unyielding set of principles that comprised an agreed upon moral code. Fighting the mine was the right thing to do.

AMAX, in its pledge for sophistication and innovation, had promised to build a "state-of-the-art" mine and to do "the best job possible." To Crested Butte, however, the Mt. Emmons Project implied the wholesale destruction of a mountain, a river drainage, a valley, a people, a spirit. Mitchell put it like this: "AMAX says it is going to do the best possible job on something that should never be done in the first place." There would be no compromise with AMAX. The conflict of values was irreconcilable.

"Quality of life" became the loaded expression that established a bulwark against the mine. It implied a "Small is Beautiful" belief system that validated Crested Butte as the outpatient clinic Rademan had described. Quality of life was seen as an antidote to the conformity of mass culture. Implied was a rural identity that stipulated living lightly on the land. Crested Butte's vaunted quality of life was fashioned from the Jeffersonian ideal of the philosopher farmer, a frontier pioneering community made up of educated, acculturated, autonomous individuals. These small town qualities of Jeffersonian America would not be co-opted by drill rigs, bulldozers, ore-crushers, tailings piles, and corporate executives wearing plaid pants.

Wes Light, in a 1979 interview, remarked that people were then attracted to Crested Butte because of high standards of living, not measured by material wealth or income, but by the comforting warmth of a small town and the blessings of natural beauty. "Some people are more concerned with money than with quality of life," he allowed, "but it would be ironic for people to come here for the money, only to have to look elsewhere for quality of life."

Crested Butte, like most communities, was neither uniform nor pure, and there were plenty of ironies. Critics routinely dismissed the town as dystopian and dysfunctional. There were feuds, bar fights, drunkenness, drug abuse, loneliness, exclusion, suicide, adultery, carousing and debaucheries of many kinds. Because of a disproportionately large population of men than women, it was said that you didn't lose your girlfriend, you just lost your turn.

Crested Butte had its share of cranks, malcontents and sociopaths. Some residents were passionate in their embrace of liberty, which they defined most openly by allowing their dogs to run free in packs and poop on your lawn. Some felt that the absence of stoplights and traffic severed all bonds to American life, that living in the midst of the mountains freed them from civic authority, the responsibili-

When the "Big Mine" closed in 1952, Crested Butte fell into hibernation, quietly slumbering on the fringe of American society.
CRESTED BUTTE CHRONICLE ARCHIVES

ties of citizenship, and from civilization itself. There was no Leviathan ruling over Crested Butte, the absence of which invited anarchy or, in the extreme, nihilism.

Independence, Crested Butte-style, could translate into carving your own set of ski tracks through deep powder snow. Freedom meant fishing in a clear mountain stream. Liberty meant mountain biking single-track trails. Quality of life in Crested Butte was a nebulous notion defined by myriad perspectives. For many, Crested Butte was a paradise. For critics, it was an absurdly faulted social experiment. For most townspeople, it wavered between the two extremes. Somewhere in the middle, at the intersection of practicality and idealism, truth and myth, was the place we called home.

But what kind of home was it? Housing was uncertain. Most jobs were neither lucrative nor glamorous. Winters lasted eight months. Roads were sometimes impassable. Snowdrifts reached higher than the rooftops. One could feel claustrophobic and isolated in the depths of the arctic chill that could hit 40 below zero. People got sick. People died. Some suffered depression, addiction, alcoholism. Some took their own lives. Most of the townspeople had to work to pay rent, cover utilities, meet medical expenses, buy a drink or an occasional dinner out, and put gas in the car. Life was real, no matter how distant one might feel from the gravitational pull of "the real world." Neighbors could be loving and friendly, charming and eccentric, despondent and hostile. There were plenty of societal castaways in this high altitude Gilligan's Island.

If you made it through half a dozen Crested Butte winters, you earned respect and were accepted. You had become a "local" by matching the stoicism portrayed by the hard bitten coal miners and ranchers. Many young immigrants aspired to nothing more than a sense of acceptance in a town where life was physically and psychologically demanding. It sometimes seemed that we neo-pioneers, with our urban or suburban backgrounds, were merely role playing on a turn-of-the-century stage set, scripted to a fantasy life.

A molybdenum mine did not fit that fantasy, but it did something surprisingly constructive. By fomenting united opposition, AMAX focused residents on a unifying need. It leavened a rough, uncultured dough and produced something wholesome from the collective ingredients. As AMAX attorney Art Biddle quipped during an interview thirty years later, "We always thought we were great intellectual stimulation for Crested Butte."

Biddle was right. AMAX prompted a serious intellectual exercise in the formerly torpid minds of many townsfolk. If anything, the quality of life improved as these fertile minds reacted to the challenge before them. The mission of defeating the mine enriched and deepened the social and civil dynamic. Apathy vanished. Emotions became more buoyant. Creativity surged. Camaraderie was infused. The crusade mentality bolstered newly empowered activists from a recondite mob to a communal outpouring for concerted action. In short, AMAX catalyzed Crested Butte into a proud, united and refreshingly eccentric adversary for whom the prevailing mood was: "Bring it on!"

11
You Wanna Do What?!

BY 1979, two years after the AMAX announcement, it seemed that the Mt. Emmons Project was on a steady march toward its goal of industrializing Crested Butte and environs. The regulatory process was judicious, but accommodating. The corporate public relations campaign was ramping up. The company presence was clearly visible throughout Gunnison County. Crested Butte was trying to get its footing on the slippery slope of appeals, public hearings, and complex legalese that seemed stacked against the town's interests and its autonomy. The AMAX proposal was repugnant to most of the townspeople, but not all of its actions resulted in community spite.

In 1980, AMAX flexed its financial muscles and performed a technological miracle that it handily converted into a major public relations victory. The corporation revealed its deep pockets and technological knowhow when it joined with the Colorado Department of Public Health and Environment and with the Town of Crested Butte to rehabilitate polluted Coal Creek, which snakes scenically through town. For decades, the creek had been sullied with toxic runoff from the Keystone Mine that had colored the river rocks fluorescent orange and had the acidity of Draino. The creek emitted a stench of sulfur and was devoid of life. Rather than provide an enhancement for Crested Butte, Coal Creek was a sensory insult and environmental liability.

AMAX put up earnest money to repair the failed tailings dams at the mine site where polluted mine effluent had been leaching into the creek. It also made plans to install a Swift Lectro-Clear wastewater treatment plant to filter out toxic impurities. The treatment plant would remove particulate pollution through an electro-chemical process first developed by the Swift meat-packing company of Chicago to purify its slaughterhouse waste water.

This much-heralded project, with a price tag of $13.3 million, would have cost AMAX considerably more had it not been for Gunnison County's support of industrial revenue bonds earmarked for the project. The Gunnison County Commissioners, in November 1979, voted unanimously to endorse the bonds at the request of AMAX, reducing the costs of corporate debt for the plant and saving AMAX $6 million over twenty years.

"AMAX has spent a lot of money in the county," acknowledged Commissioner David Leinsdorf during the bond discussions, "and it's in the best interests of the county to stop them from spending as much money as possible to provide us some bargaining power in the future."

From the time the water treatment plant was activated in 1980, it was a laudable success. It seemed that AMAX had worked magic akin to alchemy. Soon, trout swam in the limpid water as Coal Creek returned to a pristine mountain stream replete with recovering aquatic riparian habitat. The taxpayers of Gunnison County had made good on the bonds and now realized the benefits of clean water in the Upper Gunnison Basin. The water treatment plant revealed the power of technology and corporate capital in repairing what man had put asunder. For many, it established AMAX as a beneficial force in the county. The wastewater plant was a public relations smash hit.

"Coal Creek was a dead stream," remarked Terry Hamlin years later, "and I would hate to think of what Coal Creek would look like today without AMAX. That was a significant investment. There was debate in the corporation to see if that would go—a $20 million investment. But it was done, and done in the good faith that they wanted to be a good neighbor and do it the right way."

AMAX needed to nurture good will throughout the Gunnison Valley in order to play out its strategy. If AMAX could not sway Crested Butte, then it would marginalize the town, sidestep its naysayers, and focus on the wider county populace where a more judicious view might gain the company acceptance, if not downright advocacy. "After a while," reflected AMAX senior vice president Stan Dempsey, "we

A triumvirate of anti-mine warriors (l. to r.) Don Bachman, Chuck Malick, and Wes Light at a public meeting in the late 1970s.
CRESTED BUTTE CHRONICLE ARCHIVES

began taking a broader look at the community than just Crested Butte. We put our office in Crested Butte first, then we realized we needed to look more broadly at Gunnison County, so we moved the office to Gunnison."

Meanwhile, work progressed at the old Keystone Mine where access drifts were tunneled into Mt. Emmons to gradually expand geologic mapping. Powerline corridors to serve an expanded mine site were mapped, survey lines were flagged, tailings dams were sited, haulage routes were identified, housing plans were submitted, permits were applied for, and numerous mitigation studies were undertaken to offset the impacts of the mine. These costs, eventually totaling $100 million, came from the seemingly bottomless AMAX war chest. As AMAX invested in Mt. Emmons and elevated its presence, it seemed that money and lawyers could overrun the ragtag troops of Crested Butte.

Incrementally, AMAX engineers, accountants, attorneys, land men, researchers, land-use planners, and social consultants were mobilized to the front. Drill rigs appeared on mining claims and bored into the periphery of Mt. Emmons to ascertain the shape of the orebody. In order to map the orebody in three dimensions, geologists performed seismic testing with thumper trucks and explosives that punctuated the daylight hours with earth-shaking tremors. From core samples and seismic echoes, geologists formed a picture of the orebody and surrounding landforms, detailing an amorphous formation that seemed always to be growing larger and expanding the boundaries of the Mt. Emmons find.

By the late 1970s, AMAX had delineated a molybdenum orebody containing 155 million tons, averaging 0.44% pure molybdenum disulfide (MoS_2). By 1980, the orebody had been reassessed and enlarged to almost 300 million tons, the majority of it low grade ore. The plan of operation grew with each expansion of the deposit and soon called for combined mine and mill facilities capable of excavating and processing 25,000 tons of ore per day, or 50 million pounds a day. The ore would be drilled, blasted, loaded, conveyed, crushed, pulverized, and chemically treated. The final moly product would rise in a grey froth on huge leaching tanks to be mechanically skimmed, dried to a fine powder, sealed into steel drums, and trucked away to customers the world over.

The waste produced in the mining process, called "tailings," made up the vast majority of the material that would be taken from Mt. Emmons. Of everything that came out of the heart of Mt. Emmons, up to 99.6 percent would be in the form of a mud-like slurry that would be sluiced into a proposed tailings pond in Alkali Basin, a montane valley between Crested Butte and Gunnison, filling it 300 feet deep. In an effort to understand the scale of such an undertaking, comparisons were applied. The tailings dumps, for example, would be held in place by a plug the size of the Aswan Dam. That was hyperbole, but it suggested enormity on an unimaginable scale.

Water necessary for the mill process would come from diverting area streams, for which AMAX had applied, or purchased, water rights. High-tension power lines from distant coal-burning electric plants would power up the crushers, sorters, conveyors and other mining equipment. The expanse of infrastructure for the Mt. Emmons Project was huge, certainly the largest scale development ever seen in Gunnison County. And it would be centered on the mine site just a few miles west of Crested Butte.

Thousands of construction workers would be employed to build the project, all of whom would need housing and services. Some 350 miners and engineers would run the mine for a projected life of twenty years. An ambitious reclamation plan was promised, except for the collapsed mountainside, which would be left as a cratered "glory hole" on the face of Red Lady. The tailings would remain stabilized "in perpetuity," vowed AMAX, a pledge that drew snickers of disbelief from mine opponents for whom "perpetuity" was a gross abstraction.

AMAX projected spending hundreds of millions of dollars in development, with a total investment of $1 billion before the Mt. Emmons orebody was fully excavated. Depending on market prices, profits would be considerably greater. Some speculated the mine could produce $10 billion for AMAX. As accountants talked in the millions and billions, the economic disparity between AMAX and Crested Butte became laughable. The town's budget for 1977 totaled $590,278, and that was being drained as more and more of the town's capital reserves were expended in legal wrangling against AMAX. It began to appear financially imprudent for the town to fight a phalanx of corporate lawyers, no matter how many bake sales were held to raise defense funds and no matter how many supportive citizens showed up at rallies wearing protest t-shirts. The result for the town was a growing sense of overwhelm as AMAX pushed blithely through its project schedules with unflagging certainty while cultivating staunch pockets of support.

Sorely in need, the town council sent out pleas for help. Crested Butte began to resemble the besieged mission in "Remember the Alamo." The town defended its stance as a crusade for self-determination. An even more universal and lofty appeal was made based on stewardship of the biosphere. Ultimately, the town strove to align itself with the broadest of all ethical parameters within the tradition of American democratic principles—the autonomous right of a community to determine its own future.

In 1980, the town government mailed out a solicitation for funds, just as any non-profit might do. It was the first time in its campaign against AMAX that Crested Butte reached out beyond its borders for help. The appeal was in the form of a letter from Mayor Mitchell:

In 1977, AMAX told us there would be no mine if we didn't want one. Last year, the Crested Butte town council adopted a resolution calling for a stop to the proposed activity on the Mt. Emmons project until: 1.) real solutions to the social problems of rapid growth are found; 2.) real solutions to environmental problems are found; 3.) a real benefit to Gunnison County and the nation can be shown.

As AMAX finds more and more molybdenum, they seem to lose interest in our concerns about our home. They announce frequently that they are drilling more holes and finding more of this 'rare' substance. In fact, AMAX's competitors are also drilling numerous holes and finding even more of the 'gray gold,' which has led analysts to report a glut on the world 'moly' market. We do, in fact, believe they will not build their proposed mine.

The Town of Crested Butte has put in a good deal of time and effort, not just fighting for its own life, but fighting for others who may not have the ability to mount the battle required when outsiders neither hear nor listen to a town that says, 'No! Stop! We love our home!'

Not only are we saving our own county from becoming one of the world's newest mineral colonies, and the valleys and mountains around us from becoming the West's newest sacrifice zone, we are actually changing the way federal and state governments are looking at how we will use our diminishing resources.

We are, for the first time, raising the question: Is the public interest being served and is the public being compensated for the minerals removed from their land?

Crested Butte has vowed to determine its destiny and is mounting a very impressive effort. The town council recently passed an ordinance to protect the quality of our municipal water supply. AMAX has sued not only the town, but the members of the town council and myself, personally, contesting the validity of the watershed ordinance.

It is going to be expensive. It's tough to keep up the fight without friends like you. Your tax-deductible donation will help ensure not only Crested Butte's survival, but will enable us to share our findings for the protection of America's backyard.

12
Resistance from the Grassroots

PROTECTING AMERICA'S BACKYARD fell, in large part, to the High Country Citizens' Alliance (HCCA–hikka). Founded in 1977, initially as a single-issue, all-volunteer group of activists, HCCA's original mission was the cleanup of Coal Creek. "We were calling attention to the orange water coming out of the mine and into town," recalled Ceil Murray, who moved to Crested Butte in 1970. "We wanted to know if there was anyone who gave a damn. The response was not overwhelming."

Like many grassroots groups, HCCA was conceived around a kitchen table. That table was in Murray's house, which she shared with retired Air Force colonel Dick Wingerson and friend Susan Cottingham. They brought in their neighbors, Chuck and Jacque Malick, Cece MacVittie, and Mary Muirhead—the founding board.

HCCA sought a template from which to act on Crested Butte's behalf. The bible on community activism at that time was, *The Town that Fought to Save Itself.* Published in 1976, this inspiring book was written by journalist Orville Schell, who passionately described the plight of a small town, Bolinas, California, just north of San Francisco. The parallels between Crested Butte and Bolinas were many: Bolinas had acted to take a stand against the threat of sprawling development in the early '70s, a challenge Crested Butte was also facing. The HCCA board had contacted Schell for encouragement and support, and HCCA used the Bolinas model as an approach to stave off development in Crested Butte, even before AMAX had arrived.

The similarities between Bolinas and Crested Butte begin with their geographic isolation from the mainstream: "Our town is a dead end," wrote Schell. "The road comes out onto this small peninsula of land and ends. One must leave by the same road on which one arrives." Crested Butte was also at the end of a road, where Highway 135 dead ends at the town limits. Town planner Myles Rademan referred to Crested Butte as a cul-de-sac, especially during winter when the mountain passes beyond the town are buried deep in snow.

In his depiction of Bolinas, Schell might have been sharing an insider view of Crested Butte: "Not only was the town physically beautiful, but there was some almost indescribable quality to it which had to do with smallness of scale, familiarity among people, slowness of pace, absence of crowding. These qualities seemed to hang in the balance." In Crested Butte, the same indescribable quality now hung in the balance with the Mt. Emmons Project.

Bolinas, just 40 miles from a major metropolitan area, remained miraculously secluded and buffered: "We are not even geographically part of the continental land mass," wrote Schell, pointing out that Bolinas stands on the Pacific Plate. Crested Butte shared a similar disconnect because of its remoteness, which often had residents saying the town was not part of the "real world."

"Our town is a microcosm," concluded Schell, implying that similar grassroots struggles were springing up globally because of a rising mood of civil unrest that was spreading virally through a dissonant, youthful, energized population, a portion of which had discovered hidden, quiet enclaves and now wanted to protect them. For Bolinas, the threat was seen as morphing into a bedroom community for San Francisco. For Crested Butte, the threat was industrialization and urbanization.

"It was happening all over," observed Murray. "In Crested Butte, we decided that somebody had to do something about Coal Creek, and it might as well be us. Coal Creek was running orange. It smelled. It was horrible. We thought, if we're lucky, what we start will perpetuate itself."

And so it did. HCCA became the canary in the coal mine. But

Ed Marston, publisher of the *North Fork Times* of Paonia, at a rally in Horse Ranch Park on Kebler Pass in 1980 describes the dystopian future of industrial mining for the Elk Range. Marston went on to found and publish the *High Country News*. CRESTED BUTTE CHRONICLE ARCHIVES

instead of its clarion call being silenced by a noxious presence, HCCA's voice rose in a crescendo advocating for social and political action against the grandiose plans of AMAX. HCCA organized to provide the radical activism that was necessary to meet AMAX head-on.

"We were ahead of the game by having an organization that could actually deal with it," said Murray. "We had fifty or sixty members when AMAX announced, and we were as ready as we could be for something that large and us being so small. One of the first things we did was to buy one share of AMAX stock so we could attend their board meetings. We actually became a shareholder to keep informed. We also held local events that made members out of everyone who attended.

"Later, when we needed a steady income, we started the St. Jude's thrift store. That was Pat Dawson's idea. I owned the space for the store and donated it. It was all convenient. We were not a big organization as far as cash went, but we were big as far as energy went. You have to wake people up, and that's what HCCA did. We had a broad spectrum of talented people with no jobs and plenty of time. People worked for free."

HCCA's bylaws spoke directly to the Mt. Emmons Project: "To preserve and protect those environmental, social, and economic

Stuart Mace, the ideologue of Ashcroft, championed Crested Butte's tireless resistance to AMAX, suggesting that "biophilia"—the love of life—was the antidote to "solastalgia"—the tragic sense of loss in the face of irrevocable change to a beloved place. DAVID HISER

values essential to maintaining and enhancing the quality of life in the mountain west for ourselves and our posterity; To oppose and prevent the commercial exploitation of our natural finite public resources in ways that are likely to result in irrevocable damage to the environment."

HCCA was free to take a harder line than the Crested Butte town government could risk and still remain politically credible, so HCCA fomented a mood of rebellion through rabble rousing stunts and provocative demonstrations. Under the leadership of Chuck Malick, the soft-spoken owner of a small retail shop, Cinnamon Rainbow Leather, HCCA organized bake sales, handed out fliers, printed bumper stickers and t-shirts, circulated petitions, performed street theater, and staged political rallies. HCCA attacked AMAX on every front. And sometimes on every back, as its t-shirts were emblazoned with: NOT A TON IN '81.

The *Crested Butte Chronicle* reported:

> Unlike in Don Quixote, the AMAX windmill is no illusion, and yet the crusade spearheaded by HCCA generates an almost storybook quality among its members. Never before have most participants found themselves involved in such a righteous fervor.

13
A War of Words

EMOTIONS AND PASSIONS do not typically deter international corporations. There were legal and regulatory processes to follow. There was precedent to consider. There were appeals and motions to file. There were hearings, records of decision, and regulatory protocol. There was the technology of mining to understand and challenge.

All of this became familiar to me as a reporter because I had the responsibility to report on it accurately. So, I and many others had a crash course in mining parlance, in legalese, in processes of every kind, and especially in acronyms that were bandied about in an alphabet soup of abbreviated identities. I also became adept at spin, the art of news reporting with a bias through subtle propaganda.

HCCA and the Town of Crested Butte appealed in concert to whomever was willing to listen in the hopes that broad-based sympathy would turn the tide of public opinion with a condemnation of what AMAX intended for Crested Butte. The town took advantage of an unlikely entity—the Colorado Energy Coordinating Advisory Committee—an obscure bureau in the State of Colorado on which Mitchell cajoled a role and eagerly testified on behalf of Crested Butte in October 1980:

> The Crested Butte of today represents a mixture of values like the Rocky Mountain Biological Laboratory at Gothic, which continues research started more than 50 years ago. Scientists and students across the nation come each year to add to the most complete body of data compiled to date about the Rockies.

No area of Colorado contains more unspoiled Wilderness. Each year, hundreds of thousands of people visit the Elk Mountains, some to fish and hunt, others to enjoy winter and summer recreation, and, as the song by Tracey Wickland about the mountain by our home says, 'Some take lots of pictures and some just take their time.'

In Crested Butte, we have taken a pretty close look at how mining would affect us. The lessons we've learned are transferable to most of Colorado and the West.

Lesson #1 is the boom town syndrome that Governor Lamm has spoken of and that I and others from Gunnison County have seen firsthand. I don't know which is less pleasant—the boom or the bust—but where you have the first, the second is sure to follow. The cost to human life and psyche is high, and unlike reclaiming land, air and water, man is not so easily mended.

Lesson #2 is the intolerable changes in the physical environment, which is something none of us can or will accept.

The only way a project such as AMAX's proposal to mine Mt. Emmons can be a reality is to permit AMAX the use of thousands of acres of public land. The public receives five dollars an acre for a placer deposit for an investment estimated to be worth $8 billion. The world is turning to the mineral-rich Rockies for a solution. 'Energy junkies' will not be easy to keep at bay. It will take an alert legislature to prepare for the future and not just to apply Band-Aids later. How can the people of Colorado, with little or no planning, with little or no idea of the potential impacts, allow America's backyard to be destroyed?

Today, I'm not just speaking for the residents of my town. I'm speaking for the people of Denver and Fort Collins and Durango and Sterling. If we are warned, but do not act, if we do not plan now, if we do not work to find the alternatives for our ultimate survival, then when pictures are shown of what used to be here, the question will be rightly asked: Why was all this sacrificed? Who benefited from such a great loss?

We promise that there will be no mine at Crested Butte until the benefit is shown, not just to a group of investors in Greenwich, Connecticut, but to the people of Crested Butte, the people of Colorado, and to the people of this planet.

Mitchell took the fight to Aspen where he drew support from Pitkin County Commissioner Michael Kinsley, who helped wheel Mitchell through the Cooper Street Mall followed by a "Save the Lady" banner.
CRESTED BUTTE CHRONICLE ARCHIVES

Mitchell's rhetoric dramatized Crested Butte's defense, as AMAX expected it would. Mt. Emmons Project executives seemed to welcome the dialogue, or at least to suffer it with equanimity as enlivened, but non-threatening, intellectual gamesmanship. As the two sides squared off, words began to fly in volleys of verbiage that expanded the debate over the Mt. Emmons Project beyond a local concern to a matter of global, even universal, significance.

In an effort to find a balance with the anti-mine rhetoric of Crested Butte's two newspapers, AMAX published its own propaganda sheet and tried to downplay the town's quality of life concerns as insignificant when compared to the larger societal benefits of the proposed mine. *The Moly News* boosted the corporation's objective by identifying molybdenum as a technological boon to the world. The AMAX PR team, headed by Terry Hamlin, launched a local campaign calculated to isolate what some considered "environmental extremists" through a reasoned appeal to the more moderate mainstream of conservative Gunnison County.

The City of Gunnison, 28 miles from Crested Butte, and the county seat, had long played the ideological counterpart to its neighbor in the north. Now, Gunnison seemed primed for the AMAX pitch. However, commercial and residential development pressures in Gunnison were, in the early 1980s, becoming a concern to the city and the county, as they had a decade before in Crested Butte.

A boom in construction of homes and apartments to fill the growing needs of Western State College, plus a boom in tourist accommodations, aggregated a piecemeal wave of developments into a critical mass that threatened to stress Gunnison's rural infrastructure. This caused the Gunnison County Planning Commission to step into the fray and launch a comprehensive land use plan.

AMAX forecast a far greater magnitude of potential growth for the county than tourism did at that time as concerns about sprawling developments across historical agricultural lands became real. Rural values suddenly appeared threatened, as was the cherished ranching culture that defined Gunnison's rustic, traditional character. Community planners were forced to wrestle with a potential future land boom throughout a county that had no precedent for such growth. The Town of Crested Butte and the City of Gunnison could exert land use control only within their borders, so the need to impress upon Gunnison County a unified approach to development became paramount in what had for decades been a laissez-faire approach.

Meanwhile, AMAX became visible in local newspaper advertisements featuring photographic portraits of Crested Butte "old-timers" who gushed enthusiastic praise for the mine. These willing subjects extolled the virtues of respectable work in a mining economy and a return to "the good old days" of a "steady payroll." This appeal to the return of a traditional mining town masked the many impacts of modern industrial mining, the specter of which would eventually clash with the traditional ranching culture of the valley. Initially, however, the two seemed simpatico, with ranching and mining living harmoniously, side-by-side, as they had in the early settlement era, 80 years before.

Both print and radio advertisements magnified the minority views of mine supporters while impassioned rhetoric against the mine swelled commensurately. As AMAX impugned Crested Butte's credibility, the town demonized AMAX all the more. These back-and-forth jabs, however, were rarely personal and remarkably civil. The ensuing war of words served as a vent that had the effect of ameliorating more radically aggressive acts like monkey wrenching, vandalism or other reprisals, which were held to a minimum during this protracted and impassioned conflict.

"I thought we had a very dignified battle," said Stan Dempsey of AMAX 30 years after the fracas with Crested Butte. "I never felt personally abused. There were a few violent incidents where I called the FBI and the Department of Tobacco and Firearms, like the time our office window at the Alpineer Building was shot out on one occasion. But through it all I made a number of friends in that community that I'm still friendly with today. Hopefully, in this world, we don't have to settle our differences with violence or abusiveness."

"I lived and breathed two or three years of controversy in Minnesota," recalled AMAX's Art Biddle of the MinnAMAX project he represented, "and the opposition there was pretty sophisticated. They knew what they were doing. From the beginning in Crested Butte, I had a sense that there were some pretty sharp people living here, people from New York who were attorneys. I can't think of any time it got nasty, personally, though I'm sure it was personal for a few people. We realized that things could get hostile and nasty, where nobody was talking. We never thought that would be successful."

AMAX representatives were accorded good-natured respect in large part because of the absence of fear. No one in Crested Butte feared AMAX because the company's representatives were, after all, men, not gods. As a result, exchanges with AMAX staff were frank, up front and, in the case of dialogues with mining engineer Ralph Barnett, downright friendly. "Barney" became a barstool diplomat for AMAX, though neither he nor AMAX would have admitted it. Barnett's ease with the townspeople was an unexpected and unique example of consorting with the enemy, and his frank and honest repartee could be very disarming. More than a miner or a corporate flack, Barnett was a human being, and he was accepted as such.

Friendship was extended to Ralph Barnett in Crested Butte because of a bonhomie tradition that celebrated geniality. The town was small, familiar and intimate, with an innate sense of polite courtesy. Sure, most citizens hated the idea of a mine, but the individuals involved respected one another in the mood of good sportsmanship where a handshake and a smile were extended even to arch rivals. Civility toward combatants was an extension of small town generosity, Crested Butte-style, and Barnett helped bring that out.

The kindnesses accorded to AMAX figureheads also signaled the town's growing confidence in its moral and legal positions, and in the ultimate outcome of the fight. The town's self-righteousness promoted good will because most townspeople assumed that, in a just society, justice would prevail. For Crested Butte, acting forthrightly would lead to the right outcome, that the mine would be vanquished. Most AMAX opponents had deep-seated faith in the cause and refused to see it any other way.

When Mike Rock joined the AMAX team in 1979, to fill Terry Hamlin's shoes as he advanced within the project hierarchy, Rock—the perfect name for a mining advocate—stepped into the middle of an ideological debate that suited his temperament and intellect. Bright, professional, corporate in style and mannerisms, Rock replaced Hamlin's more down home persona with polish, wit, and managerial skill.

"I worked on the people side of the project," explained Rock from his city manager's office in Lakewood, Colorado, 30 years later. "I looked at where people would live, what the impact on the existing communities would be, how AMAX could accommodate everything from transportation to housing in a relatively small area.

"I was working for Governor Dick Lamb as the Western Slope Growth Impact Coordinator when we thought oil shale was going to be the answer to our energy concerns. I was then approached by Art Biddle, who offered me a job with AMAX. The issues were pretty similar—allocation of scarce resources, conflict resolution, balancing diverse interests with complex solutions—so it wasn't a big move for me going from government to industry."

Rock learned quickly that Crested Butte was an island of liberalism on the conservative Western Slope, and he found the debate both enlivening and frustrating. "There was a lot of rhetoric, and some of it was overblown. Sometimes there was a lack of respect between parties and a tendency for over-simplification: like all those opposed to the mine were 'trust fund hippies,' and all the miners were 'drunken spouse-beaters' who lived in trailer homes.

"I'm a strategist—I enjoy strategy; it's what I do best, trying to understand an opponent's perspective. I could articulate the legitimate concerns people had about the mine, and I could also speak to the overarching argument that resource development is a fundamental underpinning to making our economy work, and that miners can be good citizens. There was good-natured poking of fun in the parades in Crested Butte, and it sometimes got personal, but it was never too offensive for me."

Rock worked for AMAX from 1979-1983, then served as Gunnison County Manager, a job he held through 1987. That role spoke to Rock's ability to not take things personally during the mining debates, in which he methodically and in carefully measured tones promoted the Mt. Emmons Project from a countywide vantage.

Rock remained personally detached from the players most active in the mine opposition, keeping an arm's length from an emotional attachment to the attractive Crested Butte community, which seemed to effortlessly convince residents and visitors to share the town's views. Where Ralph Barnett let down his guard, Rock never did. But the powerful attractions of Crested Butte played on all who encountered them. These attractions could never be overshadowed by the Mt. Emmons Project because industrial mining could never measure up to the town's alluring, informal, organic culture.

"We got to know people in town pretty quickly," reflected Art Biddle, "and over time, some of us came to like and enjoy those people through mutual respect. For a little town, the mayor and the planning department had some sophisticated people. We could fight it out during meetings and then go out and have a beer afterwards. To be able to develop those kinds of personal relationships was unusual, and they can get you in trouble in your own company when outsiders see you getting too friendly. 'Are you really representing us the way you should with the adversary?' There wasn't always full agreement in our company about how to deal with that."

In answer to an AMAX bumper sticker, "Moly Makes Your Tool Harder," Crested Butte stamped its own brand using Climax to refer to the AMAX moly mine near Leadville. Later, when AMAX pulled out, one observer called it an "anti-Climax."

Ralph Barnett was an example of this unintended rapport. He argued his points and expressed his views at meetings and hearings. He did his work for AMAX. But when it was quitting time, Barnett's humanness surfaced. He bellied up to the bar with a broad cross-section of Crested Butte in a backslapping kind of conviviality that blurred the line of his loyalties and sympathies. The locals who drank with him felt that the town's magic was rubbing off, that it could override corporate coldness with community warmth.

"Ralph had a good sense of humor that helped on the firing line and in the company," recalled Biddle. "Down deep, he was a hard-nosed engineer who liked getting the job done. It was an unusual mix of people on both sides."

"We buried Ralph Barnett about a year ago," said Stan Dempsey in 2008. "He was a good man and a good friend."

There are many on the Crested Butte side of the battle lines who would echo Dempsey's sentiments. Barnett had become one of the guys. In a heartfelt way, he had become a "local."

14
Water Fight

WHILE THE WAR OF WORDS fired salvos of ideology and propaganda over a battlefield mined with studies, permits and processes, the real battle lay in the law. Impassioned speeches could sway the populace and occasionally the media, an elected official or a policy maker, but the real arbiters of the Mt. Emmons Project were select bureaucrats within the U.S. Forest Service permitting hierarchy who served under the auspices of the U.S. Department of Agriculture.

These bureaucratic public lands managers are swayed, not by emotions, but by studies, land use policies and legal guidelines. The issuance of mining permits is a cold, calculating process by which public lands are granted for private use, but only if the required conditions are met. The benefit of the doubt, however, usually lies with proponents for which "the land of many uses" has long been intended. Such has been the tradition ever since the "wise use" concept was advanced by Gifford Pinchot during the administration of Teddy Roosevelt.

AMAX officials knew that the law was on their side so long as they could prove that the Mt. Emmons project was economically viable, that it "penciled" in the black, that AMAX would make a profit from the extraction of molybdenum. The right-to-mine was based on the economic bottom line as prescribed by an historic and arguably archaic law from over a century and a half before: the Mining Law of 1872. That law seemed, at the time of the Mt. Emmons Project, immutable to challenge, an established institution that defined the American heritage in a land of cornucopian resources and historic land giveaways.

As a reporter trying to explain a bureaucratic morass to my readers, I felt like an interpreter translating a foreign language. Writing about the process caused me to glaze over, so it's no wonder that it caused the same for readers, despite the import. Crunching numbers was not my forte, but it was for others who pursued the viability of the mine in hard financial metrics. As the process ground on, those metrics began to reveal two opposing curves for AMAX: the price of the mine was increasing with every mitigation measure while the price of molybdenum on the international metals markets was decreasing with every new global discovery and every downturn in metals production.

Throughout the proposal stage, and long before significant development, the numbers on the Mt. Emmons Project were in constant flux. The calculus for AMAX and the regulatory agencies depended upon the potential profits of the mine as weighed against the costs of mining, milling and a growing list of expenses that would ameliorate identified "socio-economic impacts," a phrase that was bandied about like a household word, which for many of us it had become. Crested Butte's strategy, which evolved to higher and higher levels of sophistication, became clear: drive up the costs of the mine and mill by forcing the regulatory agencies, especially the U.S. Forest Service, to impose impossible or extremely costly mitigation measures.

Picturesque Coal Creek gave Crested Butte legal leverage against AMAX, while the mining company gave new life to the stream. SHUTTERSTOCK

The municipal water supply for the Town of Crested Butte was at the top of that list. Defending the town's true lifeblood fell to town attorney Wes Light, whose combative approach applied research, skill and chutzpah to spar effectively with AMAX attorneys on myriad legal positions. Despite his nickname—"Les Bright"—a friendly chide he would rue good-naturedly, Light was the shining example of a dogged lawyer. Without Light's persistent research, which he would mine from volumes of case studies with the same determination as a gold-bug prospector, the town would not have had the legal clout to hold AMAX at bay for as long as it did.

Wes Light had earned his undergraduate degree at the University of Wisconsin, after which he applied for a graduate degree from the University of Colorado Law School. He became the first recipient of an environmental law fellowship sponsored by the National Science Foundation and the Ford Foundation. With degree in hand, Light moved to Crested Butte in the early '70s for what he imagined would be an easy, peaceful lifestyle with reasonable demands on his legal career. He assumed that the town attorney job would allow plenty of time for skiing and hiking. AMAX changed all that.

As the town drew up a battle plan against the mine, Light realized that water rights would become a keystone in the town's defense. He studied water law with a passion, and his research culminated in the Crested Butte Watershed Ordinance, passed by town council in the summer of 1980. That single legislative act created a legal blockade to any degradation to the town's water supply, both in quality and quantity. If the battle with AMAX were related to a game of chess, water rights played the queen.

The town's primary water source was, and still is, Coal Creek, a small stream originating at Lake Irwin and fed by tributaries and small point sources along its stream course. Coal Creek flows below the Mt. Emmons mine site and parallels the Kebler Pass Road. A relatively small, burbling stream in summer that is capped by deep snow in winter, the creek meanders through Crested Butte between hand-built stone walls and joins the Slate River in a wetlands near the town cemetery. During peak runoff, usually the second week of June, the creek roars through town in a torrent.

In the 1970s, two events temporarily imperiled the town's water source. The first occurred when a flood of mine tailings from a failed impoundment dam at the Keystone Mine washed over the Kebler Pass Road and down into Coal Creek, forcing the town to shut down its historic water supply and build a pipeline to bypass the fouled section of the creek. This is when the town permanently moved its water intake upstream to guard against effluent from mine workings that continued to foul the lower portion of the creek until AMAX installed the Swift-Lectro Clear water treatment plant in 1980.

The second interruption of water flow to the town's taps occurred when the new pipeline froze during what locals referred to as, "The Winter of Un," in 1976-'77, when there was a dire shortage of snow. That winter, a hastily built pump house that kept the town's water flowing burned down. The water no longer moved, and without the insulation of snow, the pipe froze and became plugged with ice. Practically everyone in town rallied to disconnect the pipes and thaw them in bonfires placed strategically along the pipeline. This was perhaps the first time the town had come together with *esprit de corps* in the face of a common need.

The town's water supply became the primary beachhead of the town's resistance to AMAX, and it was fought in a series of public hearings. While public hearings are often dull and laborious, those that took place during the water issue were often filled with the excitement and drama of courtroom theater, and I was on hand for every episode. Watching the town staff stand up as equals against specialized corporate lawyers was heartening for Crested Butte citizens who recognized a David-and-Goliath scenario in every confrontation. As the town jousted successfully with AMAX on water, the townspeople were buoyed by an emergent sense of pride in the home team, the star of which was Wes Light.

The Watershed Ordinance was initially proposed in 1979, and Mitchell brandished it like a shield as he addressed a critical watershed meeting in June of that year between the town, AMAX and the U.S. Forest Service. "I am asking that AMAX stop its activities in our watershed, which have already been proven to be endangering the Town of Crested Butte," announced Mitchell with unblinking candor.

Despite his nickname—"Les Bright"— town attorney Wes Light mounted a brilliant defense for the town.
CRESTED BUTTE CHRONICLE ARCHIVES

"The unwillingness of AMAX to follow our request has already resulted in serious damage to our watershed with the recent forest fire."

Mitchell referred to a blaze that had broken out in 1979, above the Kebler Pass Road on public lands adjacent to the Keystone Mine. At an AMAX job site, a welder's spark had ignited a wildfire that scorched 55 acres of lodgepole pine forest and threatened siltation in Coal Creek due to erosion from the scorched earth. On a U.S. Forest Service tour of the fire site, as Mitchell and others surveyed the blackened trunks of burnt trees, the mayor had quipped from his wheelchair, "If this is the price for progress, we're paying too much."

Anticipating the town's new clout with its watershed, AMAX proposed alternative municipal water sources. This suggestion was brought up by the Gunnison National Forest's Taylor River District Ranger Mike Curran at the same meeting where Mitchell had issued his ultimatum. Wes Light, then acting as special attorney for the town, answered that the request was beyond the jurisdiction of the U.S. Forest Service. "That is the town's decision," he emphasized. "The U.S. Forest

Service is not in the business of making decisions for municipalities. The U.S. Forest Service is supposed to manage the existing watershed, not find alternatives." A U.S. Forest Service hydrologist in the room affirmed Light's point, saying "The Forest Service is, by law, charged with protecting water supplies."

Here was affirmation of a crucial precedent that would give the town enormous leverage and put all parties on notice. This finding gave Crested Butte a new sense of legitimacy, and it put AMAX on the defense, which was not a position this powerful corporation and its phalanx of executives and attorneys had anticipated.

Later, the U.S. Forest Service review team suggested that the Mt. Emmons Environmental Impact Statement (EIS) should include a watershed study. Crested Butte protested, stating that the study could be skewed in favor of AMAX because the mining company was, in effect, paying for the study by funding the EIS. "We should not have one of the private parties in the watershed, especially one in an adversarial position, supplying important empirical information," argued Mitchell. "The engineers that AMAX uses make me nervous. They get their livelihood from the corporation."

When a U.S. Forest Service Program Director for Watersheds continued pushing alternatives to Coal Creek, Crested Butte Town Planner Susan Cottingham (who succeeded Myles Rademan) pointed out an important linkage. She stated that Oh-Be-Joyful Creek, a tributary to the Slate River four miles north of Crested Butte, could not be considered a primary watershed alternative because it was just as vulnerable to degradation as Coal Creek. "Oh-Be-Joyful basin," explained Cottingham, "has been proposed for wilderness designation, but was recently withdrawn due to heavy lobbying by mining interests."

It was a matter of record that AMAX had exerted political influence in Washington with the U.S. Forest Service and the Department of the Interior to derail wilderness designation on lands adjacent to its mining claims on Mt. Emmons. Cottingham concluded: "We are suspicious because of that."

Mitchell added another caution when he asked how the town could count on any adjacent river course being secure with AMAX as a neighbor. "How could we be sure that AMAX wouldn't want to build a mine there?"

Wes Light added another barb. "Would AMAX support us on lobbying for wilderness in that area?" he asked, suggesting that support of wilderness protection as a lasting solution to the town's water supply would be a good faith effort by the mining company.

"Putting AMAX in charge of our watershed is like putting Dracula in charge of the blood bank," quipped Mitchell. "I want good, clean water for the town and I want it economically. We have that now, and someone is going to have to show me how we will benefit by changing our watershed."

Months later, in an October 1979 watershed meeting before the Colorado Joint Review Process (CJRP), Art Biddle attempted to do just that. Biddle again argued the AMAX line that Coal Creek was a poor choice as a watershed, this time basing his rationale on what he called "natural problems of turbidity." He charged that natural siltation in the creek degraded the town's water quality below state standards. Biddle advised the town to explore "underground water sources," implying that wells would enhance the town's water supply and reduce its dependence on turbid Coal Creek.

Biddle reasoned that since the 12,000-acre Coal Creek watershed was 44% covered by AMAX mining claims, watershed alternatives would be prudent in the likely event of future mining plans. Meanwhile, the town had directly petitioned the U.S. Department of Agriculture and Department of Interior for a withdrawal of AMAX mining claims within the town's watershed to erase that 44% of AMAX holdings. Such a withdrawal would have effectively prohibited any mining development within the watershed boundaries. In a public meeting, Biddle chastised the town for what he considered an end run by going beyond local review agencies and directly to federal agencies.

"We felt we had a right to act as quickly as possible." emphasized Wes Light, his umbrage raised. Light said that the water quality of Coal Creek was more than adequate, and he quoted a recent study by scientists from the Rocky Mountain Biological Laboratory (RMBL). "Water quality," he said, "has never been an issue in town tap water and, in accord with Forest Service regulations, the town has the legal right to condemn private property if that is the only means of protecting its watershed."

The town had gone directly to Washington, said Light, because local review agencies did not have the wherewithal to address issues as complex as watershed administration. Acting outside of local jurisdictions, he concluded, was an act of responsibility. Unilateral action was taken as a protective measure for its citizens, who have a right to clean water.

"The town went completely outside the normal procedure," charged Biddle, who went on to accuse Crested Butte of subverting the review process and overstepping its boundaries by using its watershed to influence land use rulings.

"That's false!" challenged Light. "Our position has been stated in the local newspapers, and I'm sure you've read every word of them. Your surprise is the result of your own failure to take the town's position seriously."

"All of this is taking place at the expense of Crested Butte citizens," interjected Biddle. "They are drinking dirty water just to develop more issues to slow down the process of the mine. We feel that government by ambush is being encouraged in this situation."

Light's umbrage was now in full flush as he took Biddle to task. "That is probably the most ridiculous statement I have ever heard in my life...that the town is allowing its citizens to drink dirty water to stop the mine. The suggestion is that there is chicanery going on, and that is not the case. We are only using the legal rights available to us."

District Ranger Mike Curran attempted to quell the high pitch of the debate by clarifying that Crested Butte had been above board on its watershed concerns. "The Forest Service is very much aware of what has been going on," assured Curran. "Everything the town has said is documented. I have provided Art Biddle with all the documents submitted. AMAX has been notified all along."

Stan Dempsey then went for the jugular, stating that he had just wrapped up negotiations with his company's capital expropriations committee for a $13 million good faith commitment to clean up Coal Creek with a state-of-the-art water treatment plant. However, he warned, if the watershed issue became a deal breaker for the mine, AMAX would be hard pressed to go ahead with a costly water treatment plant. Dempsey added that the only reason there would be no trout fishing in Coal Creek after the AMAX stream cleanup would be because the town diverted so much water to fill its municipal needs that stream levels were being imperiled.

Light was now seeing red. "AMAX," he seethed, "is not interested in a fishery in Coal Creek." The reason the company was installing a water treatment plant at the mine site, clarified Light, was because of litigation AMAX had assumed when it purchased the Keystone Mine. Their action, said Light, was far from benevolent; it was predicated on legal leverage.

Frustrated by what he considered the town's obdurate position against the mine, Gunnison County commissioner George Means, a rancher from White Pine, took up the AMAX mantle and agreed that Crested Butte had overstepped its bounds by appealing directly to Washington for intervention. He portrayed the town in a nefarious light for what he described as an inappropriate use of its influence and for subverting county authority. That's when Town Planner Myles Rademan, who had been sitting calmly through the proceedings, exploded.

"I have been coming to planning commission meetings since 1973 to discuss problems with our watershed," said Rademan, his voice shaking with emotion. "I don't feel that the commissioners have ever taken our concerns seriously. We have the absolute right to maintain our water quality. I have asked you to stop building roads at the Mt. Emmons Project, which are affecting our water supply, but nothing has happened. The town of Crested Butte is a large part of the county population, and it needs protection."

"And I object to your jumping to the United States government!" retorted Commissioner Means. Now his ire was up.

"Remember, George, that AMAX has Washington lobbyists," cautioned county commissioner and Crested Butte resident David Leinsdorf in a conciliatory tone that prevailed throughout the Mt Emmons Project and won him praise as a mediator. "If they want something, they don't come to us and ask permission first."

With this brief statement, Leinsdorf had captured the realities of political power, acknowledging that the Mt. Emmons Project was bigger than Gunnison County and that roles were being played on the federal level that were often invisible from the local perspective.

Crested Butte and AMAX had widened the playing field to include influence at the highest levels of government. The battlefield had elevated to the furthest reaches of power in America.

In the end, Crested Butte prevailed. The Watershed Ordinance was passed by town council in 1980, and the town dealt itself a high trump card in the gamble that mine activities would reduce municipal water quality and quantity. The town would hold AMAX to a high discharge standard. Additionally, all of the company's activities within the Coal Creek watershed would fall under the permitting jurisdiction of the town.

AMAX promptly filed a lawsuit challenging the controversial Watershed Ordinance. The suit listed individual council members and the mayor in what amounted to the strongest personal attack the company would foment against its Crested Butte opponents. The suit charged that local government had no legal right to override the federal "right-to-mine," on which AMAX staked the legitimacy of its project and the tens of millions of dollars it had already spent. That lawsuit was proof that the stakes were, indeed, very high.

During the court hearings that followed, Wes Light relied on a state statute from the 19th century that protected municipalities on watershed issues. He cited a precedent in Durango, Colorado, where a mine was shut down to protect that city's water source. Crested Butte's Watershed Ordinance was upheld in District Court.

AMAX appealed until the case was heard by the Colorado Supreme Court, which ruled in favor of Crested Butte. Not only was AMAX legally bound against degrading the town's water supply, the mining company was forced to file for a water discharge permit with the town. That permit would be issued conditionally on guarantees by AMAX that it would protect the town's water quality and quantity in perpetuity.

It is a wry truism in the West that water flows uphill to money. Crested Butte had reversed the flow by ensuring water, in quality and quantity, to its citizens. The town now basked in a victory that lit a bright light in the hearts of its cagey defenders. Keeping up this positive momentum would be a continuous challenge as even more pressing legalities surfaced.

15
The Right-to-Mine

AFTER WES LIGHT had established Crested Butte's bona fides in the watershed cases, his motivation grew stronger. He had gained credibility as a player in a big arena, and he enjoyed the role. Still, the legal deck was stacked against him with the single, most implacable, legal hurdle to Crested Butte: the Mining Law of 1872.

This federal law, which the town argued to be antiquated and obsolete, provides a major boon to mining companies engaged in large-scale land acquisitions. The Mining Law is akin to the Homestead Act, Timber Act, and Railroad Act, federal giveaways of the 19th Century that deeded enormous tracts of public lands into private hands to encourage westward expansion for any developer able to exploit public lands for a profit—and to further settlement and development of the American West.

Wes Light disparaged what he called the "right-to-mine steamroller." He challenged it through the U.S. Forest Service, under whose review and ultimate decision the Mt. Emmons Project was subject. Light suggested a litmus test for the Mining Law, with Crested Butte as a test case.

"When the process of establishing an AMAX mega-mine next door to Crested Butte began in 1977," Light explained years later, "a majority of residents sensed that such an undertaking would destroy the town and physical environment which make our businesses tick and our lives enjoyable. Common sense was enough to tell people of experience and good will that they were under attack from a proposed environmental disaster. We couldn't believe," said Light, "that a law existed that left the Forest Service no way to deny the use of the public's land for some purpose that might be destructive, unnecessary, unpopular and unwarranted. Surely, the protector of our public lands must have some mechanism to say 'no' to such a vast proposal."

In an effort to explore the right-to-mine mandate, the High Country Citizens' Alliance sponsored the Crested Butte Mining Law Conference in 1980. Lawyers attended from around the country representing conservation groups, including the Sierra Club and the National Resources Defense Council. Harvard University participated, using the conference and the Mt. Emmons Project as a legal case study. Light said the findings of the conference revealed that the right-to-mine applied to lodes and veins, but not to vast porphyritic deposits like the Mt. Emmons orebody. The Law designated only one mill site per lode and had no provisions for aggregating multiple claims as a consolidated prospect, which AMAX had done.

"We looked carefully at the reasons the Mining Law was adopted," explained Light. "We studied its intent, how it had mutated, and how the Department of the Interior had a different view of it than the Forest Service. Basically, we found that the old law was simplistic, relegated to the pick and shovel days, that it had originally been drawn up in 1866 to reward miners and prospectors in California who had helped underwrite the costs of the Civil War."

Like a vein of precious metal, the Mining Law appeared simple on the surface, but became complex the deeper one went. There were no guidelines for land exchanges, ore conveyor routes, power line corridors, tailings dams or water rights. These contemporary issues proved enormously complicated for the U.S. Forest Service to weigh against the public good, for which the Mining Law was purportedly written.

Light traveled to Washington, D.C. for meetings with then Interior Secretary Cecil Andrus and members of the Jimmy Carter Administration, appealing for a favorable interpretation of the law that would favor Crested Butte and the protection of small town autonomy. "We challenged the right-to-mine wherever we could," said Light.

Still, the U.S. Forest Service claimed that its hands were tied: If AMAX could prove it had an economically viable project on Mt.

Emmons, it had the "right-to-mine." The caveat was that AMAX would be forced to mitigate whatever negative impacts, on- or off-site, occurred during the mining process. Here was another toe hold on which Crested Butte would mount its defense against the mine.

The town claimed that AMAX should be responsible for mining impacts on roads, air quality, housing, wildlife habitat, schools, police and hospitals. If those corrective costs exceeded the value of the orebody, then the project would not be economically viable, and the Mining Law would not apply. If that cost/benefit ratio could be proven not to pencil in the black for the Mt. Emmons Project, then the legal framework of the Mining Law would work for the town, not against it.

By raising the bar for mitigation, said Light, Crested Butte and Gunnison County could force the project into bankruptcy before it even got started. Since the U.S. Forest Service was mandated to safeguard local communities, the bar for mitigation went up to an all-time high. Serendipitously for the town, as mitigation measures mounted, and the cost of building and operating the mine also soared, there occurred a gradual drop in molybdenum prices throughout world markets. Though legal precedent assured AMAX the "right-to-mine," escalating mitigation costs would reduce its viability under the sway of collapsing metals markets.

Facilitating Crested Butte and Gunnison County in their collective efforts to assess the costs of mining, the State of Colorado enacted a novel review mechanism early on in the Mt. Emmons Project. The Colorado Joint Review Process (CJRP), launched in 1978, was a new multi-agency forum providing a larger sounding board on which to weigh the cost/benefit equation of the Mt. Emmons Project, while providing greater review oversight and evaluative resources.

"The Mt Emmons Project was our first effort, our maiden voyage," explained Harris Sherman in a 2012 interview when Sherman was Undersecretary for Natural Resources and Environment at the U.S. Department of Agriculture in Washington, D.C. At the time of the contest with AMAX, he headed the Colorado Department of Natural Resources.

"It was a project ahead of its time," recalled Sherman. "It was novel. It was the first large scale effort taken by state and federal governments to coordinate a large-scale natural resource project. The goal was to find a clear path for a variety of review steps. We wanted to have a better way to involve the public at an earlier point than had been typical with such projects. The stakeholders came to the table early on rather than typically at the EIS stage. It was a healthy step in educating the public."

The CJRP evaluated how an Environmental Assessment (EA) could be most beneficial, how an Environmental Impact Statement (EIS), a far more detailed study, should proceed, and how permitting reviews could go on simultaneously rather than sequentially. "This was the first time we focused on a more coordinated approach," reflected Sherman. "It wasn't perfect, but it was helpful. We were able to raise issues that would have gone unnoticed otherwise."

Looking back on the Mt. Emmons Project, Sherman saw it as a supreme regulatory challenge. "You had a high quality recreation-based community that was very intent on protecting its quality of life, and you had one of the most sophisticated mining companies in the world focused on a world class molybdenum deposit. You had local and state governments that were trying to reach out and find a way of reconciling these vastly different interests. It was an unusual project in that sense. There was also an interesting cast of characters, locally and nationally. My recollection was that all these parties, notwithstanding their differences, made a good faith effort to try an entirely new process of environmental permitting review that had never been done in this country before. There was a certain amount of good will between these parties."

Sherman marveled at the convivial nature of the participants in the CJRP as described in one stand-out evening of Crested Butte-style diplomacy. "I remember when David Leinsdorf, the Chairman of the Board of County Commissioners, hosted a dinner at his home where he personally cooked a Chinese meal for all the stakeholders. I was amazed he had the talent and ability to become a Chinese chef and bring all those people together in one evening."

David Leinsdorf was a global sophisticate whose Austrian father was the renowned maestro, Erich Leinsdorf, of classical music fame. David Leinsdorf's gourmet Chinese dinner typified his role as medi-

Dick Wingerson, a retired Air Force colonel and founding board member of the High Country Citizens' Alliance, points out to US Senator Floyd Haskell the path of destruction AMAX would cut for a powerline corridor through Horse Ranch Park. CRESTED BUTTE CHRONICLE ARCHIVES

ator. He brought together in his modest apartment the AMAX team and members of the CJRP. Included were county commissioner Rocky Warren and County Manager Dorothy Johnson. AMAX was represented by Mike Rock, Art Biddle, Ralph Barnett and Gunnison attorney Dick Bratton. "I just thought it made sense to get adversaries and decision makers together in a social setting," said Leinsdorf. "That was my thing at the time: I did a lot of Chinese cooking. There were no focused conversations. We drank and talked and had a party. It was about opening lines of communication."

Seeking a compromise to the Mount Emmons Project, Leinsdorf advanced a "small mine" alternative. "It seemed to me that a small mine would be more in keeping with the history of Crested Butte," said Leinsdorf in retrospect, "that it would have been an industrial mining facility more compatible with the tourist economy, that wouldn't have overwhelmed the town the way a big mine would have. I was meeting with a group of people in Gunnison who thought a small mine was a viable compromise."

While Leinsdorf opened new channels of communication, Harvard University took up a scholarly study of the social, economic, and environmental regulatory processes being advanced in Crested

Butte. A team of Harvard law students was assigned to Crested Butte to study the Mt. Emmons Project as it unfolded. These young collegians, along with their professor, Dr. Carl Steinitz, were soon swept up in the emotional appeal of Crested Butte's defense.

Steinitz was quoted in the *Crested Butte Chronicle* as describing the greater Gunnison Valley as an integrated whole. He said there was no way to separate what is done in the upper part of the valley from what happens in the lower part, that the two are inextricably linked. "You don't have to accept a degradation in the quality of life here," concluded Steinitz in his summary. "The citizens have a chance of winning between corporate profits and public disaster."

Winning against corporate profits in Crested Butte now elevated to an exercise in faith, and it fostered a religious approach against the mine led by a group of anti-mine zealots who invoked the Quaker tradition. Wes Light, in his search through the antiquities of federal land grants, had discovered a little known phrase in the National Forest Organic Act of 1897, stating: "Settlers may use land within the national forests for schools and churches."

Light reasoned that if the 1872 Mining Law applied to miners, then a church claim for religious purposes on National Forest Service land should have similar clout. The Rocky Mountain Biological Laboratory (RMBL) in Gothic had its origins with founders from Swarthmore College, which was formed by Quakers in the 19th century, so it wasn't difficult to find Quaker adherents in the scientific ranks of RMBL. Some of them had already combined with another Quaker group in Paonia, a farming, ranching and coal mining town 40 miles west of Crested Butte. Together, they formed the nucleus of a Quaker "Meeting," which elected to file a church claim in Alkali Basin, on the flank of a proposed AMAX tailings impoundment site.

Alkali Basin, a sage-covered depression between Flattop and Red Mountain, 10 miles south of Crested Butte, had two access routes. The primary road came up a draw from Highway 135. This route had been gated by Spann Ranches, a Gunnison cattle ranching family that held grazing leases there. The only vehicles they allowed to pass their gate belonged to AMAX survey crews, so there was little doubt about the Spann's sentiments regarding the proposed mine. The Quaker

Meeting group opted not to challenge that access, but rather to come in from the west, on a rugged four-wheel-drive, two-track road from Ohio Creek that had no closure.

An initial Meeting, or service, was announced in the summer of 1981 to assert the Quaker claim. It was sparsely attended, but the following was fervent. As the "faithful" were performing absolutions in Alkaki Basin, registered surveyor, Will Reid, a Quaker who owned the Elk Mountain Lodge in Crested Butte, methodically staked a five-acre church claim. It all seemed too simple, too easy. Buoyed by the success of its inaugural visit to Alkali, the Meeting was reconvened the following Sunday, but not via the rough and rocky road to salvation from Ohio Creek.

Imbued with righteous zeal from the spirit of their new calling, the Quaker votaries decided to notify rancher Lee Spann that they would be coming in the following Sunday to conduct their Meeting over the much easier route up his gated road. At the appointed hour, cars and pickups loaded with the devout, plus a journalist or two, drove up to a knot of ranchers standing with the Gunnison County sheriff at the closed gate.

The *Crested Butte Chronicle* reported: "Most of us were there out of curiosity over the stance taken by this unpresupposing [sic] religious group, and by curiosity just to see this disputed piece of earth that was threatened to be submerged by mining excreta. Guarding the gate were three men—Lee Spann, the County Marshal, and George Volk—presenting as defiant a pose as their crossed arms and, in one case, holstered gun, could convey."

Don Bachman was among the Quaker throng, and recalled the scene: "After the requisite scuffing and spitting and awkward but cordial conversation, we were turned back. Subsequently, we met that day up the Taylor. I believe some came in on the dreaded road from the west one more time that summer, but we had made our point and got some press. I believe the claim was actually filed in the courthouse, and some of us agnostics damn near got converted."

The church claim had creative merit, but it was never taken seriously, though there was talk of seeking divine intervention. The fervor in Crested Butte had taken on quasi-religious overtones for what many felt was a spiritual crusade. Moods were lifted to a fevered pitch as the town seemed to be gaining ground on the industrial giant. Even if both sides were stalemated, the pleasure many derived from "sticking it to AMAX" became a potent dynamic for community solidarity. Fighting an external threat had unified and empowered a citizenry that had never considered itself capable of steeling itself for a long-term fight with an intractable foe.

Still, opponents to the mine understood that mitigation remained the only reasonable recourse for ameliorating industrial impacts in the East River Valley and beyond. The rapid population boom of thousands of construction workers forecast for the proposed mine became a key impact. An enormous, itinerant mining work force was perceived as a threat to limited community services and governmental infrastructure. Historically, in fast-growing boom towns, taxation rarely caught up to the costs of social needs. Raising local taxes to pay the spin-off costs of a corporate incursion would spell disaster for those on fixed incomes— the poor and senior citizens—of which Crested Butte and Gunnison had many.

According to sociological studies included in the EIS research, small, intimate communities like Crested Butte and Gunnison thrive

The Crested Butte Quaker contingent had a boot-scuffing standoff with the sheriff at the entrance to Alkali Creek that ended in at least one religious conversion. CRESTED BUTTE CHRONICLE ARCHIVES

only on a delicate social balance that evolves over time, a balance dependent upon the stability of gradual change. The explosive growth that AMAX portended would quickly alter the stability of these communities, both of which had assimilated values and identities over nearly a century of formative influences. The challenge of mitigating intangible social values came from the intuitive knowing that the AMAX mine would forever change something that resisted definition and could not be replicated. Mitigation could not remedy the irrevocable damage done to a spontaneous and profoundly vital sense of community. Once that natural ambiance was lost, there were no instructions on how to reinvent it.

Defending Crested Butte from AMAX, the town had adopted defensive tactics appropriate to a community under siege. That stance changed nearly four years after the AMAX announcement of 1977, when the town chose to formalize its stance against the mine in a full frontal offensive against its adversary. Maintaining political neutrality in order to remain a viable player in the first years of the review proceedings was prudent. Crested Butte town council waited until 1980 to officially declare war, when its position was solid and community support was assured.

The High Country Citizens' Alliance, meanwhile, had taken the activist role with radical undertones by orchestrating formal challenges, filing legal appeals, and taking a hard line in its media outreach. The town and HCCA were clearly in collaboration, but that was kept under wraps until a decisive public meeting was held at the Crested Butte School in 1980, when the town's planning department strongly recommended that the town council vote against the mine. The council did just that, voting unanimously to become an overt adversary to AMAX.

When the unanimous vote was cast, cheering and applause filled the room. In the spirited moment immediately following this landmark vote, councilmember Claudia Richards dramatically tore off her blouse, revealing a HCCA t-shirt reading, "NOT A TON IN '81." More cheers erupted as a rebellious mood swept through town. From that day forward, Crested Butte would no longer conform by probity to the niceties of political correctness. The gloves were off against an avowed evil. The good fight was on.

16
'The Best Mine in the World'

A T THE ONSET, AMAX made a sincere overture to Crested Butte: We will build you the best mine in the world, a state-of-the-art molybdenum producer that will represent "a new generation of mines." That pledge was echoed throughout the Colorado Joint Review Process as a recurrent theme. It was embraced by the U.S. Forest Service, the Department of the Interior and the Mined Land Reclamation Board, all of which aligned in making the Mt. Emmons Project a source of pride and innovation through novel processes that stretched the oversight of governing bureaucracies and enlarged the responsibilities of the permittee. For many of those involved on both sides, the Mt. Emmons Project became an innovative career opportunity.

AMAX had achieved this mark of excellence once before in a project for which the corporation was castigated by its mining competitors because it had willingly upped the ante in reclamation and environmental controls, all of which translated to higher costs of production. AMAX now took a leadership dare in Crested Butte by pledging to go where no mining company had gone before. In its way, Crested Butte had already succeeded in elevating the obligations of extractive industries.

What does the best mine in the world look like? For AMAX, it looked like their Henderson Mine, billed as an outstanding environmental achievement and the role model for Crested Butte. At Henderson, new ground had been broken a decade before Mt. Emmons came on line, when AMAX fashioned an unlikely partnership with local, regional and national environmental groups. The instigator of that landmark collaboration was Stan Dempsey, Senior Vice President of AMAX, a recognized industry environmental reformer who now assumed that role with the Mt. Emmons Project.

"I was probably the first VP of Environmental Affairs in the whole mining industry," said Dempsey in a 2008 interview. "That made sense because AMAX pioneered more emphasis on environment than most other companies, which was a difficult transition for a mining company. At Henderson, I got the environmental interests together because I knew that the Henderson mine would require doing something different than the way things were done in the past. We put together five former chapter presidents of the Sierra Club and five people from AMAX who set up an advisory experiment called, 'Experiment in Ecology'. It was very successful."

According to Robert Cahn's 1978 book *Footprints on the Planet*, Dempsey took quite a risk at the Henderson Mine:

> This unique effort had grown out of a chance meeting one blustery winter evening in 1967. Stanley Dempsey and Roger Hansen arrive simultaneously outside a locked gate in Denver to attend a meeting both thought was scheduled for that night. They went to a nearby tavern to phone and found that their meeting was not until the following week, so they sat down for a beer.
>
> They discovered immediately a shared interest in hiking and the outdoors, and both were lawyers. But Dempsey worked for AMAX, considered an enemy of the environment. Hansen was executive secretary of the Colorado Open Space Council and had helped to lead several successful fights to preserve Colorado's scenic areas from developers such as AMAX.
>
> As they talked and sipped their beer, Dempsey decided to go out on a limb and broach to Hansen an idea that had been in the back of his mind for a long time. "Roger, what if a major mining company came to you and said: 'We have found a big ore deposit in a scenic mountain area. If we are willing to do completely open planning with some responsible environmentalists, would the environmental community be willing to make constructive suggestions, or would they jump on it and try to kill it?'
>
> Dempsey was treading on very risky ground. Details of the company's plans were a closely held secret, and he had not cleared

his idea with the top brass. He chose his words carefully. "Could a team of company people and environmentalists possibly work together to develop a major mine on the soundest possible environmental basis?'

Roger Hansen was quiet for a moment, thinking about the hazards involved in cooperating with a mining company. He could expect accusations of 'sellout', or worse, from environmental colleagues. But the idea was intriguing. 'I don't know. Maybe,' Hansen finally answered. 'It might be possible. Tell me a little more.'

Dempsey revealed to Hansen that AMAX had discovered a huge molybdenum deposit on the east side of the Rockies, within the Arapaho National Forest. He suggested that it might be even larger than the company's flagship Climax mine, the huge deep-pit scar on the Western Slope of Colorado, ringed with tailings ponds. The Climax mine, however, was not the poster child to trot before a conservationist—or was it? Cahn described how Dempsey's gamble paid off as Hansen signed on to his proposal.

> The Climax operation was a constant reminder to the company of an era when mines were operated without concern for the pollution they caused or the lands they despoiled. *Times* had changed, though, and now Dempsey wanted to bring in environmental considerations at the concept stage, nine or ten years before mining operations would begin, and make the Henderson mine a model of environmentally sound planning.
>
> The 'Experiment in Ecology' would bring consensus to an otherwise hostile tradition. These two ordinarily opposing groups were pooling their knowledge to come up with methods of mining and ore processing that would do minimal harm to the forests, streams and wildlife of this scenic area straddling the Continental Divide 40 miles west of Denver.

Rather than fighting a pitched environmental battle, Dempsey had negotiated an enduring peace. Instead of acrimony, he nurtured harmony and trust. Dempsey said he wanted to avoid the waste of time it would take "slugging it out" with opponents. To Dempsey, the agreement with Hansen was clearly a matter of expedience, of building a mine with the least expenditure of resources, as Cahn explained.

When working with AMAX managers and engineers, Dempsey does not talk about saving the environment just for the environment's sake. He seeks rather to frame the problems and solutions in terms of cost effectiveness. He tries to show the manager how the environmentally correct way will pay off in the long run even if it costs more in the immediate time frame. Dempsey's chief argument is that doing the right kind of environmental homework can prevent years of costly delay.

Years later, Dempsey described Henderson as "a done deal" that was simple by comparison to Crested Butte. There was no nearby town with a promising and potentially conflicting recreation-based economy, so a huge potential obstacle was removed from the Henderson equation. The environmental impacts at Henderson were mostly groundwater issues, not intractable socio-economic upheavals. At Henderson, environmentalists had little choice but to cooperate with AMAX because the corporation had already successfully acquired the necessary permits. That meant that the mine was accepted as a fact, not a theory. Conversely, in Crested Butte, opposition coalesced almost immediately because, from the beginning, there was no acceptance of AMAX, which had the entire permit process to wade through. Despite Dempsey's impressive track record at Henderson, the Mt. Emmons Project was no slam dunk.

Still, Dempsey was confident that he could engage Crested Butte as he had engaged the opposition at Henderson, whom he had won over through the rational argument that compromise would provide mutual benefits and create ultimate acceptance of the mine. "Working with ecologists and environmentalists has made our engineers and our management more sensitive to their interests," Dempsey is quoted in Cahn's book. "And I think that the environmentalists, by working with our people, have found that some of their own ideas were not practical."

Dempsey held out hope for a methodical approach to convincing Crested Butte of the wisdom in moving toward acceptance, cooperation and practicality. So did Art Biddle. He had made strides similar to Dempsey's when AMAX encountered environmental challenges at the MinnAmax Project in northern Minnesota, near the Boundary

Waters Wilderness Area, several years before the Mt. Emmons Project. Like Dempsey at Henderson, Biddle's challenges at MinnAmax were mostly environmental, not socio-economic.

"Community relations were not quite as significant there because there was already extensive mining in the Iron Range," explained Biddle. "Still, we were the camel's nose under the tent, and there were twenty-five environmental groups aligned to fight the project. We prevailed in winning approvals for a small test shaft. That took a couple of years to get through the permitting process, and we worked real hard with the Sierra Club. Our goal was to do it right."

Every project is unique, so when the AMAX team approached Crested Butte, it was with strong environmental credentials represented by Dempsey and Biddle. Crested Butte, however, was not about to move into a Zen-like acceptance of the "practicality" AMAX put before the town. Crested Butte successfully and forcefully expanded the mining issue to socio-economic impacts and mitigations on which Dempsey and Biddle were as yet unproven. Having found AMAX's Achilles's heel, it was on this front that the town waged a tireless campaign.

"I wasn't surprised," said Dempsey of Crested Butte's anti-mine stance. "That's a first knee-jerk reaction anywhere. You could have that happen in Cleveland. I was hoping it would be more like Henderson, so I was disappointed when it wasn't. But we were not surprised."

Biddle thought Crested Butte missed an opportunity to make history with AMAX, which he characterized as a forward-thinking, progressive mining company striving for a high measure of social and environmental responsibility. Working with AMAX would not only have been expedient for Crested Butte, it would have stepped up industry standards. To Biddle, social and environmental impasses were not deal-breakers; they could be resolved through the Joint Review Process (JRP) and safeguarded by a scrupulous mitigation plan. Biddle believed that Crested Butte's future lay in paving the way toward a "new generation of mines" in which AMAX and the larger Gunnison community would have been co-leaders.

"Recognizing that mining companies usually come in with a black hat, we were trying to change that color," explained Biddle. "The

Billows of smoke on Mt. Emmons came from a fire at the AMAX mine site and gave the town an early premonition of a pending environmental disaster.

CRESTED BUTTE CHRONICLE ARCHIVES

bottom line was to do the right thing, and AMAX was pretty advanced in this area, compared to most mining companies. A lot of that had to do with Stan Dempsey's leadership and with the 'Experiment in Ecology.'

"I'm a Colorado native," pointed out Biddle, "and it seems like mines in this state tend to be in the more scenic places. This country runs on minerals and development, and there's got to be some way to do it right. The JRP was a model of public/private planning that was supposed to be a tool for oil shale development. We worked long and hard on that process with the Mt. Emmons Project, and it motivated local and regional governmental people to see the value of that process. We got some awards for that. It challenged everybody. It was, like: the train is rolling, so you'd better get on board and participate."

Crested Butte was on a different track altogether, which AMAX executives seemed unwilling to acknowledge. Cooperating with big business was contrary to the town's core values. Crested Butte was new to the overtures of an international mining company, and so was the mining company new to the deeply entrenched values of a small mountain town. What AMAX considered rationally practical, Crested

Butte considered irrationally impractical. The two entities appeared to be intractably antithetical. Crested Butte was intent on derailing the AMAX train even before it left the station.

"If you're a purebred environmentalist who wants everything pristine and undeveloped, Crested Butte was a place to take that position," allowed Biddle. "Crested Butte was a ski area, an historic town, a beautiful spot. I don't think it was irrational to think there shouldn't be as big a mine, or no mine at all. You have to respect that position. But our goal was to move beyond that to do the best job of planning and to minimize the impacts from the environmental and growth and population standpoints. We would try to make people prepared so there wouldn't be a boomtown with problems. We wanted to solve the groundwater issue, and we started on that with Coal Creek. Having a polluted stream running through town, people could point to what they were going to get with a big mine. Eventually, as the process moved on, we had to look at a smaller mine option."

To most citizens of Crested Butte, the AMAX pledge to develop a mine with sensitivity was an oxymoron. There was no appropriate way to extract millions of tons of molybdenum ore from Mt. Emmons, process it, mill it, and dump the waste. This is where a huge gulf of perspective loomed. AMAX sincerely wanted the town to work with it to prove that a modern mine could protect wild nature and delicate social values. Such was Dempsey's appeal.

"You don't have to destroy everything to get moly," he reasoned. "I've worked on many reclamation techniques, and I'm still not satisfied that the industry has reached its full potential in developing those techniques. There's more we could do. But if everyone worked together, with the premise that the mine will be built, like at Henderson, where the environmental community willingly helped us, it can be done without destroying everything. Henderson is a good example that it can work. But as long as people have power to stop it, they will."

Dempsey appreciated the tenacity of his environmental opponents, and he was also aware that these ranks were growing. Crested Butte became a focal point for thwarting future mining proposals everywhere, just as it could have become a focal point for mining solutions anywhere. All things are susceptible to trends, as Dempsey opined years after his retreat from the Mt. Emmons Project.

"I had the benefit of perspective from having worked in places all over the world with moly and aluminum. I went through thirty of these kinds of battles. Being both a lawyer and a mining guy, I was very involved in the institutional frameworks we developed. In the thirty years I was involved, I observed that the power of the environmental community has expanded enormously. But the resource demands will be so great in the future that there will be a balance of power between development and environment."

AMAX had tipped that balance of power before. In Catlin, Illinois, residents objected to an AMAX coal strip mine proposed in 1974, because they said it threatened productive farmland. "Nowhere has it ever been proved to us or anyone else that you can restore farmland like this to its original productivity," Catlin Mayor Terry Dolan was quoted in Cahn's book. "We're not environmental radicals here, but AMAX has taken the basic attitude that they will do what the state law requires, and nothing more. And that is not satisfactory. A poll shows that 96 percent of the people oppose the AMAX project. But they have gone right on."

In 1975, AMAX Coal applied for a permit to strip mine 20,000 acres on the Cumberland Plateau in East Tennessee. The plan met with opposition from "Save Our Cumberland Mountains" (SOCM), a group formed in 1972, to challenge coal strip mining. Over time, SOCM expanded beyond the original five counties it defended and reached onto the Cumberland Plateau to fight the AMAX permit. On the plateau, SOCM discovered the widespread separation of surface and mineral rights where surface owners had few or no rights over mineral extraction on their lands. At one community meeting, SOCM packed a schoolhouse for a show-and-tell on strip mining in Catlin, Illinois, which had been fighting AMAX for three years. Because of concerted opposition from local and state entities in Tennessee, AMAX left the state in 1977. Another AMAX property, the Delta Strip Mine in Saline County, Illinois, one of the largest strip mines in the region, shut down in the mid-1990s because it couldn't operate under the passage of the Clean Air Act Amendment of 1990.

AMAX defended another of its beachheads, a copper mine in Puerto Rico, where environmentalists challenged the company on the impacts of copper production. The head of mining operations for AMAX there refuted what he called "wild statements." He argued, "We can talk for six hours about copper's effect on the environment. The effect of copper is actually minimal."

Opponents also questioned whether Puerto Rico would receive economic benefits from copper mining. They pointed to the controversial AMAX-owned Tsumeb copper mine in Namibia, where, between 1967 and 1975, the company reportedly made profits of $38 million from an original investment of $1.11 million (source: The People's Grand Jury). The Tsumeb mine and a Cheyenne coal mine, also owned by AMAX, were the subjects of a report published in 1977, titled, "The AMAX War Against Humanity: A Case Study of the Multinational Corporation's Robbery of Namibian Copper and Cheyenne Coal."

Published by an activist organization called, The People's Grand Jury of Washington, D.C., the study issued an indictment against AMAX for what it called industrial imperialism. The corporation was charged with "insidious parallel activities in Namibia and the Northern Cheyenne territories" where it exploited natural and human resources with little financial reward for the native peoples and disregard for environmental impacts.

The People's Grand Jury claimed that AMAX was part of an overbearing economic structure of international reach. As a typical international corporation, it had no loyalty to anyone or anything other than to promoting its own bottom line. "Western society has created the multinational corporation as a means of maintaining domination of the world economy by the wealthy nations by insuring a constant finance-capital flow to those nations," read the conspiracy-laced charges. "AMAX's board of directors is a typical slice of America's ruling class. They are all white, exclusively male, wealthy and privileged, and earnestly seeking to maximize profits while enlarging their control over the economic, political, and social affairs of society."

The 1970s was a contentious decade for AMAX as it expanded and diversified. AMAX partnered with Japan's Mitsui Company in the mid-'70s to build an aluminum smelter. Called the Alumax Pacific

Corporation, the project was targeted for Astoria, Oregon. Environmentalists and the Oregon Environmental Quality Commission were opposed because of concerns about the unavoidable fluoride emissions from an aluminum smelter and the potential for pollution in Youngs Bay Estuary adjacent to the proposed smelter site. Alumax withdrew and decided instead to build the $300 million plant in Umatilla County in eastern Oregon where there was apparently less opposition.

In 1980, according to "Rethinking Resource Management: Justice, Sustainability and Indigenous Peoples," a study by Richard Howitt, AMAX experienced another setback when it retreated from exploration and development of oil and gas resources in Australia. A conflict with Aboriginal natives and their supporters occurred on a drill site at a place called Noonkanbah. Protests were staged and confrontations with police occurred. These hostilities forced AMAX to pull back and revise its strategies by refocusing its interests in the U.S. The eviction of AMAX was called "a sign of the times" as Aboriginal rights triumphed over "industrial imperialism."

"To some extent," mused Dempsey in retrospect, "the people in Crested Butte were conceited to think they were the only ones fighting us. It was colorful, and it made a hell of good story, but there were a couple of places where the people actually beat us. Still, I'm fond of the memories. It was like a chess game."

Where AMAX had deftly played the game elsewhere, Dempsey's attempted checkmate failed in Crested Butte. Still, he pointed to *Footprints on the Planet* as a testament to the success of his vision as it played out at the Henderson Mine. Cahn's portrayal of Dempsey is a favorable example of what a mining professional could achieve with good faith by addressing environmental concerns. Cahn, however, set a cautionary tone. His book's forward, written by Jacques-Yves Cousteau, was a call to arms for civic engagement in resource issues:

> For short-term conveniences, we are taking away from future generations the vital options they would need to exercise in order to survive decently. But there is hope at the horizon: If yesterday, such blind behavior of the decision-makers was not even discussed, today, on the contrary, public opinion is awakening and irresponsible decisions are openly challenged.

The 'Glory Hole" of the Climax Mine nead Leadville is what AMAX wanted to lay at Crested Butte's doorstep. DAVID HISER

The Henderson Mine was challenged, and Stan Dempsey rose to that challenge with a bold, new environmental initiative that brought critics into the fold and empowered them within a novel, inclusive process. Still, large scale, industrial mining leaves "footprints on the planet." No matter how sensitive are the miners, no matter how embracing are the collaborations, there are costs, as Cahn concluded.

> Dempsey feels the Experiment in Ecology at the Henderson mine cannot be repeated in all situations. But he believes a number of general lessons learned from it can be applied in other cases: 'The first thing is that people in the mining business have to admit that any sizeable operation is going to cause change in the area—it can't be the same as before. Next, any industry should try to identify citizen groups that can assist in the design of the property to minimize this impact.'

Buoyed by Dempsey's spirit of cooperation at Henderson, AMAX sought consensus rather than conflict in its initial dealings with Crested Butte and Gunnison County. This led to an ambitious campaign to introduce potential adversaries to all aspects of the mining process—to give the decision makers an insider's view. Rather than positively influencing public opinion, however, the campaign produced a very contrary result that became another nail in the AMAX coffin.

17
The Belly of the Beast

SEVERAL YEARS into the Mt. Emmons Project, AMAX had made no real progress in breaking the logjam of local opposition that was spreading from Crested Butte into Gunnison County. Relations with the community appeared to be at a stalemate. AMAX had won converts, but had not aligned a critical mass to its cause.

While AMAX launched PR campaigns countywide, Crested Butte stuck closer to home. The town had not actively sought a larger base of support in the county because the more conservative elements there either favored the mine, seemed ambivalent about the impacts, or felt alienated from Crested Butte's alternative lifestyle and therefore marginalized the town's stance. For many Gunnison retailers and ranchers, there was no love lost for the hippie contingent they associated with Crested Butte. Geographical distance also played a role. Gunnison County spans 3,260 square miles and covers many drainages where scattered neighborhoods were far removed from Crested Butte and AMAX. Mt. Emmons is a long way from W Mountain, and the further away people lived, the less invasive and threatening the mine seemed.

In what AMAX senior vice president Stan Dempsey had termed a chess game, the corporation made a daring move that was characteristic of Dempsey's risk-taking calculus. This gambit, while well-reasoned to the industrial mindset, failed to win adherents, and instead galvanized opposition to the mine throughout the greater Gunnison Valley. A more dire miscalculation could not have been made as

AMAX blithely moved itself into checkmate, at least where community relations were concerned.

In January 1980, in an overture to allay the community's fears of a mine, AMAX invited representatives from Crested Butte, the City of Gunnison and Gunnison County on what became known as the "Boom Town Tour." In an effort to show local decision makers that they and their constituents could live and prosper with a mine in their backyards, AMAX orchestrated a tour for 30 guests who would visit "model mining communities" in Craig, Colorado and Rock Springs, Gillette, and Wright City, Wyoming, towns whose economies and social structures originated in rural ranching and agriculture, but now revolved around coal strip-mining and coal-fired power plants.

Preliminary to the Boom Town Tour, a select group of local elected officials and government administrators had been hosted on a pilgrimage to the polished side of AMAX with a whirlwind visit to corporate headquarters in Greenwich, Connecticut. Sparkling offices, impeccably attired executives, and an urbane sense of institutional prestige and stature had been communicated on that trip a year before. Now AMAX would show the nuts and bolts of mining by exhibiting real mining communities. AMAX would unveil a vision of how Crested Butte and Gunnison County might look with a molybdenum mine overlay.

As one of the local journalists included on the junket, I filed a series of articles for the *Gunnison Country Times* describing the conditions witnessed in these modern industrial centers. Surprisingly, AMAX had underestimated the fearful message resulting from the tour as participants recognized the real plight of these once quiet, rural communities. Mining and power plants had not delivered a boon of glad tidings; just the opposite. Crime, drugs, alcohol abuse and domestic violence overwhelmed municipal services and brought on traffic congestion, crowded schools, noise, pollution and community disintegration; these were the issues described by grim-faced local sheriffs, teachers, doctors, reporters, and town administrators.

A somber tone of dystopian gloom was conveyed when the Boom Town Tour met with Arnold Evans, Sheriff of Wheatland, Wyoming, home of a coal strip-mine. This soft-spoken country sheriff appeared

The author at work: Public hearings can be long and tedious, but during the AMAX fight they were rife with drama as the town's case against the mine became more and more promising. CRESTED BUTTE CHRONICLE ARCHIVES

apologetic and uncomfortable as he stood before his intent visitors in a motel conference room and described an incident on a recent Saturday night when a deputy received a call about disturbance at a local bar: "There was a wildcat strike by construction workers, and that prompted a parking lot brawl that involved about a hundred construction workers. We've got fourteen cops, and ten of us showed up, including myself. All we could do was watch and wait. It was terrifying," confessed the Sheriff. "It made us all reconsider our jobs and what our community had become."

The sheriff's grim demeanor mirrored George Bailey, the character Jimmy Stewart portrayed in *It's a Wonderful Life*, the Frank Capra film that depicts the moral collapse of a small town. Sheriff Evans gave such a portrayal as he explained how the boom town cycle had spun out of control, bringing on dramatic increases in armed robberies, prostitution, drug abuse, child abuse and suicide. As the police department had to focus on increasing emergencies, other services were dropped, like checking on vacation homes or writing minor traffic violations. "I wish you guys better luck than we've had," concluded the taciturn sheriff, adding that the flight of long-time residents, as a result of the new industries, had left a noticeable void in his community.

The AMAX representatives with us on the tour appeared blindsided. They blanched at the sheriff's disclosures, but it was too late to change the play. The sheriff's sobering confessions had driven the message home. Company towns appeared to be thriving with growth, development, regular payrolls and hard-working people, but at a huge cost to community. The Boom Town Tour revealed an underbelly of decadence that had poisoned the spirit of these communities and sobered a fearful and somber populace to the tradeoffs of industrial development and economic prosperity.

Beyond the deeply shaken towns in which the coal mines had exerted their influence were the strip mines themselves, enormous rents in the earth where super-sized excavators and giant earth movers gouged the earth and shook the ground. As the railroad coal cars lined up on sidings and moved off in snaking lines toward the power plants, it was apparent that the casualties of such a gargantuan industrial scale were not only in the decay of communities, but in the irrevocably altered landscape. All of us on the tour were as sobered as the soft spoken sheriff when we realized that we were witnessing the sacrifice zones to which Mitchell had referred. These now desolate-feeling places were expendable within corporate economic equations. Once industry had gained dominance, there was no going back to quieter times and rural values. The physical and psychic landscapes had been forever altered.

AMAX assured Crested Butte and Gunnison County over the course of the Mt. Emmons Project that socio-economic impacts could be managed to make them negligible. Mitchell soon shared his personal experience from the tour with remarks at a public meeting: "We've seen other guinea pigs and they all died. We don't perceive a new experience here. We are being asked to be reasonable, but AMAX says that there is no higher purpose than building a mine. They originally said that, if we didn't want the mine, they wouldn't build it.

Since that time, their position has consistently been that there will be a mine."

Not only were eyes opened over the course of the Boom Town Tour, but participants on the tour who came from different walks of life in Gunnison County became friends. We shared airplane cabins, tour buses, hotel rooms, dinner tables, and drinks. We talked, got to know one another, laughed, and revealed quietly held preferences for the quiet, pastoral place that each of us called home. On our last night together, in Wheatland, Wyoming, Crested Butte town manager Terry Hunker and I staged a comedic awards ceremony that not only poked fun at each other, but revealed a newfound solidarity, county-wide. Participants began the tour as strangers and ended as neighbors confronting a unifying threat that each of us clearly recognized.

This was a far different outcome than AMAX had intended, yet Art Biddle defended the tour years later as a goodwill gesture: "That tour was an effort to be open on an important issue and gain some measure of credibility. We wanted to help community leaders by going out and talking to people in other towns. We wanted to get them thinking about their issues and concerns. We didn't expect growth issues to go away. It was just another step in trying to do the right thing."

The findings of the Boom Town Tour did the right thing for Crested Butte by inspiring the widest resistance yet to AMAX. Rather than ameliorate local concerns, the Boom Town Tour heightened caution and steeled community resolve. Decision-makers on all levels now knew, first-hand, how traditional community values could be forever forfeited to invasive industries that took on the domineering role of an occupational force. These findings not only tainted AMAX plans for Crested Butte, they sullied the modern mining industry as an agent of community ruin.

"The AMAX strategy," explained Terry Hamlin, "was to look at impacted communities. The Boom Town Tour was to show that these were impacted communities, to show the problems and ask how to deal with them. But if people had made up their minds, they would see only the negatives."

Those negatives now aggregated into perceived contradictions.

"We won't open a mine if you don't want us." "Our tailings dams will last forever." "We will give you a new generation of mines." Such assurances now had the air of duplicity. They relied on faith instead of proof. They were negated by a groundswell of empirical evidence that said just the opposite.

On another AMAX-sponsored tour, guests from Gunnison County were toured through the massive Henderson and Climax mines. We felt the drama of a 3,000-foot elevator plunge into the bowels of the earth where seemingly endless mine tunnels stretched out like spokes from a central shaft within an extensive subway. We watched diesel-powered ore carts hauling crushed rock to the mill, heard the din of "bell crushers" and "ball crushers" smashing rock into powder, saw the gray scum of molybdenum disulfide floating on huge vats of chemically-treated sludge, witnessed toxic tailings pouring from huge pipes into vast and reeking tailings ponds. We stood before the Climax "glory hole" near Leadville, where Bartlett Mountain had been reduced to a crater, and wondered about the "subsidence" predicted for Mt. Emmons. In a strange way, the abhorrence we felt for Climax served to steel our resolve that nothing like this would ever be tolerated in Crested Butte. Climax became the ultimate inspiration to wage a ceaseless battle against AMAX.

The deeper the people of Gunnison County journeyed into the mining industry, the more fault was found with it as a mismatch for community values. Instead of an embrace, there was growing repugnance. In response to the prurient AMAX t-shirt, "MOLY MAKES YOUR TOOL HARDER," a Crested Butte bumper sticker admonished: "DON'T CLIMAX IN CRESTED BUTTE." The so-called "new mine" had become old and tired, and was looked upon as a sham. The all-caring AMAX image seemed hollow and transparent as it became common knowledge that the first allegiance of any corporation is not to local stakeholders who will suffer the industrial ills, but to shareholders with investment interests who are looking for a strong return.

Cahn's book, *Footprints on the Planet*, had praised Dempsey and AMAX for its progressive efforts, but Cahn's own words were far more telling:

> As a nation and as individuals we are finding that our decisions and the steps being taken by leaders in government and business and by average citizens are making footprints on our planet that will scar it perhaps for centuries. What was being called the advent of the environmental era was really the dawning realization by millions of Americans that we need to consider the impacts of our decisions. I wonder what responsibility we have—whether as writer or banker or government official or corporate president or secretary or homemaker or student or mechanic or architect or scientist—to tread lightly wherever we go and leave footprints that do not mar our planet.

Many began to understand that AMAX would always stand aloof from Gunnison County, that it represented an invisible cadre of managers, accountants and executives whose interests lay in the gut of Mt. Emmons, not in the well-being of the communities surrounding it. The approval process became stale and bureaucratic, producing a blizzard of reports, a tsunami of numbers, a flood of studies too boggling to comprehend. Following the issuance of yet one more institutionalized study, the *Crested Butte Chronicle* mourned:

> We speak of losing our quality of life; we bemoan the damage to the environment; we fear the social chaos that accompanies boom towns. Yes, they are all realities we should be concerned about. But they are not the biggest loss. As we study reams of information from a computer readout we understand that we are losing one of our inalienable rights. That right is our identity as human beings, no matter how imperfect we are. All of a sudden, we are statistics. We are manpower units, welfare loads, unemployment charts, public opinion polls, body counts, computer printouts. We are no longer you and me in our imperfect and crazy uniqueness. All of a sudden, we are the faceless by-product of mass processing.

18

Save the Lady!

AS A SLOW BUT RISING TIDE turned against the AMAX Mt. Emmons Project, there occurred a fraying of the social fabric in Crested Butte. As the town grew more and more strident in its attacks on AMAX, a deepening gulf of alienation and long-buried hostilities formed between those who took pride in the town's mining legacy and the new wave of young, anti-mine residents—a classic rift between old-timer and new-timer.

A small and embittered cadre of the town's former coal mining families now stridently supported AMAX. Their allegiance to mining drew a line between them and what some in their number considered shiftless newcomers who sponged off tourism, a dishonorable source of income. To these mining traditionalists, AMAX meant the revival of Crested Butte's legacy and the time-honored tradition of extracting a modest living from the earth through hard, honest labor. Perhaps AMAX could reinstate the old values, bring back the old ways, turn back the clock, purge the hapless ne'er do wells, and even reinvigorate polka dancing at local bars.

Rarely outspoken, but bitingly opinionated, this faction of beleaguered old-timers scorned the liberal dissidents who had taken over their town. They formed a political alliance calling themselves, "The Concerned Citizens," and they ridiculed Mitchell's administration for hiding behind the federal protection of Crested Butte's National Historic designation, which the town had secured in 1975. They and their forebears had built the town, and now its historic significance was being used as an obstacle to stop the return of traditional mining.

Old dislikes crept into whispered conversations. Backyard gossip became terse and inflammatory. Curses were flung around the coal stoves in winter and over the back fences in summer.

Arguments broke out during city council meetings, in the bars, the post office, the shops. Civility disintegrated. Threats were made against town officials. Town planner Myles Rademan kept a loaded gun by his bed as protection against his nemesis, a hardened, old rancher who glared at him through Coke bottle glasses and made vocal threats. Wherever people gathered, debate sprouted like skunk cabbage in the spring. Alliances were formed, hatred was cultivated, and grudges were established that would last decades, lifetimes.

The *Crested Butte Chronicle*, for which I reported on AMAX and anything else that could be called "news," was rebuked for its extremist approach to environmental issues on which the newspaper railed in every issue. Journalistic objectivity had been compromised by a deep-seated distrust of AMAX and disillusionment of the corporate world. The *Chronicle*, for which I had left the Gunnison paper in 1979, had hired me to share editorial duties with editor Gil Hersch. Gil's wife, Marion, sold the ads, financing the paper to serve as a propaganda organ for our blatant anti-mine crusade.

The *Chronicle*'s editorial bias also railed on the status quo as represented by corruption in American politics and business, much of the antipathy targeting the amorality of the Vietnam War and America's complacency with racism. In the early '80s, the *Chronicle* issued an editorial defending its position as a left-leaning periodical, written by Gil Hersch:

> Most of us were brought up in a society that emphasized one thing: productivity. We were sent to elementary schools nine months out of the year to be trained to fit into the system. High schools and college were the same. Few questioned the system. It was part of life. Suddenly, we opened our eyes and looked around to see that our society was falling apart. The biosphere is sending out danger signals of an imbalance.
>
> Acid rain, cancer, species extinction, deforestation, pollution of oceans, and smog are becoming apparent problems. And a raft of social ills has turned our cities and industrial centers into living nightmares. In Crested Butte, the *Chronicle* has followed the 'back-

Swedish songbird, Tracey Wickland, and author Paul Andersen formed a duet to sing songs of protest against the AMAX mining proposal. CRESTED BUTTE CHRONICLE ARCHIVES

yard' perspective. We have looked to our own backyard and applied it to a larger picture until the entire nation appears as a backyard to us all, even the planet, in its interwoven complexities. We at the *Chronicle* are not dreaming up imaginary crises. Nor are we misrepresenting the facts. We care about our community. We live here and love the land that supports us.

Gil and Marion and their two children were newcomers to Crested Butte, having fled their native New York City in the mid '70s when Gil, an attorney, was disbarred from practicing law while working for his uncle's law firm, representing interests in South America. According to Gil, one of his clients mailed him a shipment of contraband drugs for which Gil was busted by federal agents. Gil escaped criminal charges but was booted from the law firm and from the legal profession. He and Marion sold everything they had, bought a mobile camper, and, with their young children, set off to discover America. Their voyage ended in Crested Butte where they discovered a small contingent of fellow

New Yorkers. This was as far as they could get from New York, and they enjoyed the removal.

Coincidentally, the owner of the *Chronicle*, Myles Arber, was another East Coast attorney who was in the process of fleeing Crested Butte. Arber had made himself unpopular to a large segment of his readers because of the editorial liberties he took with the paper by venting personal vendettas. He had repeatedly lampooned the owner of the ski area, Howard "Bo" Callaway, on the unproven charge that Callaway had used his influence as Secretary of the Army under the Ford Administration to appropriate permits for the ski resort from the U.S. Forest Service. A boycott of local businesses loyal to Callaway threatened to bankrupt the paper, so Arber desperately handed it over to Gil and Marion on a lease arrangement while he relocated to Boulder. Until I came along, Gil had written the entire newspaper each week. He displayed credible journalistic skills, sharp insights, clear moral instincts, editorial courage, and a carriage of aloofness that could border on arrogance.

Regarding Arber's style of journalism, his first edition, after having purchased the paper from its founder, George Sibley, in the late Sixties, featured a restaurant review of the Way Station. This popular bar and restaurant sported a sign at its doorway: "WE SERVE NO LONG HAIRS HERE." Such blatant exclusion of hippies evidently tweaked Arber, whose restaurant review opened with, "The Way Station actually does serve long hairs. I discovered one in my soup." Feisty, contentious, and often hilarious, Arber's approach to the news was not appreciated by everyone, and the community in effect blackballed him into vacating town.

The *Crested Butte Pilot*, under Jane and Lee Ervin, was the other weekly paper serving Crested Butte. Ervin was a hard-drinking, heavy smoking editor who portrayed the newsman archetype with all his being and was beloved as a man of the people. Clever with words, unfazed by conflict and a favorite with the bar crowd, Ervin was diligent, hard-working and popular. Everyone in town read both papers, which you could pick up from unlocked wooden boxes scattered around town. It was expected that readers would drop a quarter into a slot, and most did. The competition between the two papers raised the ante for reportorial élan, and both papers rose to the occasion with literate and well-crafted prose written to inform and influence. Both papers were clearly biased in favor of the town and against AMAX.

The newspapers were not exactly in harmony, however, given stiff competition for advertising dollars, and there were personality clashes between the owners. Still, the papers fought the mine in chorus, and their editorial slants were simpatico. Journalistically, there were two mouths to feed in Crested Butte, and I had increased the *Chronicle*'s appetite with my $250 per week salary.

Following every town council meeting, a strategy and bull session was held at Mitchell's Victorian home over cold beer handed out from a cornucopian refrigerator, gratis of Mitchell. Often, a pipe circulated, filling the air with a pungent reminder that this was Crested Butte and the peace pipe was a social custom. Gathered around Mitchell's dining room table, where a Vermont Castings wood-burning stove crackled on frosty nights, anti-mine strategists strengthened our resolve and boiled the issues down to a clear conflict in ideology. Bothersome incongruities had to be ignored if the fires of passion were to burn brightly, and burn brightly they did. Through these informal strategy sessions came a broader understanding of what this battle meant.

If Crested Butte could be overrun, then so could any town, any ideal, any value. AMAX was not the only industrial antagonist active in the world, and Crested Butte was not the only community mounting a defense. The exploitation of natural resources and rural communities was occurring worldwide. The AMAX battle in Crested Butte foreshadowed the nascent challenge to globalization that would explode decades later in 2019 at World Trade Organization protests in Seattle. Crested Butte represented early rumblings of the new millennium when large scale corporate malfeasance would be challenged by local communities, native peoples and indigenous cultures.

Crested Butte took seriously the responsibility to "think globally and act locally." This was the Sixties generation fighting the same entrenched powers that had fronted the Vietnam debacle and sanctified dubious incursions of the military/industrial complex. Crested Butte was standing firm, without compromise, united on issues of global significance.

"We do not inherit the earth from our fathers," the *Chronicle* opined in a paraphrase of Chief Seattle's famous speech. "We borrow it from our children."

Chief Seattle's words rang truer than ever:

> Teach your children that the earth is our mother. Whatever befalls the earth befalls the sons of the earth. If men spit upon the ground, they spit upon themselves.

Those manning the barricades in Crested Butte knew well what this fight was about. We had hiked the high ridges to glorious mountain peaks and surveyed distant ranges. We had walked alpine basins carpeted with wildflowers. We had sniffed the fragrance of lupines in bloom. We had tasted pure water from mountain streams. We had camped at high mountain lakes beneath a celestial dome of sun and stars. We had experienced the majesty of nature. We had witnessed the perfect harmony of wilderness and were enriched by it.

Tracey Wickland, Crested Butte's poet laureate and beloved folk singer, articulated this shared experience in "The Mountain Song." Strumming a guitar, her long blonde hair a bright contrast against the deep tan of her bronzed and attractive features, Wickland was the archetypal mountain woman—a backpacker, mountain biker and telemark ski goddess. Her laughter was contagious, and her sweet soprano bore a message of transcendence.

> I came here from the city a thousand miles away
> I came just for a little while, I never meant to stay
> I meant to take my pleasures, have a good time and be gone
> But I fell in love with the Lady, now I sing the mountain song.
>
> I listened to the music of the night wind in the pines
> I saw the quiet splendor of a field of columbines
> I skied a crystal pathway to a mountain peak so tall
> And walked the mighty summits with the One who made it all
>
> CHORUS:
> Then I fell in love with the Lady
> 'Cause I've seen her at her best
> When I walked her wild and rugged paths

Through her open wilderness
And now I never will betray her
Steal her riches and be gone
'Cause when you love the mountain Lady
You will sing the mountain song.

People come from everywhere to see what they can find
Some take lots of pictures, and some just take their time
And there are some who take her beauty that can't be bought or sold
And they think of only money while destroying wealth untold

CHORUS:
But when you fall in love with the Lady
When you've slept upon her breast
When you've walked her wild and rugged paths
Through her open wilderness
I know you never will betray her
Steal her riches and be gone
'Cause when you love the mountain Lady
You will sing the mountain song.

Tracey Wickland sang about love, which ultimately was at the heart of the townspeople's deep affection for "the mountain lady" and for Crested Butte. Love was the message of Myles Rademan's coalescing slide show at the Grubstake. Love, as it spread through Crested Butte, could become more contagious than the annual flu. Love is uniting. Love is deeply personal. Love is empowering. There was nothing in the AMAX strategy for diminishing this depth of love, and there was no greater fervor for Crested Butte than this most powerful of all emotions. Call it airy-fairy and touchy-feely, but love was palpable here. Photographer Sandra Cortner would convey that message picturesquely decades later in her book, *Crested Butte: Love at First Sight*.

> My generation's horror was the Vietnam War. Haunted by the death they had seen, some found a safe haven here. Others sought adventure and the beauty of the mountains. Many were on their way elsewhere and stopped to visit a friend or to go skiing, but after driving onto Elk Avenue, they never left. Almost everyone describes that arrival as "love at first sight."

Love for Crested Butte stirred a timeless fervor, and we at the *Chronicle* took the AMAX battle very much to heart. Propaganda became an acceptable weapon in defense of that which we loved. The editorial staff of two—Gil and I—dug for every bit of dirt we could find on AMAX. We printed examples of negligence by other mining companies and exposed horror stories of apocalyptic strip mines. If there was a shortage of news, we filled the paged with editorials, ridiculing AMAX promises and deriding the corporate vision. Given the size of the AMAX war chest and the tiny budget of the newspaper, we figured it was a fair fight.

When the mine site on Mt. Emmons broke out in a forest fire in 1981, I raced up to cover it, risking my life in a foolhardy attempt to photograph flaming conifers so I could display them prominently on page one. Such photojournalistic heroics were yet another effort to fan the flames of controversy. Talk about inflammatory prose! My newspaper article about the fire read as if AMAX had intentionally torched a grove of giant sequoias.

A self-imposed assignment took me to Marshall Pass, on the Continental Divide, where, in the early 1980s, the Homestake Mining Company had opened a uranium strip mine. I visited the site with a mine representative where we observed a front-end loader "sorting" uranium ore as it was stripped from a mountainside. The operator lowered the huge bucket toward a man on the ground wielding a Geiger counter. Depending on the reading, the man waved the machine to the left or to the right. To the left was a growing pile of ore that would be loaded onto trucks. To the right was an unprotected stream course. As I watched the bucket dump its load into that drainage, a tributary to the headwaters of Tomichi Creek, I speculated that the half-life of the low-grade uranium in that watercourse would be far longer than a hundred generations of my successors and that Tomichi Creek was a tributary to the Gunnison River which was a tributary to the Colorado River.

Many in Crested Butte practiced civil protests with modest guerrilla antics. We hiked through public lands where AMAX claims laid out powerline corridors, roads and waste dumps, and we dutifully and methodically pulled survey stakes and collected wads of fluorescent

The Red Lady Salvation Ball became a town tradition where red ladies (and sometimes men) strutted their stuff in a ribald, high-spirited celebration that kept the town's mood high in more ways than one. Marilyn Leftwich shows how it's done.

CRESTED BUTTE CHRONICLE ARCHIVES

survey flags, innocently suggesting that we were cleaning up litter. There was street theater in July Fourth parades featuring HCCA floats depicting demented AMAX "tailings monsters" raping the "Red Lady."

The Red Lady Salvation Ball, HCCA's annual fête and one of the most popular parties in town, began in 1978 as a way to celebrate Red Lady, just as AMAX was preparing to defile her. Begun as a dance contest with a ribald theme, the ball soon featured flamboyant, cross-dressing, scarlet-clad men and women cavorting and gyrating before a panel of well-lubricated judges. Gender has long been inconsequential as contestants, encircled by cheering onlookers, whirl and gyrate to a rock band in a frenzy of crazed pandemonium. Through the decades at each Red Lady Salvation Ball a costumed Red Lady has been selected and celebrated with celebrity acclaim. Once chosen purely for a sensual dance spectacle, the Red Lady is now honored for additional attributes like devotion to community and environment. The honoree represents for the following year the embodiment of pagan spirit and the soul of the mountains, presiding in costume at various occasions and bringing new talent and energy to a growing "sisterhood."

On a more whimsical note, musical satires were performed by Tracey Wickland and me costumed in playful guises. Tracey portrayed "Mina Orebody," a blonde bimbo with huge falsies stuffed beneath her blouse. My stage persona was "Coal Portal," a rough-and-tumble miner wearing soiled coveralls and wielding a pickax. We sang the parodies we wrote over cocktails in local bars, belting them out in two-part harmonies. Appearing in hard hats and anti-mine t-shirts, Mina and Coal mocked AMAX miners who wanted to "give Crested Butte the shaft." Our songs played on mining vernacular, turning the euphemism "subsidence" (the collapse of a mountain), into a satirical ditty.

Subside by Subside
(Sung to the tune of *Side by Side*)

Oh, we just got a barrel of moly
That's why we're happy and jolly
Just to tunnel along
'Til the mountains are gone
Subside by subside

Oh, we don't know what we'll find tomorrow
But we'll leave a permanent scar-oh,
As we tunnel along
'Til the mountains are gone
Subside by subside

Through our mighty efforts
What if the mountains fall?
As long as we make profits
It doesn't matter at all

When we've ruined your town and departed
We'll find a new place to start it
And we'll tunnel along
'Til the mountains are gone
Subside by subside

"Save the Lady" ski tours were launched from Crested Butte to Aspen over 12,700-ft. Pearl Pass as we skied with heavy, overnight backpacks through twenty-five miles of stunningly beautiful winter scenery. These epic treks over the Elk Range were led by the inimitable Roy Smith, an outdoor adventurer who had been among the first wave of Outward Bound instructors brought to the US from Great Britain in the 1960s.

With Smith waving us on, we protest skiers trudged stoically above timberline through radiant, snow-covered peaks on a skiing crusade against the greed that could destroy it all. Smith, a staunch wilderness advocate, campaigned for Oh-Be-Joyful wilderness designation by introducing a lofty and soulful approach to conservation in a guest editorial in the *Chronicle*: "We might look at the need for wilderness as providing a reservoir of thought and spiritually evocative experiences where we can re-create and emerge with a better sense of human priorities."

Smith led the Save the Lady skiers into places we had never been before. We slept in snow caves far above tree-line when the mercury plunged to ten below. We weathered blizzards among snowbound summits in whiteout conditions. We arrived, glowing with messianic fervor, in Aspen where our Aspen comrades, Pitkin County commissioners Michael Kinsley and Bob Child, organized demonstrations of support on their side of the Elk Range. Smith, dressed in woolen knickers, leather boots and a knee-length anorak, led his backcountry acolytes in a parade through Aspen with Mitchell in his wheelchair, flanked by Kinsley and Child. Mystified Aspenites looked on as the Crested Butte demonstrators marched arm-in-arm through the Hyman Avenue Mall bearing a banner: "SAVE THE LADY: HANDS OFF, AMAX."

In the early '80s, hale and hearty Roy Smith led another ski crossing, this time with Colorado Governor Dick Lamm and a small contingent of Crested Butte skiers on a two-night, three-day tour over East Maroon Pass. We skied to Gothic for a first night spent in the comfort of heated cabins, gratis of Rocky Mountain Biological Laboratory. The next day, we plodded with heavy packs up past Copper Lake and over East Maroon Pass (11,824 ft.) where we dug snow caves and huddled to keep warm through a bitter cold night. Lamm suffered a sleepless vigil beneath the snow and was thoroughly spent by the time we reached the trailhead at Maroon Creek late the next afternoon. Smith had lost the trail down E. Maroon Creek, so we thrashed through thick willows along the snow-covered creek for what felt like hours. We were met by the governor's anxious staff and a few reporters who were witness to the beleaguered and good-natured governor hobbling in with a broken bamboo ski pole and the last of his strength. Standing there with my camera to shoot the good governor's triumph, I could not in good conscience snap the shutter on this bleary-eyed man in his final staggers to civilization.

Taking backcountry protests to the extreme, a group of daring backcountry skiers scaled Mt. Emmons on the night of a memorable Flauschink celebration in 1979, for their own display of solidarity. At an appointed time, long after sunset, revelers in town were called out of the Tailings bar onto Elk Avenue. Attention was called to Mt. Emmons where, emblazoned in pink flares across Red Lady Bowl, was the flaming epithet: FUCK AMAX. Cheers resounded throughout town to the peeling of church bells.

The local posse that did the deed had skied that afternoon to a midpoint on Red Lady Bowl at 11,000 ft. They carried heavy packs and traveled over the snow on cross-country gear comprised of lightweight skis, three-pin bindings and leather boots. The original intent had been to spell out STOP AMAX, but bolder minds prevailed thanks, in part, to the imbibing of strong drink, so the message was enhanced to make the best use of the 300 road flares one of the group had purchased in Denver, where such a quantity would not be traced back to the perpetrators.

"The group fueled themselves on Jack Daniels and other substances," described Sandra Cortner in *Crested Butte: Love at First*

"Save the Lady" ski tours were launched from Crested Butte to Aspen over 12,700-ft. Pearl Pass as we skied with heavy, overnight backpacks through twenty-five miles of stunningly beautiful winter scenery.
CRESTED BUTTE CHRONICLE ARCHIVES

Sight, "then dug a snow pit in which to relax after they had spent the afternoon placing the flares. Spelling the message in a legible manner was achieved by using a long rope knotted at regular intervals designating where the flares would be placed. The letters were 50 feet wide and 100 feet tall."

At dusk, with everyone in position, one of the conspirators lit a flare in the snow pit. That was the signal to light all the flares and also to notify an in-town conspirator to make sure the act was seen. Sandy Cortner was alerted, so she got set up for a photo. As the flares caught, church bells tolled throughout town. At the appointed moment, the streets filled and a wild cheer went up for the message on the mountain that echoed the simplistic sentiments felt by so many. The flare crew packed up and made a wild, nighttime ski descent, buoyed by inebriation and the spirit of derring-do. Returning to town, the conspirators quietly filtered inconspicuously into the Wooden Nickel saloon to the grins of clueless revelers who told them feverishly about what they had just witnessed.

"Thirty plus years later," observed Cortner, "these former hippies are short-haired family men driving SUVs instead of decrepit pickup trucks. Many have moved away." One of the flare crew, she wrote, "is surprised that today's young people protesting the mine haven't come up with a similar stunt and advertised it through social networks. 'It would go viral, man!' he enthused with the same sparkle in his eyes as shown that auspicious night on Red Lady Bowl."

While activism and street theater reached a high pitch, there was a noticeable lack of serious monkey wrenching: the willful act of destructive sabotage. Monkey wrenching is the result of desperation, and there was little of that in Crested Butte. The mood was naively optimistic. Activism, Crested Butte-style, was civil, impish, and honored an unspoken code not to break the law or destroy property; that kind of recklessness could harm the town's moral standing.

The prevailing strategy was to challenge the law and its precepts with sound, rational, legal arguments while vilifying and satirizing those who would destroy paradise. Orchestrated protests were methodical and choreographed. Individual protests were uniquely spirited and often filled with merriment. Crested Butte wanted to win hearts and minds and eventually to win the ensuing legal battles that would ultimately decide the issue. These dual approaches caused a complementary resonance within the community where everyone got to play a role.

AMAX had an enormous war chest, but Crested Butte had a far deeper and more enduring resource in the strength of its convictions, in the loyal ranks of the grass roots, in the cohesion of community, and in the town's commitment to counter-culture values. The mine opposition took on a noble aura. Defeating AMAX wasn't about boosting professional careers, enriching bank accounts, or self-aggrandizement; it was about virtuously defending one's beloved.

Fighting the mine was about preserving the values on which lives and community were based, values that transcend money and status, values that were sacred then and remain so today. If you fought AMAX, it wasn't just about being against the mine; it was about being for the town, for the self-determination of a community and its future generations. When taken to this higher plane, the fight against AMAX had all the attributes of a spiritual crusade.

19
Celebrity Reinforcements

B<small>Y THE EARLY</small> 1980s, Crested Butte had gained credibility and critical momentum for a full court press. AMAX, meanwhile, worked feverishly to sweeten its image. The corporation's PR campaign portrayed itself as an economic powerhouse of global stature, a good corporate citizen striving to serve its stockholders by producing valuable commodities to supply the industrial supply chain with the raw materials necessary for human progress. AMAX drew its conviction from the belief that reasonable people would embrace a reasonable project within a reasonable community for a reasonable and inevitable outcome.

To improve its stance, AMAX made overtures to purchase thousands of acres of ranchland in Gunnison County. These holdings would serve as prime trading parcels for acquiring key public lands on which AMAX planned to mine molybdenum, mill the ore, and dump the tailings. Many of these acquisitions came with senior water rights that AMAX would apply to the immense water requirements of ore slurries and milling. The company proposed residential housing units and commercial developments to support its work force and create a community overlay built for mining. Every parcel of land purchased or under contract by AMAX raised the ante for property owners who stood to realize financial gain.

AMAX spent an estimated $100 million on the acquisition of land, water rights, exploration, orebody delineation, mine planning, metallurgical testing, and myriad ancillary activities. Hundreds of bore holes in Mt. Emmons produced a detailed map of the orebody, while seismic testing revealed the deeper geology by shaking the ground around Mt. Emmons and sending tremors, both real and figurative, beneath the town of Crested Butte. The Mt. Emmons Project was literally earth-shaking for residents of the Upper Gunnison River Basin.

Crested Butte sought land acquisitions of its own. The town proposed and eventually won a Congressional Wilderness designation for nearby Oh-Be-Joyful, a well-named expanse of glorious alpine basins abundant with wildflowers. The town successfully established legal protection for its municipal watershed in Coal Creek and also in Oh-Be-Joyful through the controversial and strategically advantageous Watershed Ordinance. To support that ordinance, the town petitioned the U.S. Forest Service for a withdrawal of 17,900 acres of mining claims from "settlement, sale, location, or entry" in order to limit activities that could degrade its watershed. By locking up wilderness and protecting water, the town's strategy was to squeeze AMAX between two restrictive boundaries.

Both issues were hotly contested by AMAX. Corporate attorneys filed lawsuits against watershed protection. In September 1981, AMAX attorneys charged Crested Butte with "claim jumping" by attempting to preempt mining rights. The company maintained that "AMAX was not given a fair opportunity to participate in the watershed hearings," that the town "totally ignored the corporation's evaluation" in which an alternative water supply was suggested.

In addition to protesting the Oh-Be-Joyful Wilderness designation, AMAX lobbied for a 15,000-acre reduction in the Maroon Bells-Snowmass Wilderness Area and a 30,000-acre reduction in the Collegiate Peaks Wilderness Area, claiming that both wilderness areas held mining potential. Thanks to strong regional support for wilderness in the Elk Range and beyond, AMAX failed on both fronts. Today, Crested Butte's Coal Creek watershed is protected and Oh-Be-Joyful is part of the Raggeds Wilderness Area. The Maroon Bells-Snowmass and Collegiate Wilderness Areas remain wild and protected, and are substantially larger today than they were during the AMAX onslaught. Visitation to these crown jewels in America's wilderness crown have climbed steadily over the years.

Crested Butte counter-attacked with assaults against other AMAX mines, especially its flagship operation near Leadville, the open pit called Climax. Crested Butte portrayed Climax as a glaring example of environment neglect, a vast and festering environmental wound that could potentially pollute two major river systems at their headwaters—the Arkansas and Colorado Rivers. The question was: Is Climax how Mt. Emmons might look in 30 years?

Looking beyond Crested Butte, it became clear that the long-term costs of industrial mining throughout the US had created a deficit on the national balance sheet and a legacy of ecological time bombs poised at various headwaters, that the environmental costs of mining would be paid by every man, woman and child living or yet to be born. Crested Butte asserted that public lands should not be sacrificed for short-term profits, but should be treasured for their beauty, purity and grandeur as a legacy to America's frontier past. The town pleaded that environmental stewardship was part of a coveted national trust that was being violated with every ton of ore extracted for corporate profit and consumer indulgence. Nature had rights, too, and those rights trumped the profits of distant shareholders who were detached from the liabilities of their gains.

Few advocates of wild nature were as convincing as Dr. Paul Ehrlich, noted author of *The Population Bomb*. A professor of biology at Stanford University, Ehrlich had spent twenty years as a summer field biologist at the Rocky Mountain Biological Laboratory (RMBL—"Rumble") in the nearby historic mining town of Gothic. This learned, eloquent critic took to task what he called the "misdirected federal bureaucracy and corporate culture represented by the Mt. Emmons Project." He warned that AMAX activities would destroy years of scientific data, and he portrayed AMAX mining plans as an "archaic and outmoded system of exploitation that would harm local ecosystems for centuries to come."

In July 1979, I finagled an interview with Ehrlich. He invited me to ride with him in his Jeep as he drove home from Crested Butte to Gothic one fine summer afternoon. I threw my mountain bike in the back, switched on my tape recorder, and was richly entertained as Ehrlich launched into a tirade about the Mt. Emmons Project. In a seamless, articulate oration, he linked AMAX to the overall downgrading

Dr. Paul Ehrlich in pursuit of butterflies for research into his ongoing studies of alpine ecosystems at Rocky Mountain Biological Laboratory.
CRESTED BUTTE CHRONICLE ARCHIVES

of the global environment with an ominous portent of impending eco disasters. Ehrlich's words on AMAX focused on the local and encompassed the global:

> Large scale mineral development is not a good idea in this valley because there are so many long term values at stake under such an exploitative action. If there is ever an emergency need for a mineral from this area, it's still there in the ground. It can always be extracted if our lives are ever at stake. But the current development on Mt. Emmons with AMAX is not based on a national or local need. Most of the molybdenum goes overseas, a great deal of it through Belgium to the Russians who put it in the nose cones of international ballistic missiles with which they threaten us.
>
> The only need that AMAX is advancing here is to keep its clod of capital growing at a given rate per annum. There is only a need for profit for AMAX stockholders. It is wrong to destroy an area like this, which has already established a strong economic base, to turn a rural sociology into an urban sociology for the benefit of a few stockholders who live somewhere else. Under the current AMAX proposal, this area will be destroyed for the profit of a few people.

Another well-known advocate for Crested Butte was the desert scribe Edward Abbey, author of *Desert Solitaire* and *The Monkey Wrench Gang*. In a 1979 article by Abbey reprinted in the *Crested*

Iconoclast Monkeywrencher Edward Abbey and Mitchell don hard hats to visit a potential timber sale near Crested Butte in the early 1980s.
PAUL ANDERSEN | *CRESTED BUTTE CHRONICLE* ARCHIVES

Butte Chronicle, Abbey decried what he called the "religion of growth" that underpinned the emerging global economy. "The industrial assault against the commonwealth, against our wilderness, the national forests, the public lands, the parks, the rivers, the seashores, the small towns and farmlands, continues unabated. Indeed, it continues on a scale larger, more determined, more ferocious than ever before against the Earth and against humanity."

Over beers on Mitchell's lawn in the summer of 1981, Abbey, who was befriended by Mitchell and happily lent his persona and gravitas to Crested Butte, proclaimed his disdain for the "minions of Wall Street" who represented AMAX. Abbey urged Crested Butte to "enjoy the mountains before the bastards have a chance to tear them down. Fight like hell!" he cheered, a beer bottle raised in his hand during a raucous toast to the Red Lady.

And yet, Abbey's call to arms was tempered with an even sterner admonition:

> Do not burn yourselves out. Be as I am, a reluctant enthusiast, a part-time crusader, a half-hearted fanatic. Save the other half of yourselves and your lives for pleasure and adventure. It is not enough to fight for the land; it is even more important to enjoy it. While you can. While it's still here. So get out there and hunt and fish and mess around with your friends, ramble out yonder and ex-

plore the forests, climb the mountains, bag the peaks, run the rivers, breathe deep of that yet sweet and lucid air, sit quietly for a while and contemplate the precious stillness, the lovely, mysterious, and awesome space. Enjoy yourselves, keep your brain in your head and your head firmly attached to the body, the body active and alive, and I promise you this much; I promise you this one sweet victory over our enemies, over those desk-bound men and women with their hearts in a safe deposit box, and their eyes hypnotized by desk calculators. I promise you this: You will outlive the bastards.

Dr. Roderick Frazier Nash, a professor and environmental historian from the University of California at Santa Barbara, visited Crested Butte in 1979, at the invitation of Myles Rademan. Nash, who later moved to Crested Butte and married Honeydew Murray, a local doyenne, came with academic credentials that were highlighted by two seminal books he had authored, *Wilderness and the American Mind* and *The Rights of Nature*. In an interview for the *Crested Butte Chronicle*, Nash described the boom and bust cycle of western mining economies.

"The only inexhaustible resources," Nash said, "are scenery and wildness. The real gold is in tourists' credit cards. The future of places like Crested Butte should be built around attractive industries, not extractive industries." Nash pointed out that wildness represents a valuable and fragile resource, important to both biodiversity and to the human spirit. He warned, however, that leaving nature alone requires a degree of self-restraint that is seemingly beyond the capacity of modern humans. "Do we, as a species, have the courage to disassociate progress from growth?" he asked rhetorically.

At the head of a chapter in *Wilderness and the American Mind*, titled, "The Wilderness Cult," Nash quotes George S. Evans, who, in 1904, issued a potent defense for wilderness, and for the American character:

> Whenever the light of civilization falls upon you with a blighting power, go to the wilderness. Dull business routine, the passions of the market place, the perils of envious cities become but a memory. The wilderness will take hold of you. It will give you good red blood. It will turn you from a weakling into a man. You will soon behold all with a peaceful soul.

The AMAX issue posed ponderous philosophical questions that incited introspection about one's place in the world and the even larger question of the appropriate role of humans on the planet.

The final paragraph of Nash's groundbreaking book touched on Thoreau, the strongest voice of wildness to come out of the American transcendentalist school. "When Thoreau wrote in 1851 about wildness being the preservation of the world, he did not mean merely the human component," wrote Nash, referring to the larger context of the biosphere. Quoting Thoreau: "What we call wildness is a civilization other than our own."

Nash concludes his book with a grand notion: "At the heart of the new ecocentric rationale for wilderness is respect for this larger community of life and process. So wilderness preservation has become, finally, a gesture of planetary humility." Rod Nash made a huge impression on me by advancing philosophical notions regarding man and nature. Twenty-five years later, Nash and I co-moderated "The Wilderness Seminar" at the Aspen Institute, a five-day immersion in wilderness philosophy at the 10th Mountain Huts of Aspen.

A man who had been in the trenches in numerous highly visible environmental campaigns, David Brower, was another of Mitchell's celebrated visitors. Considered by many to be the father of the modern environmental movement, Brower was a well-respected advocate for Mother Earth. This world-class mountaineer with more than 70 first ascents to his credit, lent his gravitas to the embattled town with elegance and style befitting the persuasive president of the Sierra Club. "Let the mountains talk, let the river run. Once more, and forever," projected Brower in an enlivening moment for the town.

The dialogue with AMAX had become an emotionally charged intellectual journey. The bigger questions were enticing to players on both sides and, in the ensuing discourse, revealed likable qualities among adversaries. Matters of intellect resulted in grudging mutual respect that began to permeate the mining debate.

The ensuing ideological debates stretched minds between the pragmatics of materialism and the sacred purity of Gaia. For me and for many in Crested Butte, missile nose cones, car chassis, strategic weapons, bicycle frames, the whole line of moly-infused industrial

Dr. Roderick Nash, consummate wilderness historian, author and close friend to Crested Butte during a ski tour to Gothic and beyond.

CRESTED BUTTE CHRONICLE ARCHIVES

John Denver came to CB to lend his moral support and later recorded *The Mountain Song*, by Tracey Wickland, on one of his albums.

CRESTED BUTTE CHRONICLE ARCHIVES

products paled before the values inherent in a virtuous crusade that questioned the very tenets of industrial civilization and human progress. Passions became inflamed with self-righteous indignation and irrepressible zeal based upon spiritualistic, moralistic and idealistic tenets in the semblance of a pagan jihad.

AMAX could not come close to touching that burning spirit and unflagging energy with all the PR overdrive it commanded on Madison Avenue. Crested Butte had more momentum than a D-9 bulldozer, and it came with the unity of body, mind and spirit.

Then the tide suddenly shifted. 🦌

The destruction left in the wake of a forest fire that scorched 55 acres after a welder's torch on an AMAX job site ignited the dry timber. Mayor Mitchell's comment upon surveying the site: "If this is the price of progress, we're paying too much."

PAUL ANDERSEN | *CRESTED BUTTE CHRONICLE* ARCHIVES

PART II

A Pyrrhic Victory

*"The Town of Crested Butte
has put in a good deal of time and effort,
not just fighting for its own life,
but fighting for others who may not have
the ability to mount the battle required
when outsiders neither hear nor listen
to a town that says,
'No! Stop!
We love our home!'"*

—MITCHELL

Mayor of Crested Butte • 1980

20

The Crash

WHEN AMAX unveiled the Mt. Emmons Project in 1977, demand for molybdenum had been increasing at seven percent per year. Two years later, in 1979, AMAX reported gross sales of $2.5 billion and earnings of $365 million, a significant portion being attributable to high returns from its molybdenum division.

By 1980, U.S. steel markets, in which molybdenum played a role, had become glutted with cheaper, more competitive foreign steel imports. A slowdown in US manufacturing compounded a falling curve in the demand for domestic steel, creating a large surplus of molybdenum. The moly market went into freefall.

By 1981, the price of moly had plummeted from a high of $35-a-pound to $4-a-pound. In the four years (1977-1981) during which AMAX had endeavored to open a mine in Crested Butte, a crash in the price of moly forced AMAX into a hurried retreat from the rising costs of the Mt. Emmons Project. AMAX responded by laying off 900 mine and mill workers in its Colorado operations at Climax and Henderson. Soon, the company's top-flight moly producer, Climax, would close altogether, plunging Leadville into yet another cycle of bust.

By 1981, despite investing $100 million to develop the Mount Emmons Project, AMAX had made little progress toward its objective other than solidifying an intractable insurgent stronghold. AMAX executives were not only battle fatigued; they were disheartened by the economics that ruled their professional lives and determined their careers.

Crested Butte had nothing to do with the downturn that snuffed the AMAX expansion. To its credit, the town had succeeded in a major stalling tactic when, in 1980, the town objected to AMAX plans to burrow two 16-squarefoot drifts, or tunnels, thousands of feet into the heart of the Mount Emmons orebody. The town prevailed with the U.S. Forest Service at this critical juncture by successfully arguing that penetration was premature, forcing AMAX to pull out before it could climax in Crested Butte.

According to AMAX officials, had the drifts been approved and opened, the Mt. Emmons Project might have gone beyond the point of no return. AMAX would have been committed, no matter the financial losses, to building the mine. By halting AMAX at that critical step, Crested Butte managed to delay the company's timetable long enough for the downturn in the metals market to terminate its local ambitions.

The town's ceaseless and spirited opposition, the rising costs of mitigation pushed by the town, the interminable regulatory processes, and the collapse of the international metals market forced AMAX to announce on August 7, 1981, that it would postpone the Mt. Emmons Project. A month later, Wes Light, then acting as attorney for the High Country Citizens' Alliance (Ron Landeck had replaced Light as Crested Butte Town Attorney), argued at a meeting of the Colorado Joint Review Process that the AMAX mining claims were no longer valid because they were no longer economically feasible.

Light was effectively turning the tables on AMAX by invoking the 1872 Mining Law. When Light suggested that AMAX was "on a permit fishing expedition" with no immediate intention to mine, AMAX spokesmen became evasive and noncommittal. "We are trying to second guess you," pressed Light, "because we don't think you're being very candid. This is supposed to be an open forum. My feeling is that you know more than you're saying. All we have been getting is a lot of double-talk."

Art Biddle assured the Colorado Joint Review Process that AMAX was acting in good faith. Mike Rock said the outcome was dependent on unknowns tied to the world market and to AMAX production figures. But Light pressed the issue: "The public pays for the application process," he said. "We need to discern between a permit expedition and a bona fide developer. We are concerned that the U.S. Forest Service is operating under the idea that the orebody is developable. We don't think it is, so there is no legitimate claim."

"The fact is that we are pursuing the development in earnest," assured Biddle. "We are serious or we wouldn't have spent a hundred million dollars on the project."

The U.S. Forest Service refused to act on Light's charges and instead took a wait-and-see attitude. But there was no deliberating in Crested Butte. In a celebratory mood, the town issued an optimistic press release:

> CRESTED BUTTE—The town government, which has been fighting a proposed molybdenum mine on nearby Mount Emmons, plans Saturday to celebrate AMAX Corp.'s decision to postpone the project.
>
> Mayor W Mitchell said Monday that the AMAX decision was a result of efforts by opponents in Crested Butte that made the giant mining company realize "they can't do the job right."
>
> When he announced the delay 10 days ago, Mike Rock, community affairs director for AMAX, cited the national economic downturn and the soft molybdenum market as reasons for the decision.
>
> Activities here Saturday will include a hike up Mount Emmons, a "re-consecration ceremony" at the summit, an ancient Ute Indian dance, and a street celebration with live music.

What seemed an interminable struggle had ended with hardly a whimper. AMAX was suddenly gone, leaving a strange and lingering void.

21
Dancing in the Streets

TWO WEEKS AFTER the AMAX announcement, on August 22, 1981, Crested Butte held what became known as the "AMAX Going Away Party." It was both an act of hubris and a release of long held tensions. No AMAX personnel attended, as this was not a going away party cheering a departing friend. This was a good riddance snub to an unwanted guest who had outstayed their welcome.

The celebration began early that morning when a group of more than thirty Crested Butte citizens gathered on top of Mt. Emmons. Many of us rode our mountain bikes to the summit, grinding it out for two hours up the steep, rocky Gunsight Pass road, which is etched across the backside of Red Lady Bowl and gave access to some of the first AMAX drill rigs. Blissfully ignoring the obvious irony that the mountain bikes we were riding were made with chrome-molybdenum steel, we reached the summit in fine fettle and very high spirits.

As we pushed and prodded our bikes to the summit, a group of hikers was making its final ascent from the front side of the mountain, strung out along the tundra-covered ridge. The clouds were low, the air was damp and cool. Occasional curtains of drizzle swept over the mountain.

When the hikers and bikers collected on the summit, we traded handshakes, hugs, tears and grins. Surrounding us in this peak experience was a sea of peaks cresting like whitecaps. What emerged on the mountaintop at 12,392 feet that morning was a strong feeling of belonging to a community that few had ever known could exist, and that fewer still have found since. We had become brothers and sisters, bonded by a unity that was deep and unshakable. We were, as Shakespeare put it in Henry V: "We few, we happy few, we band of brothers..."

Suddenly, the air reverberated with the wop-wop of a helicopter. Some thought it might be an AMAX chopper sent to harass the revelers, but as the chopper flew nearer, heading straight for the mountain, the Channel 7 News logo came into view. The chopper hovered overhead, then settled in for a landing at the top of Red Lady Bowl. The whine of the engine slowly died. The long blades lazily chopped the air and came to a gradual stop.

When the door flew open, Mitchell's face beamed an indescribable smile. He raised his fingerless fist to the heavens, and a deep cheer went up. His gleaming chrome wheelchair was unfolded and moved into position below the open door. Several friends hoisted the mayor into the chair and wheeled him across the tundra. Mitchell had never thought it possible that he would somehow ascend Mt. Emmons and cheer a personal victory, not only against AMAX, but against the impossible odds he had personally surmounted in his eventful life.

Mitchell was on the mountain, wearing a "Bye-Bye AMAX" t-shirt. By simply being there, he disproved the naysayers who claimed that what he had done, what the town and all of us had done, was impossible. Stuart Mace was there, having come over from Aspen, a bold ideologue with Druidic notions who loved the Elk Range holistically and applauded Crested Butte's resistance with a brief benediction:

> We know how to run a bulldozer, we know how to destroy, but we don't know how to build and live peacefully with nature; we've always seen it as an adversary. Let the whole Family of Beings speak to you of harmony, balance, empathy, humility, frugality, gentleness. Let them explain that Life is a gift; that we are guests at that Banquet.

Those who were there will never forget that day, a day in which the little guy had won, a day that honored the vitality of community and small town autonomy. Right had spoken to power, and right had prevailed, or so it felt to this gathering, at this time, on this sacred mountaintop.

Marylyn Leftwich, Siste O'Malia and Laura Godfrey cavort as ladies of the night during a raucous moment at an early Red Lady Salvation Ball.
CRESTED BUTTE CHRONICLE ARCHIVES

Never mind the irony of our bikes frames and that both the chopper that flew Mitchell to the mountaintop and the wheelchair he used were made with chrome-moly steel produced at other mines in other places of which we were then ignorant. Never mind the overarching incongruity implicit in the way many of us in Crested Butte demonized industrial development and natural resource extraction while enjoying the fruits of an industrialized society and the consumption of natural resources that even a seemingly modest American lifestyle entails. An even deeper, more personal irony was revealed to me decades later when I learned that molybdenum is on the ingredients list of the Spiru-tein protein powder I add daily to my smoothies; I am part molybdenum. On that glorious, celebratory summer day of our victory over the evil foe, the dichotomies were forgotten or simply denied. This was not a time for self-recrimination but rather a time for joyous celebration of our heroic commitment to a cause bigger than ourselves.

When a community stands up against all odds for its deepest values, there can flourish an intractable and empowering sense of euphoria. No matter how unrealistic or impractical the contest, there is nurtured in a besieged community the rare fervor of self-determination that lies at the very heart of human liberty and in the foundation of the democratic institutions that birthed this nation. Separated in many ways from the American mainstream, Crested Butte expressed an all-American ideal.

The majority of the town's citizens had united against AMAX, marshaled their homespun resources, and shouted an emphatic "No!" Right or wrong, enlightened or disillusioned, naïve or visionary, NIMBY or globally connected, Crested Butte had revealed that an impassioned community has a right and a responsibility to take up the challenge against a corporate juggernaut and, aided by good fortune and unpredictable circumstances, prevail in defending its soul, the pure and radiant essence of a time and a place and a people.

On that beatific afternoon, a block of Elk Avenue in downtown Crested Butte was closed off to traffic. A flatbed truck was pulled up on the sidewalk where a stage was set up for a local band, the Crested Butte All-Stars, starring Robert J. As the band tuned up for its hit

Elk Avenue was closed, the music played, and the people danced into a mine-free future. Tracey Wickland and Bruce Blackwell (foreground) shake their booties with Crested Butte Mountain rising up behind.

CRESTED BUTTE CHRONICLE ARCHIVES

song, *Molly Be Damned*, the sun broke through the wispy clouds of dawn. With the first guitar chords and the first drum beat, there was dancing in the street. The music resounded across town, and everyone who had cause to celebrate the defeat of AMAX came out to rock and roll in the shadow of Mt. Emmons.

Sue Navy, a founding member of High Country Citizens' Alliance (now High Country Conservation Advocates), fondly recalled coordinating the day's events: "I had long envisioned and dreamed of the day we would celebrate AMAX's departure with a community climb to the top of Red Lady. Even as the battle with AMAX seemed interminable, my hope sprang eternal. Having Mitchell appear by helicopter was more than I could have imagined, as my dream of this day came true. We were celebrating our win, and our future, on a mountain we so revered. The street dance that followed allowed four years of pent-up energy to explode in jubilation. I'll never forget that day and the exhilaration we all felt."

Mitchell was lifted to the stage. He took the microphone and made a few remarks to noisy cheers. Here was a victory speech in which Mitchell described his sense of accomplishment and pride. He applauded Crested Butte for the good fight, the noble cause, for its vaunted values and ideals, its vision and commitment. There were tears in his eyes as he imparted his deep appreciation. "May we always have glory days instead of a glory hole!"

Those were tears of gratitude and cheers of spiritual ebullience. They burst from the love that had grown, first in the minds, then in the hearts of the people, an all-encompassing love that was given, first to the town and mountains, then to each other. Love was perhaps the most important byproduct that AMAX ever produced in Crested Butte.

When it was break time for the band, "Myna Orebody" and "Coal Portal," wearing our hard hats and coveralls, climbed onto the stage. In a vaudeville rendition, Tracey Wickland and I gave the final benediction with our popular AMAX parody, sung to the tune of George M. Cohan's *Hello, Tootsie, Hello*. We called our version, *Bye-Bye, AMAX, Bye-Bye*, and accompanied the lyrics with tambourine and kazoos.

Tracey Wickland at a peak moment atop Mt. Emmons singing *The Mountain Song* for a TV film crew. That song became a rousing anthem for Crested Butte and was later recorded by John Denver. High Country Citizens' Alliance president Chuck Malick is on the left, with Mitchell at lower left. CRESTED BUTTE CHRONICLE ARCHIVES

Bye-bye AMAX bye-bye
Bye-bye AMAX, don't cry
All we can say is 'golly'
We're sorry but the bottom just dropped out of moly

Bye-bye drill rigs, aw, shucks,
Bye-bye to all those trucks
We wish we could say,
We'd like you to stay
But all we know
Is that we're glad
You're goin' away

And so it's
Bye-bye AMAX bye-bye
Bye-bye AMAX bye-bye

22

In Retrospect

CRESTED BUTTE CELEBRATED as if things were final, that AMAX had been routed for good. The mining giant had walked away, but in Crested Butte, there was still work to be done.

When Chuck Malick, founding president of HCCA, stepped down in 1981, he handed the reins to Don Bachman. Malick lavished credit for the AMAX defeat in his outgoing address to the High Country Citizens' Alliance and its supporters, but cautioned about dropping the HCCA guard:

> The indefinite postponement of AMAX's mining project is an unqualified victory for Crested Butte, for HCCA, and for those who believe in local determination everywhere. But the AMAX battle is not over. We have the momentum, but not the victory. More importantly, our challenge of the 1872 Mining Law must not be allowed to drop. The national and local importance of Wes Light's attack on this archaic law and the inequitable application of that law can hardly be overestimated.

Over the next two years, activity at the old Keystone Mine and within the regulatory process ground to a halt. All eyes were on the metals market, which alone would determine Crested Butte's future and that of the mine, or of any mining company that might follow, and others did. In 1982, the Wall Street Journal reported that AMAX was crippled by $1.7 billion in debt and had posted a $350 million loss that year. In 1983, AMAX reported losses of $489 million, the company stock dropped to $7.74 per share, and AMAX closed up its local offices in Gunnison County and took its losses back to Greenwich, Connecticut. In 1984, the price of moly bottomed out at $2.50 per-pound and AMAX issued a final statement on the Mt. Emmons Project: "We're physically in possession of the property, but it no longer has any value on our books. It's delayed indefinitely."

AMAX senior vice president Stan Dempsey pointed out in an interview years later, "Mt. Emmons is one of the major undeveloped ore bodies in the world. Ore bodies like that are few and far between. There are others, but not high-grade, primary deposits. We reckoned that Mt. Emmons was a national level resource. Ironically, at the end of the day, we could have received the permit to mine, but by then the market fell out from under the project. We actually turned down the permit. By that time, I was managing AMAX operations in Australia."

Art Biddle also reflected, decades later, on the project he had spent four years advancing: "The EIS was completed and essentially approved by the U.S. Forest Service. From our perspective, that was a big step leading toward permitting. We felt we were pretty much on the right track. If moly prices hadn't tanked, we would have proceeded on and would have been successful. There might be some who would say they could have delayed us forever, but we had a foundation to defend ourselves in court with a good case."

According to Susan Cottingham, a HCCA co-founder who succeeded Myles Rademan as Crested Butte town planner, the town recognized early on that the price of moly was in decline. "We had enough access to financial information to predict this decline, and our idea was to hold them off long enough for the market to change. We're not taking credit for a change in the nation's economy, but we were perceptive enough to know what was happening."

"I know a lot of people take credit for having defeated the mine," analyzed former Gunnison County Commissioner David Leinsdorf, "but I view the defeat as happening because AMAX themselves misplayed their cards as far as the market was concerned. They were monopolistic for a long time, and they allowed the price of moly to rise to the point where it became cost effective for a lot of other mining companies to exploit marginal ore bodies and for copper companies to retrieve moly as a byproduct of copper. When the price was lower,

A close-knit community is one thing AMAX could never hope to defeat. The battle against the mine cemented friendships and formed alliances that would be lifelong. (l. to r.) Marcia Dowell, Sue Navy, Glo Cunningham, Herschel Augsburger and Annie Starr. CRESTED BUTTE CHRONICLE ARCHIVES

at $8 or $9 dollars a pound, AMAX had the market to themselves. But AMAX let the price go to thirty bucks, and all these other companies came in, and the market collapsed as a result. Once the price of moly plunged back down, it didn't really make sense to invest hundreds of millions of dollars in Mount Emmons, so it was really AMAX's greed and misreading of the market that defeated the project."

Chuck Malick minced no words in disparaging the fallen giant as a victim of a fickle economy that had driven the beast all along. "The cold cash morality prevailed," he concluded. At the time of Malick's retirement, HCCA membership totaled 350, of which 240 were Crested Butte locals. With the mine seemingly thwarted, Susan Cottingham suggested that limiting growth and development in Gunnison County required an equally unflinching stand to that taken against AMAX. This would, in effect, return HCCA to its root mission of protecting the ambiance of the town against over development.

HCCA member Roy Smith suggested a more conciliatory stance: "We don't want to be an organization that looks for something to fight," he said, foreshadowing a shift of tactics and a new approach to the future. "We should try understanding the issues instead of just fighting something. Ski expansion on Snodgrass Mountain is one issue that is going to need some careful evaluation. If we want any credibility, we should focus on a reasonable approach." In this overture for peace, Smith was extending an olive branch instead of waving a protest placard. He recognized the toll of prolonged war on the psyche of the community.

Don Bachman credited HCCA with creating a successful template for grassroots activists everywhere. The organization had gained a credible footing with federal agencies through the fight with AMAX and had become part of the input process in Gunnison County. HCCA was funded mostly by local donations and took its finances seriously. "Looking at our budget," said Bachman, "we spent about $75 a day to oppose AMAX, while they were probably spending $75,000 a day to keep the project going. Our fiscal management was better than theirs."

Bachman, who served on the HCCA board, explained that AMAX had failed because of hard economic facts driven by the rising stakes of social and environmental mitigation, for which HCCA campaigned relentlessly. "HCCA had the benefit of an economic analysis and forecast which clearly showed the proposal was uneconomical at the commodity prices of the time and into the future. The price of production was driven up by regulatory imperatives and topographic realities that limited infrastructural options, especially for waste disposal and for assuring public land management values which produced satisfaction and economic stability for our communities. External costs to AMAX were also rising, including equipment and labor, and there was more viable competition for moly production elsewhere."

Wes Light had long reasoned that since the price of molybdenum had fallen, the Mt. Emmons Project was no longer economically viable. "There is no right-to-mine," Light concluded, "and the U.S. Forest Service can best serve its public trust by not allowing the use of special and sensitive public lands for such an environmental, economic and social disaster."

To Light, the AMAX retreat vindicated concerns expressed over the pitfalls of the boom-and-bust cycle of industrial mining. "This

Gunnison County Commissioner David Leinsdorf was a skilled conciliator who favored a "small mine" option. CRESTED BUTTE CHRONICLE ARCHIVES

calamity with the moly market could have happened after we were sucked into the boom. We could have been into the construction phase of the operation by then, and a thousand people could have been out of work. AMAX was a victim of conflicting curves on the financial chart. While the cost of the project was rising, the price of molybdenum was dropping. By putting the price curve where it belonged, we made the project too expensive for now and maybe forever."

Gunnison County Planning Commission member and founding HCCA board member, Dick Wingerson, dubbed the AMAX announcement an "anti-Climax" to a long and pitched battle. Humor still held sway in a dénouement that began to slowly cast a cloud over Crested Butte and Gunnison County.

23

The Damage Done

STEFANIC'S GROCERY STORE was one of the first places where I felt at home in Crested Butte. Tony and Eleanor Stefanic were friendly and helpful, always with quick smiles and eager to please. I sensed that their kindness was not predicated merely on customer relations, but implied a larger sense of welcome and accommodation to this new resident of town. When I first lived in Crested Butte in 1970, Stefanic's is where my roommates and I shopped for all our provisions. If we felt like splurging, we would ask Tony for a beefsteak, which he would butcher from a large hunk of red meat, slicing off a steak or two on his large, round, wooden butcher block.

The Stefanic's employed their friend, June Krizmanich, who offered equally friendly service while happily chatting in a way that made the store feel familial. June, like the Stefanic's, came from a mining background with a long family history in Crested Butte's coal mines.

During the midst of the fray with AMAX, I had written for the *Chronicle* a particularly condemning editorial about the proposed mine. The paper had just come out on the streets when the office phone rang. It was June asking with apparent nonchalance that I stop by the store. "Sure," I said, "I'll be right over." In two minutes I was there. But instead of the smiling, friendly face I had known, I was confronted by a glaring June, who dressed me down publicly for what I had written. She scolded that my editorial was mean-spirited and had done an unpardonable wrong to her and all of the old-timers in Crested Butte for whom I had shown a complete lack of respect.

The old storefront of Stefanic's Grocery where the author became persona non grata after publishing an editorial condemning AMAX.
CRESTED BUTTE CHRONICLE ARCHIVES

During her tirade, I felt the conspicuous absence of Tony and Eleanor, who had abandoned me to June's anger. Her words and affect caused something deep inside me to shrivel with shame and hurt. June and I never spoke again, and Stefanic's was no longer a place I went without feeling guilt and recrimination for my perceived betrayal.

AMAX was gone, but not forgotten. The divisiveness and bitterness of opposing and sometimes hostile segments of Crested Butte and Gunnison County had opened a festering wound that would not soon heal. The AMAX conflict magnified a mostly dormant social division and cultural rift that now threatened to splinter Crested Butte and compromise the delicate sense of community many residents, old and new, considered to be the town's greatest asset. Crested Butte had saved itself from the mine, but now faced a period of long pent up acrimony.

The local pro-mining minority, made up of old-timers, charged that Mitchell's combative zeal had driven out the only chance Crested

Butte had to regain its historic integrity as a mining town, an honorable and respectable working man's community. They labeled the town's leaders and environmentalists pseudo-intellectuals, obstructionists, and spoiled trust funders whose motives were selfish and ill-conceived. Some derided mine opponents as degenerate drug-users whose brains were addled by narcotics, indolence and altitude. They maligned us as slackers who had abandoned the Protestant work ethic and demeaned the town's political process with a warped, vision.

No one stated this with greater vituperation than John Paul Pitts, the publisher of the *Gunnison Country Times*, the ideologically conservative newspaper in Gunnison where I had begun my career as a reporter. Pitts had been imported from Midland, Texas during the early years of the mining battle by the owner of the *Times*, Perkins Sams, an oil-rich Texan notorious for having fenced off seven miles of Taylor Creek as his private vacation domain. It was Pitts' role to stand up to the liberal faction of Crested Butte and defend conservative values.

Pitts was strident in his role as caustic critic of Crested Butte. When he took over as publisher, he weighed in with his first editorial by dividing the human race into two types: Type A was productive and positive. Type B was destructive and lazy. In Pitts' opinion, the majority of Crested Butte fell into "Type B".

In the immediate aftermath of the AMAX pull-out, Pitts titled his condemning editorial: THEY WILL DANCE IN THE STREETS AS CHILDREN WEEP.

> Like modern day medicine men, Mayor W and the rest of the High Country Aliens have come into the streets to dance their dervish—probably in costume, as usual, and proclaim that their Red Lady parties, balls, treks to Aspen, fist shaking, news making, and semi-intelligent incantations had driven the bad spirit out of the mountain.
>
> As the postponement party goes on in Crested Butte and Wes Light dances in the street with Mayor W, Gil Hersch and the rest of the "*Chronicle* Crowd," there will be children in Gunnison saying good-bye to their friends, who thought they would be going to school here this year. Tearful wives will be packing away dishes and saying

good-bye to friends, and despondent husbands will be looking down the road toward new jobs. Losing your job and having to pull up your family and move on is no cause for dancing in the streets.

As a product of boom towns, I can definitely say that boom is better than bust. Boom meant that my daddy had a job and my momma didn't cry over the bills. Boom meant that there was show money on the weekends and shoe money at the start of school every year. Boom meant that there wasn't a constant parade of loaded down cars heading out of town and friends and relatives stopping out front to say good-byes as they moved on to find jobs.

The loss of families in the Gunnison Country as a result of the AMAX pull-back will be 20 to 50, and I can tell you one thing. Most of them would rather be staying than going. Also, I am sure that the merchants who sell them groceries, gasoline, shoes, homes and furniture are not that anxious for them to leave.

I do not share any of the joy of the "*Chronicle* Crowd", Mayor W or the High Country Aliens, and for the record, I count it a distinct honor to be counted an enemy of that bunch.

'Mayor W' wrote back with fire in his belly:

> Dear Mr. Pitts,
>
> In a recent column you wrote of your latest speculation about how long it would take Crested Butte to dance in the streets. You asserted, "Well, it has happened and I lost."
>
> JPP, you've won and so have the rest of the people of this area. Whether it was a soft moly market or the efforts of Crested Butte and Gunnison citizens to oppose the AMAX proposal, or a combination of the two, all of us involved are better off for the AMAX decision.
>
> Can you imagine how many children would be weeping, how many wives tearfully packing, if AMAX had maintained its position to proceed with a construction phase on the Mt. Emmons Project?
>
> And what about the merchants who would have expanded and enlarged, and the influx of new businesses based on the projected growth from the mine? What about the shells of the towns of Gunnison and Crested Butte, left like hollow monuments to an aborted whim of a company that cares more for its profit margin than it does for its country and our environment?
>
> As the product of a boomtown, perhaps the problems that ac-

company them have become commonplace to you; the housing shortages, over-taxation of public facilities at the expanse of long-term residents, increased alcoholism, crime, wife and child abuse.

I would suggest that you try to look beyond the naiveté of a 10-year-old who equates boomtowns with "show money on the weekends." The weight of such a fate for a community goes far beyond the short-term financial implications you would suggest.

You call yourself proud to be our "enemy," a classification that you, and no one else, have placed yourself in. Our fight is not meant to make enemies, but to uphold values and resources for posterity—for our children's children who may "weep" for want of open space, wilderness and clean air.

Unlike an enemy's, yours is an attitude which offers a threat to no one but yourself.

Sincerely,

W Mitchell
Mayor of Crested Butte

Disparagement for Crested Butte's "new guard" poured forth from a small cadre of old-timers who resented us young upstarts for overpowering their traditions. Sedmak, Stadjuhar, Krizmanich, Verzuh, Tezak, Gallowich, Kovanic; these were among the names on a list of 45 signatures on a damning petition:

> Editor,
> There are many people in Crested Butte who do not share the views of Mitchell and followers which have been presented to the world. We are, however, reluctant to speak out, having a feeling of hopelessness, since we are in the minority; having the reluctance to chance ridicule by those who consider themselves intellectually superior; and some have even (mistakenly, certainly) expressed fear of reprisal.
> We, too, love Crested Butte and its surroundings, and are very much concerned. It would take much recital of facts to reveal conditions as they really are in Crested Butte, and the reluctance or refusal of those in charge to rectify matters. Those whose opinions differ are ignored.

Terry Hamlin had been both a long-time Crested Butte local and a mining advocate for AMAX, working within the Mt. Emmons Project since it began. His vantage was therefore unique. More than twenty years after leaving Crested Butte, then engaged in a Christian mission, Hamlin considered it all from a distance and spoke his truth in a telephone interview:

> It's not my right to judge, but you wonder how you enjoy benefits of technology, industry, and science in the world we live in and not know that, somewhere, trade-offs have been made to enjoy that. If I'm part of the community, trade-offs are part of being a citizen.
>
> In Crested Butte, AMAX was held to a higher standard. They didn't intend to steamroll the community or they wouldn't have invested in land planning with state-of-the-art computer-generated information. They also looked at smaller mines with order of magnitude studies. There were a lot of very talented people on the AMAX side, offering to work with Crested Butte. At times I was perplexed that people would turn it down flat. But in the end, it was the economy that killed it.
>
> There were a lot of people in Crested Butte and the county who could see the economic benefits of the mine. All the people I worked with at AMAX were caring people who wanted to see it done right. Unfortunately, civility has been lost in the public debate arena. People take on personal attacks as opposed to differing viewpoints. Some can separate that, but the majority gets caught in the passion of the moment and the engagement. It's a great disappointment to see civility lost when people have different points of view that could work toward a compromise.

24
Post Mortem

NOW THAT THE BATTLES WITH AMAX were over and the saber rattling silenced, Crested Butte fell into a malaise, a post-war blues. The glue that had so tightly bonded the mining opposition had suddenly disappeared, and there was no returning to normalcy, if there had ever been any normalcy in Crested Butte.

The town seemed diminished, perhaps exhausted, by the fight. The ultimate casualty was the intangible, delicate, serendipitous sense of frivolity the townspeople had enjoyed before battle lines had been drawn. Four years in the trenches changed all that. The Elysian Fields had become a war zone rife with divisiveness. The politics of exclusion and alienation weighed heavily on an already strained social fabric.

The same national recession that had hurt AMAX also crippled Crested Butte and the Colorado resort industry. The town now scrambled to secure its own financial future and provide a living for its people. Tourism promotions, which had been shunned in the early '80s as a great evil that would "Aspenize" Crested Butte, were now fostered by none other than Mitchell, who finished out his last term in office under pressure to advance the town's bottom line. A better fighter than a promoter, Mitchell lost his re-election bid six months after AMAX pulled out when realtor and banker Thom Cox, a native of Kansas, was elected.

"I've never promoted Crested Butte for tourism," said Mitchell explaining his stance as mayor, "but we had a bad winter and a tough spring. Sales tax was low and we needed a shot in the arm. My aim was not to become another Aspen, but to get a share of the tourism."

In the years immediately following the departure of AMAX, Myles

Chuck Malick, leather shop owner and president of the High Country Citizens' Alliance. CRESTED BUTTE CHRONICLE ARCHIVES

Rademan converted his breakthrough Grubstake slide show into an infomercial he called "Illuminations." The images were similar to those that had won the hearts and minds of Crested Butte in 1977, but the audience was different. Rademan used the show as a soft promotion for Crested Butte, targeting tourists eager to glimpse the character of this unusual community. Customers paid to see what Rademan had artfully crafted. With this visual tool, Rademan had helped save the town from AMAX. Now he used the same tool to help sell the town to an audience that included tourists, businessmen, second home-owners, speculators and land developers.

"There was a general feeling that we wanted more business in town," allowed Rademan. "But how much were people willing to invest to gain that end? Each public investment was an act of faith in the future of Crested Butte. We were not limited by one future; there were a lot of futures we could create."

The war was over and Mitchell was out. He suffered the General McArthur syndrome of sudden powerlessness. Atonement was the dues he paid for those years of heroic adulation. The Crested Butte town council, which had been waging a lofty, ideological battle for the soul of the town, returned to the pedestrian concerns of dog control, repairing pot holes, expanding sewage treatment capacity, and budgeting for snow plowing and trash removal. Such business-as-usual matters were plodding and dull compared with the excitement of standing off the foe with fiery rhetoric. The town's warriors experienced a letdown that was enervating. Where resistance had pushed them together, a comparative vacuum now drew them apart. The end of the AMAX drama ushered in an emotional letdown, a kind of post-traumatic stress syndrome.

"Crested Butte has gone through a series of booms and busts," Rademan explained shortly after AMAX had withdrawn. "Some people leave and others come to fill the vacuum. In a lot of ways, we are experiencing a painful process. Any period of transition is that way, because some of the glitter is gone. That forces people to look at their lives and their personal state of affairs. They have to decide to get out or stay and dig in."

In an AMAX post mortem, Susan Cottingham laid out the challenges for Crested Butte in a letter-to-the-editor printed in both local papers:

> Through these tumultuous times, the positive goal of the majority of our citizens has been clear: preserve the social and environmental values which have made Crested Butte a special place to live. This means a continuous commitment to clean air and water, to the preservation of the beauty of our land and our wilderness, to a healthy and sustainable local economy, to a thriving and safe social and cultural environment. We have weathered the AMAX controversy. We have made our case, clearly and successfully, and we have made the largest mining conglomerate in the world aware of our strength and determination.
>
> Where do we go from here? Do we abandon our policies endorsing quality of growth and high standards in the face of a national economic picture over which we have no control? Do we no longer believe in the special nature of Crested Butte and eagerly prepare to join the American mainstream? Do we breathe a collective, smug sigh of relief and consign AMAX to the back burner while they continue business as usual? I believe that the answer is NO."

Celebrating AMAX with a "going away" party initiated a complex transition from the fray of the fight to the return of normalcy, or whatever that meant for Crested Butte.
CRESTED BUTTE CHRONICLE ARCHIVES

Gradually, many of the principals in the fight, those who had argued most passionately against the mine, moved away. Mitchell relocated to Denver, then to Santa Barbara and occasionally Hawaii, promoting himself as a motivational speaker. Rademan took a city planning job in Park City, Utah, where he later helped the city accommodate the winter Olympics there. Chuck Malick, Susan Cottingham, and Don Bachman—the HCCA mainstays—moved off to further causes in conservation, regulatory administration, lobbying, and legal research elsewhere. Malick became a lobbyist in Denver. Cottingham and Bachman relocated to Helena and Bozeman, Montana, respectively. Wes Light moved to Aspen and served as Pitkin County Attorney, then returned to Crested Butte and resumed his role as town attorney, during which he won a major pollution lawsuit against Louisiana Pacific. He later served as Crested Butte mayor before moving to rural southern New Mexico and vacationing at a second home in Costa Rica.

"They had had their five-year stint in an idyllic setting," reflected Art Biddle, dismissively. "They were talented enough to find other places. That was certainly one of the great career experiences for me."

"After AMAX left, a lot of the people fighting the mine left, too," reflected Mike Rock. "There's something telling in that: Life goes on, we all grow up. One thing we need to be sensitive to is that we move on, but that people are left to live in the aftermath of what we have done, whether it's protesting a mine with self-righteous indignation or working for a mining company and making an impact that will last well into the future. It seems like a bump in the road now, but if you continue living there, those decisions have far greater impacts."

Denis Hall, who had reported on AMAX for the *Crested Butte Pilot*, did not leave Crested Butte. He stayed to eventually assume leadership of HCCA and continue in local journalism with his "Earth Matters" column for the *Crested Butte News*. In a March 2006 column, Hall revisited the AMAX record in light of new mine activity. "To think that we actually stopped a mining project with the momentum of economic development and the force of law behind it was hubristic," he wrote. "Economics stopped the mine, pure and simple. The myth that we stopped the mine made us feel good. We were the little town that could."

"Crested Butte is a very small, isolated community which attracts people because it's a great experience," summed up Terry Hamlin, "but there are perspectives that we hold when we are thirty years old that, as we go out in the world, we understand that things are different. It's like when I was on ski patrol, I spent a lot of time on top of the mountain looking out over the peaks. Those peak experiences are few and far between. Most of life is lived in the valleys. We enjoy an amazingly prosperous lifestyle compared with other parts of the world. If we live in isolated communities that are unwilling to change, then, when we go into the world, we see different realities."

Hamlin's remark about peak experiences and life being lived in the valleys stuck with me for years. It's true that life is lived mostly in the valleys. But spirit thrives on the mountain peaks where the air is thin and the sky seems closer to heaven. The AMAX fight had awakened a soaring community spirit that had looked down from a lofty perspective over the more mundane aspects of life. For many, returning to life in the valley was a spiritual letdown, and for some, like me, that meant a search for new horizons. Of all places, I chose Aspen.

The author pushing his 35-pound chrome Mongoose over
West Maroon Pass to Aspen before bikes were banned in wilderness.
PAUL ANDERSEN COLLECTION

Mt. Emmons as pictured with a molybdenum mine Photoshopped as a worse-case scenario. IMAGE BY DENIS HALL

PART III
An Onslaught of Suitors

"U.S. Energy wants to put lipstick on a pig and dress it all up in frilly clothes to try to attract another partner and scare those living near the potential mine into taking action no matter what the cost."

— MARK REAMAN

Editor | *Crested Butte News*

AUTHOR'S NOTE

LANDED A JOB with the *Aspen Times*, moved into a small downtown apartment, and began reporting on what felt like big city life. Aspen, despite its worldly image, is geographically still a small town, but the scale was considerably larger than where I had come on the other side of the Elk Range.

As embroiled as I became in the Roaring Fork Valley, my rear view mirror was filled with Crested Butte where I retained a soulful connection that will never leave me. So, I looked back often and took notes on a succession of mining proposals that confronted the town over the next several decades. Looking back from Aspen, I followed these new overtures by talking often with Crested Butte friends and from informative reporting in the *Crested Butte News*.

What follows resumes the chronology after the AMAX capitulation where Crested Butte rejected the advances of five other mining companies, including a resurgence by U.S. Energy in what seemed like a final, desperate act of umbrage against the town.

My hope, and the hopes of Crested Butte, are that the current owner of the Mt. Emmons Mine properties—Freeport-McMoRan—will continue in a joint effort with local activists and municipalities to end the threat of a mine on the Red Lady forever.

25
Phelps-Dodge Devours AMAX

THE FIGHT AGAINST AMAX seemed to resolve in 1983 when the corporation announced it had scratched the Mt. Emmons Project from its books. But that surrender marked only one battle in a much larger campaign. AMAX was gone, but the molybdenum in the core of Mt. Emmons was still there to be reawakened like a sleeping giant, or more like the Loch Ness Monster, stirring menacingly beneath the surface.

"This is one of the longest running mine fights in the country," assessed Wendy McDermott, executive director of HCCA in the early 1990s. "We've been working for years to keep a mine off Red Lady, and nothing has changed."

In December 1991, AMAX resurfaced when it announced plans to develop a "small mine." Plans called for excavating 10,000 tons per day of the highest grade ore: 0.7% molybdenum. (This compared with the original estimated projection of 25,000 tons per day of low-grade moly.) Fists were immediately raised in Crested Butte as new anti-mine strategies began to stir, but AMAX rescinded its proposal before a first punch was thrown.

It seemed as if the company were testing the waters of a community it hoped had changed after the original Mt. Emmons Project had been dead and buried for almost a decade. Perhaps the community had sobered up from the intoxicating tussle. Perhaps the uncertainties inherent in a tourist economy would make a mine look more attractive. Maybe a gradually changing population had become ambivalent about a mine. Crested Butte had changed in many ways, but it was not even close to altering its course on condemning an industrial mine—of any size.

The AMAX proposal to "high grade" the Mount Emmons orebody contradicted a 1979 report from independent mining consultant Stan Michaelson, who was hired by the Gunnison County Planning Commission to evaluate an earlier small mine proposal for economic viability. This idea had been championed by then county commissioner David Leinsdorf. Even at 20,000 tons per day, concluded Michaelson, such a mine would be only "marginally feasible." A more financially realistic Mt. Emmons project would be in the range of 30,000 tons per day, he had said. Any speculation would, of course, be determined by the fluctuations of the international metals market. This may have been yet another permit fishing trip for AMAX.

As another decade passed and the new millennium advanced, AMAX went through internal changes. In the early 1990s, the company had been renamed Cyprus-AMAX, representing its union with another huge mining conglomerate, Cyprus Mineral Company. In 1993, the joint venture filed for a patent application to keep the Mt. Emmons Project alive. The re-enlivened corporation also commenced securing water rights for eventual production. In 1996, Cyprus-AMAX threw down the gauntlet and filed for conditional water rights. The Town of Crested Butte and HCCA joined with Gunnison County, the Western Slope Environmental Resource Council, and others to protest. The water rights application went to trial in 1998. Crested Butte and its allies won a hard fought decision.

In 1999, Cyprus-AMAX was acquired by mining behemoth Phelps-Dodge in a hostile takeover. This transferred ownership of the Mt. Emmons Project to the world's biggest copper and molybdenum miner, an operator for whom Mt. Emmons was manageable. An appeal from Phelps-Dodge to the Colorado Supreme Court on the water rights decision was heard on September 19, 2001, but with no change in the Court's earlier decision. This keystone issue—water rights—appeared intractable as the strongest defense against a mine in Crested Butte.

A psychological setback for the town occurred in 2004, when Phelps-Dodge was issued 155 acres of mining claims atop Mt. Emmons by the Bureau of Land Management (BLM) for $5 an acre. This absurdly discounted value on public lands was predicated on the Mining Law of 1872. The issuance stirred considerable local resentment since the lands were also valued as backcountry ski terrain and public open space. There was something highly symbolic about the top of Red Lady Bowl being handed over to an industrial behemoth for a song.

Crested Butte and the High Country Citizens' Alliance filed an objection in 2005, but District Court dismissed the allegations and held that the plaintiffs had no right to challenge the BLM's issuance of the patents. The case ended its upward trajectory with the U.S. Supreme Court in 2006, which upheld the lower court's dismissal of the case. Phelps Dodge paid the government a nominal $775.00 and took possession of the 155 acres.

On February 28, 2006, a legal finding allowed Phelps-Dodge to return the Mt. Emmons property—and the costly water treatment plant—to U.S. Energy Corporation, the same company that had sold its interests thirty years before to AMAX. The transfer included 25 patented and 520 unpatented mining claims totalling 5,400 acres. The contested 155 acres atop Mount Emmons were included in the return.

"We are very excited about re-acquiring the Mt. Emmons molybdenum property," stated Mark Larsen, president of U.S. Energy, in a press release. "We view this property as a potential 'company maker.' We are now engaged in the active pursuit of a sizable mining industry partner to co-develop and mine the property." The new prospect was called Crested Butte Corporation.

It all came back like a bad dream, yet another threat to capitalize the Mt. Emmons orebody. But there was a caveat that would create a long-term financial liability for U.S. Energy. By taking back the Mt. Emmons property, U.S. Energy also took back the Coal Creek wastewater treatment plant, a $1 million-per-year expense that was mandated by law to protect the quality of Crested Butte's water.

Meanwhile, the price of moly was dramatically rebounding, as columnist Denis Hall reported: "Crested Butte Corp. owns 5,400 acres of patented mining claims... They own water rights, maps, delineations, mine plans—everything AMAX accomplished—and the orebody itself. In the high-grade deposit alone, there is $6.4 billion worth of molybdenum up there under the rocks of Red Lady Bowl. The good folks at U.S. Energy intend to get that $6.4 billion out of the ground."

"Rarely are mineral deposits of this magnitude discovered," noted U.S. Energy's Larsen, "and we now own it in a very favorable pricing environment." U.S. Energy CEO Keith Larsen (Mark and Keith are brothers—nicknamed in Crested Butte "The Larceny Brothers.") added: "Today we find ourselves in a robust commodities market driven by the economies of China, India and the United States. We believe that the price of molybdic oxide will remain strong compared to historical prices. In light of this, we have decided to move forward with permitting the property in an effort to tap its tremendous value for our shareholders."

U.S. Energy conceded that the majority of the permits required to take Mt. Emmons to production had expired and needed to be updated and re-filed with federal, state and local agencies. A consulting group that specializes in drafting and obtaining mine project permits estimated that it would take up to five years to secure the necessary permits for a revisited venture on Mt. Emmons, at a cost of $5 million.

U.S. Energy made an overture in March 2006 that echoed AMAX assurances from 30 years before: "As we move forward, we intend to fully engage the local communities and to work closely with all agencies involved in the permitting process. This will be aimed at minimizing environmental impacts and to also educate the public at large about the significant economic benefits that could be realized when the mine is brought into production. We look forward to presenting our ideas and business plans to community leaders and the public at the appropriate time. Our long-term strategy is to make this project a win/win situation for all parties involved to the maximum extent practical."

Coincident with the Larsens' optimism came an announcement in April 2006 from Phelps-Dodge, stating that it would reopen the Climax mine near Leadville after almost 20 years of inactivity. While some Leadvillians cheered the announcement, others wondered what the boom/bust cycle of mining had in store for them with yet another reawakening of the sleeping giant in Mt Bartlett. Leadville had been crippled by crime and social upheaval when AMAX closed the mine in the mid-'80s; this in reaction to the downturn in molybdenum prices. After Phelps-Dodge made the announcement to reopen, Leadville residents appeared hopeful that the current rebound would last.

As U.S. Energy positioned itself to move forward on Mt. Emmons, the Coal Creek wastewater treatment plant came back to haunt. A report by the Securities and Exchange Commission warned: "The company does not have the required capital resources to maintain and operate the water treatment plant long-term and develop the Mt. Emmons molybdenum property. Management of the company is therefore aggressively pursuing industry partners and other venues of financing for the property."

On March 3, 2006, the price of molybdenum was $25 per pound, down from a high of nearly $40 a year before. At $40 per pound, the potential value of the Mt. Emmons orebody was over $10 billion. Even at $25 per pound, the value was placed at $6.6 billion.

On March 10, 2006, in answer to U.S. Energy's renewed interest, a headline in the newly published *Crested Butte News* announced, "Local Officials Vow to Fight Plans for Mt. Emmons Mine." Crested Butte Mayor Alan Bernholtz said, "We all feel that we're on the same page in fighting the mine from opening in our community." A unifying voice came from Chris Morgan, Mayor of Mt. Crested Butte: "Mt. Crested Butte does not support the mine. Mining and becoming a great resort don't fit together; that's pretty obvious."

The *Crested Butte News* had now become the voice of Crested Butte and a growing portion of Gunnison County. This resulted after the town's two competing papers—the *Chronicle* and the *Pilot* — merged following a long, drawn out negotiation between Pilot owners Lee and Jane Ervin and *Chronicle* owner Myles Arber. Now, with just one newspaper in town, journalism gained a level of sustainability and viability it had not had before. The new media organ was consigned to the capable hands of editor Mark Reaman.

26

'Lucky Jack' Strikes Out and so does Thompson Creek Metals

IN APRIL 2006, as the towns of Crested Butte and Mt. Crested-Butte girded for a fight, U.S. Energy announced it had found a new partner. Kobex Resources, Ltd., of Vancouver, Canada, put a strong new face on the Mt. Emmons Project when it renamed the project "Lucky Jack." Kobex opened the project by hiring a community relations firm headed by former Greenpeace leader, Patrick Moore, an eco-apostate who was considered the right person to assuage Crested Butte's environmental concerns.

"He's hired to sell us something that the town doesn't want," reacted Wendy McDermott, executive director of the High Country Citizens' Alliance. Kobex also hired former Gunnison County Commissioner Perry Anderson as its local spokesman. Battle lines quickly formed as the community dug in for another siege.

Two years of stalemate, complicated by the same Gordian knot of regulatory challenges that had beleaguered AMAX, forced Kobex to announce it was abandoning the Lucky Jack project: "The decision was made reluctantly since the Lucky Jack molybdenite property is still considered to be one of the best undeveloped primary molybdenum deposits in the world. However, the regulatory and legal uncertainties which currently exist at the federal, state, county and municipal levels have become too great to justify the necessary time and major predevelopment expenditures that are required to advance this property."

HCCA's mineral resources director, Bob Salter, told the *Crested Butte News*, "We welcome this departure as a strong indication of how effective local efforts have been in stopping the development of a mine on Mt. Emmons. It's clear that Kobex Resources and their highly experienced CEO have made a wise decision to cut their losses here in Crested Butte."

"Kobex had underestimated resistance to a mine on Mt. Emmons," editorialized the *CB News*. "Of course, there is no rest for the weary. The threat of mining on Mt. Emmons still exists, and the need for reforms has not diminished."

The Town of Crested Butte again rejoiced. This time, HCCA made ambitious overtures to forever end the threat of a Mt. Emmons mine with a proposal to purchase the key 365 acres at the U.S. Energy mine site, take over the operation of the Coal Creek water treatment plant, and facilitate the withdrawal of 5,000 unpatented mining claims surrounding Mt. Emmons.

"Life is Fine Without a Mine" read a full-page advertisement in the *Crested Butte News* soliciting support for a "final solution" to industrial mining on Mt. Emmons. "Don't let corporate mining interests destroy the health and beauty of our mountain communities! Together we can prevent a molybdenum mine and the industrialization of the Gunnison Valley!"

This appeal seemed overly ambitious at first, but given the growing number of resort-based capital investments in the Upper East River Valley, the local and regional economy was at a tipping point for valuing a successful and assumedly sustainable resort scenario over that of a one-time mining venture with the potential for environmental and socio-economic disruptions. There was now greater buy-in on the anti-mining stance as Mt. Crested Butte sided fully with Crested Butte in a pledge of solidarity based on the mutual interests of the upper East River Valley.

Then, in August 2008, Crested Butte felt another shock with U.S. Energy's announcement that another partner had been found. Thompson Creek Metals Company USA reportedly signed option agreements that would give it 75% of the Mt. Emmons Project. "It's what we were hoping for," announced Perry Anderson, the former Gunnison County Commissioner who had remained the local spokesman for U.S. Energy. "They are a good, solid company and they have the assets and knowledge to see this project through. It is very positive for U.S. Energy, it is positive for the project, and it is positive for the community."

Thompson Creek Metals and U.S. Energy boasted that the dawning of a new day would be illuminating Mt. Emmons as the end-of-the-rainbow pot of gold the world had been waiting for. "Thompson Creek Metals Company is one of the largest publicly traded primary molybdenum producers," wrote Thompson Metals CEO Kevin Loughrey in a full page newspaper ad placed as a letter to the community. "We have a strong record of success in our other operations, and we look forward to bringing our excellent reputation, proven methodologies, and long range vision to Gunnison County."

The company launched a website and promoted itself with regular newspaper ads reassuring the community with promises for "a reduced footprint, worker safety, better precision, stability, and a lasting legacy." One ad asserted that the newly formed Mt. Emmons Moly Company would "provide a natural resource that plays a role

As new mining companies elbowed their way into Crested Butte, none had the financial capacity to underwrite a new mine given the history of strident opposition from the town and the high prices of mitigation.

ARIZONA GEOLOGICAL SURVEY

in local, state and national commerce while providing significant economic benefits to the local community."

It was "déjà vu all over again," but the courtship lasted only four months when another house of cards collapsed and Thompson Creek Metals shook loose from the Crested Butte tar baby. On April 25, 2011, CEO Loughrey announced, "We made the strategic decision to step back from the Mount Emmons project and focus our efforts and resources on our Berg exploration property located in British Columbia." Here was yet another example of resource imperialism, where a company facing daunting prospects on Mt. Emmons shifted development ambitions to a path of less resistance.

HCCA reacted with a celebratory, but cautionary, press release: "We need to be mindful that U.S. Energy Corp. remains the sole owner of the mine property, and that the company intends to continue efforts to develop a mine and find a new partner. HCCA continues to be concerned about existing water quality impacts on Mt. Emmons. As we have for years, HCCA will continue to fight at every step of the way to protect our environment, economy, and way of life."

The conflicts that arose over Mt. Emmons are popularly told as corollaries to struggles throughout the history of the West, wherein various traditional archetypes are depicted doing battle over the land: independent homesteaders vs. ruthless cattle barons. . .a lone settler vs. a domineering timber company. . .a quaint frontier town vs. greedy speculators for oil, gold, silver, uranium, coal, copper, lead, water, and molybdenum.

One of the most sobering lessons from the AMAX fight was an epiphany I gleaned in 1987. This was several years after I had moved across the Elk Range for a newspaper reporting job in Aspen. While attending a memorial service at the Aspen Institute, a top tier global organization dedicated to international policy and values-based leadership, I fell into conversation with a trio of Institute trustees, all dressed in business suits. I mentioned my recent move from Crested Butte, and two of the trustees said they recognized the name, having served on the board of directors of a company called AMAX. I told them, somewhat haughtily, that I had lived in Crested Butte when the Mt. Emmons Project was a hot topic. "We fought the mine. . .and we won," I boasted. "Oh, yes," one of them nodded in reflection, "that's when our moly division moved to Africa."

The fact that AMAX shifted its operations to Africa and that Thompson Creek Metals focused on British Columbia reflects the reality of the global economy and global markets: Extractive industries will seek the path of least resistance to extract economic gains and enrich their shareholders. Crested Butte said "No!" so Africa became a global sacrifice zone for molybdenum. Crested Butte put up a struggle, so Thompson Creek Metals exploited the mineral wealth of British Columbia.

Not all communities have the wherewithal to resist the entreaties of industrial capitalism. Centuries of resource colonialism answer with resounding finality that such has not been the case during colonial epochs of grand scale, which include the thirteen original American colonies. Today, many communities succumb to what the late desert scribe and ardent social critic Edward Abbey referred to as the "iron glacier" of capitalism. Abbey's visits to Crested Butte during the AMAX fight allowed him to witness a modest exception to that grinding, inexorable force.

Meanwhile, U.S. Energy ramped up its commitment to open a mine in an announcement by CEO Keith Larsen: "While we are disappointed with Thompson Creek's departure from the project, we remain committed to moving the project forward on our own behalf as well as reaching out to other potential partners, including those outside of our borders. Looking forward, we will be reaching out to the Chinese, who have expressed an interest in the project in the past. They tend to have a longer term view regarding resource inventory."

The *Crested Butte News* cheered Thompson Creek Metals' departure with a front page color photo of—what else—a celebratory bicycle parade down Elk Avenue. Smiling participants were dressed characteristically in red and carried a HCCA banner. A placard on one townie stated: "MOUNTAINS NOT MINES."

Still, the suggestion of a Chinese intervention brought on sober headshaking in Crested Butte. Beneath the newspaper headline—"U.S. Energy loses major investor in moly mine"—was a gallows humor subhead: "What's Mandarin for molybdenum?"

27
The Rogue Returns with a Vengeance

JUST WHEN CRESTED BUTTE thought it was safe to wade into the deep waters of a final solution to end mining on Mt. Emmons, U.S. Energy, the rogue wildcatter, resurfaced in 2012.

It began with what seemed like a feint as described in a newsletter from HCCA:

> You've heard the good news. HCCA, along with the Town of CB and the Red Lady Coalition, is engaged in active discussions with U.S. Energy to create a permanent solution that will end the mining threat on Mt. Emmons. Let me say that again—negotiations are underway to create a permanent end to the threat of mine development on our Red Lady! We are confident that such a solution is possible, but it will require a concerted commitment from the entire community.

The idea of removing the risk of mining was a heady, almost unbelievable, notion. Plans called for three key conditions: 1.) ensuring that the AMAX-built mine water treatment plant would be operated affordably, in perpetuity; 2.) exchanging U.S. Energy's land and mining claims with land owned by the Federal government elsewhere and of equitable value; 3.) protecting Mt. Emmons from future mining claims through a federal Congressional mineral withdrawal, which would remove the threat of a "Climax" in Crested Butte.

Water, again, was the critical issue. The *Crested Butte News* reported in Sept. 2012 that the State of Colorado had mandated stricter standards for water quality in Coal Creek.

> The portion of Coal Creek running through the town of CB will be reclassified by the state as a water source and mandated to meet drinking water standards. This means stricter standards for mine effluent treatment at the Mt. Emmons mine, owned by U.S. Energy, specifically calling for lower levels of toxic metals and chemicals like arsenic. The plan requires U.S. Energy to determine the point source of those toxic agents. U.S. Energy is seeking more leniency in its water discharge.

Then came a major shakeup as U.S. Energy stepped back from overtures to end the threat of mining with an opposite approach. Two months after the state mandate, in November 2012, U.S. Energy announced a scaled up mining proposal for Mt. Emmons that ignored any compliance with the town's values and stood in complete ignorance with experiences from the past.

An alarmed HCCA learned of the plan and petitioned the U.S. Forest Service for information. The request was denied on the grounds that the plan contained "confidential business information." HCCA filed a "Freedom of Information Act" (FOIA) request, explaining that any new mining plan was of great importance to the community and that there was a legitimate need for public disclosure. The U.S. Forest Service refused a second time.

"The impact of these operations on the community's clean water, wildlife and quality of life are significant and should be available for public consumption," appealed Jennifer Bock, HCCA's Water Director. HCCA was working towards a permanent solution to prevent mining on Mt. Emmons, and now came an enormous mining proposal by the recalcitrant owner. While the proposal was not AMAX-scaled, it was no trifling venture.

The finally released U.S. Energy proposed Plan of Operations spelled out what was in store for Crested Butte:

- A large scale mine running 24-7-365 for 33 years
- Mining and processing 12,700 tons of ore per day (about half of what AMAX had proposed)

- Producing a total 143 million tons of high grade ore (AMAX had targeted 300 million tons.).
- Employing 335 miners, with a workforce of 1,000 for four years of mine development and mill construction.
- Upgrading Kebler Pass to an all-weather surface for year-round truck traffic to the railroad line in the North Fork Valley.

Gunnison would not be spared, nor would Ohio Creek, Carbon Creek and Splains Gulch, through which powerlines would run to the mill and mine. Water would be diverted from the Slate River and Carbon Creek to fill new reservoirs at Carbon Creek, Mill Creek and Elk Creek, stored for industrial purposes with decreed water rights of 3,600 acre feet. In an end run around the mine's biggest obstacle, the plan said the Town of Crested Butte's watershed would not be denigrated by operations.

"This proposal," announced an alarmed and incredulous Greg Dyson of HCCA, "cannot be measured on a scale of anything the Gunnison Valley has previously experienced. Mining Red Lady would fundamentally alter the economy and lifestyle of Crested Butte. It would result in the loss of the scenic, recreation, wildlife and water quality values we enjoy today." Bill Ronai of the Red Lady Coalition, charged, "No studies have been done with respect to environmental or socio-economic impacts, and there is no mention of any studies looking at cumulative impacts, which could potentially be critical given the lifespan of the proposed project."

U.S. Energy had just set the clock back to 1977, either as a stubborn last ditch effort or as a ploy to instill shock and awe in Gunnison County and improve its bargaining power. Then came a strange disclaimer in a U.S. Energy announcement: "Although a temporary shutdown of operations is not planned, circumstances beyond the control of the project may require a temporary cessation of operations based on severe weather or unfavorable economic conditions." In other words, the nature of this extractive process would bring a boom and very likely, a bust, so prepare accordingly.

Six months later, in June 2013, HCCA fired a warning shot at the U.S. Forest Service by seeking affirmation that the Wastewater Treatment Plant at the old Keystone Mine would continue operations at $2 million per year, which U.S. Energy said it was paying to keep Coal Creek alive and the water plant functioning. If U.S. Energy did not act in accordance, charged HCCA, the U.S. Forest Service would be in violation of the Clean Water Act. "We fear," wrote HCCA, "the U.S. Forest Service and U.S. Energy are playing Russian roulette with the water quality of Coal Creek."

HCCA went further and protested U.S. Energy's proposed "Voluntary Clean-Up Plan," (VCUP), a stop gap measure that proposed to cork the old mine portal. HCCA deemed this grossly insufficient for the long-term, as HCCA's Water Director, Jennifer Bock, stated. "Unfortunately, we can't just plug a hole in the mountain and hope that everything will be okay. There is no understanding of groundwater flows on Red Lady, and we don't want to see what happened in Silverton happen here, where a mining company plugged an old tunnel only to have water that was even more polluted come out of another part of the mountain."

U.S. Energy showed its true colors by misleading the public because the mine site was neither eligible for a VCUP, nor had the U.S. Forest Service permitted the corking of the portal. The mine effluent could not be negated in U.S. Energy's plans because the effluent contained dangerous levels of cadmium, copper, zinc and arsenic—the heavy metals that had poisoned Coal Creek before AMAX stepped in with a timely fix.

Jennifer Bock laid out HCCA's resolve: "A clean-up on Red Lady may be a good idea, but with our clean water at stake, we need to know for sure. The state is now requiring real transparency. U.S. Energy will have to explain how development of a mine could be compatible with a cleanup plan, and there will be meaningful review from technical experts within the state government."

Water again provided a lever by which Crested Butte moved its world. As for the proposed Plan of Operations, *CB News* editor Mark Reaman took U.S. Energy to task:

> It wasn't that long ago that U.S. Energy was in a lawsuit with mining energy giant Phelps-Dodge, and the loser essentially had to take the mine. U.S. Energy lost and now has the mine. . .which comes with an annual expenditure of close to $2 million to run the

water treatment plant. I understand why U.S. Energy wants to put lipstick on a pig and dress it all up in frilly clothes to try to attract another partner and scare those living near the potential mine into taking action no matter what the cost. They are running out of money and opportunity. . . And did I mention that the price of molybdenum is now about $11 a pound? And there is no shortage of moly around the world.

Greg Dyson of HCCA wrote in the newsletter of August 2013 about bearing witness to one of the largest, most heinous legacies of large scale industrial mining in Colorado:

> I was hiking a section of the Colorado Trail recently, from Copper Mountain to Camp Hale, and was enjoying the beautiful trail above tree-line near Kokomo Pass, when suddenly the Climax Mine loomed into view. I had a bird's-eye view of it and it wasn't a view I wanted. I stood there for a good long time and took in what a 100-year-old molybdenum mine looks like. Bartlett Mountain has part of its face missing, as if a giant bear had been clawing at it. There is a massive tailings pond looking an ominous orange color. And the noise—I could hear machinery operating from miles away.

Dyson warned that U.S. Energy now represented the most serious threat to the sanctity of Red Lady since AMAX. HCCA insisted on a bond to lock-in U.S. Energy's responsibility for water quality in Coal Creek. "Everyone and everything downstream of the plant is at risk until a sufficient bond is imposed," he said.

Then came a measure of intrigue in Crested Butte politics. In October 2013, Crested Butte mayor Aaron Huckstep and town council held mine discussions in closed meetings with U.S. Energy and later reported substantial progress on the mine proposal. Because the Crested Butte town government had gone rogue by closing doors to the town's interested NGO parties, division and acrimony split the ranks. HCCA founding board member and attorney, Jim Starr, fired off a letter-to-the-editor:

> It appears that Huckstep is being less than honest or that this so-called coalition is really no coalition at all, but rather a unilateral effort by him and perhaps the Town Council to cut a deal without involving the Red Lady Coalition and HCCA. . . It is time to set

egos aside, stop playing Lone Ranger and genuinely engage at least the coalition partners in creating and successfully negotiating the terms of an acceptable agreement.

Meanwhile, the Voluntary Clean-Up Plan (VCUP) proposed by U.S. Energy had gained regulatory adherents in the State of Colorado who appeared willing to throw Coal Creek's future into the hands of the Larceny Brothers. An alarm rattled Crested Butte.

"The mine issue blew up over the weekend," reported Mark Reaman in the *CB News* in November 2013. "Through some quick local action and common sense review by the state, the situation appears to have calmed, but the communal blood pressure sure went up fast. Understandably."

Reaman charged U.S. Energy with a duplicitous, behind-the-scene subterfuge in seeking the Voluntary Clean-Up Plan without disclosure to Crested Butte and other interested parties.

> U.S. Energy is a wolf in wolf's clothing. Don't forget that. It seems obvious they don't like the liability of operating the wastewater treatment plant and want out. But the best thing would be to get the threat of a future mine out of our realm. If U.S. Energy wants out, we should help them. But it will take honest and open dialogue, and this latest incident should remind us of that as we move forward.

HCCA, the Red Lady Coalition, and the Town of Crested Butte petitioned the Colorado Department of Public Health and Environment to rescind its approval of the VCUP it had granted U.S. Energy in 2012. The petition charged that the application was incomplete and misleading and could endanger the East River and Gunnison River watersheds.

In a separate action, in February 2014, the Colorado Water Conservation Board voted to set minimum water levels for Oh-Be-Joyful Creek and the Slate River. This measure was intended to create improved habitat for trout in streams that have long suffered toxicity by heavy metals from historic mining activities. This measure mandated higher seasonal flows in Oh-Be-Joyful and set yet another value for high quality water at sufficient quantity.

In March 2014, U.S. Energy agreed to sit down at a negotiating table with HCCA, Red Lady Coalition and the Town of Crested Butte. Instead of firing shots across each other's bows, they met to call a cease fire and strive for cooperation. That peace-making gesture was a breakthrough that had taken only 37 years since AMAX first appeared on the scene in 1977.

The *CB News* reported that U.S. Energy's portfolio was shifting from hard rock mining to oil and gas, a more potentially lucrative and less capital intensive endeavor. "There is plenty of moly everywhere," wrote Reaman. "There is honestly no immediate threat of a new start-up molybdenum mine anywhere in this country, let alone the middle of the Rocky Mountains three miles west of Crested Butte."

U.S. Energy, Reaman astutely surmised, finally realized that trying to develop a molybdenum mine on Red Lady came with a $2 million per year liability. Given moly prices, Mt. Emmons was not going to guarantee the company a profit. "That just won't happen, given the high cost of infrastructure and regulatory mandates," he editorialized.

In a conciliatory move, and perhaps to save face, U.S. Energy withdrew its Voluntary Clean-Up Plan and appeared to give in to the pushbacks from HCCA. The Town of Crested Butte signed a confidentiality agreement with U.S. Energy that opened a door to communication and negotiations. The possibility of ending the threat of mining became a hopeful panacea.

AMAX was gone, but the vast store of molybdenum beneath Mt. Emmons remains as a magnetic attraction enticing a succession of industrial suitors to Crested Butte. ARIZONA GEOLOGICAL SURVEY

28

Fighting a Mine is Hardwired

SINCE AMAX FIRST ANNOUNCED plans to gut Mt. Emmons, Crested Butte's resolve against a mine has been steadfast. The anti-mine constituency is no longer made up of an insurgency of irregulars, but rather a new and refreshed team of professional advocates who receive salaries. The ensuing mining battles have continued with fresh energy, not necessarily because of a more spirited, idealistic and activated community, but in part because of the higher stakes the community now holds—financial stakes.

The steadily rising trend in prosperity and property values today in Crested Butte paints a far rosier economic picture for the town than it did when AMAX reared its head in 1977. The resort economy then was modest and lacked sustainability. Crested Butte held the promise for prosperity, but it wasn't money that motivated the front liners who stood up against an industrial peril. The old guard was fortified more by idealism that by economics. There existed the rationale that one kind of economic development—recreation—was mutually exclusive from another—mining.

The battle with AMAX was originally framed by the sincere belief that it was the right thing to do. There was a sense of social justice and moral fervor to "the good fight." In the midst of the battle, Crested Butte and HCCA came to a new alignment based, not solely on moral and ethical judgements, but on economic realities. As wilderness scholar Rod Nash had pointed out, recreation and scenery underpin the only truly sustainable economy. "Instead of mining molybdenum, the town should mine the credit cards of tourists."

The town's moral crusade became overshadowed by the prosperity of recreation, which gave credence and pragmatism to the town's protestations against mining overtures. The focus on economics as an argument for preserving the environment was far more mainstream than saving the world. The argument against mining was more about speaking the parlance of the "real world," from which Crested Butte had so adamantly distanced itself.

This ideological shift also began to frame the future of Crested Butte more in terms of its resort economy, where moral and ethical arguments are ambiguous. Despite this shift, the image Crested Butte continually conveyed was that of a bucolic retreat. That identity was best defended, not with profit and loss statements, but with words and pictures, and in the most nuanced way, through poetry and song. The character of the community, the soul of Crested Butte, emerged as an emotional force that defied definition and belied sociological labels.

In the December 2018 *Winter Guide*, a seasonal insert in the *CB News*, the cover featured an iconic photo of a "local" riding a "townie" with skis over their shoulder. The opening words painted an idealized picture with warm hues: "There's something about a fresh coat of white covering the rooftops of downtown. The brightly colored wood buildings along Elk Avenue pop with their electric color. It feels surreal as you walk along the streets...It's a storybook that's come to life..."

When Vail Resorts acquired Crested Butte Mountain Resort in 2018, Mark Reaman observed the financial impact. "Local real estate got a bit of a lift to its already upward trajectory." Sales tax receipts in Crested Butte and Mt. Crested Butte were also on an upward track. The possibility of a substantial downturn in resort property values due to an industrialized mining venture would threaten much more than it did in 1977. The second home market alone would tally large in that equation, as would retail investments and resort infrastructure. All would undergo a downturn if the region fell under the thrall of a mining economy and culture, or so was the belief.

"The same kind of conflict that occurred in Crested Butte with

AMAX will play out again and again, not only here, but across the country," predicted Mike Rock. "People will get better at working toward peaceful co-existence. There will be mines and there will be oil wells. At the end of the day, you've got to find some places where you can accommodate these activities. But in Crested Butte today, it is inconceivable to me that the mine could open. There is so much invested in second homes that there's a strong vested interest. It would be as difficult as opening a mine in Aspen or Telluride. Why would you do that in such beautiful places?"

Rock had the answer to his rhetorical query: "Well," he said, "the geology that makes it beautiful is what makes the mining viable. And all of those towns started as mining towns. Those early mines left damage that will never be repaired, and the industry bears the responsibility and the stigma for that. You can't be unobtrusive with mining, but you can be less obtrusive. Disparate activities can co-exist, but that ship has sailed in Crested Butte."

If a mineral withdrawal is not achieved, and if the Mount Emmons orebody ever becomes hugely profitable by decree of the metals market, then the right-to-mine could again become the driving force for whatever company—or government—owns it. The Chinese? The Russians? The Brazilians? The US Department of the Interior? Inherent value will summon the necessary capital and, more important, the will to face off against the *enfant terrible* that is Crested Butte. Whether private or public, corporate or state, whomever or whatever reaches for the gleaming molybdenum ring from the spinning carousel of capitalism had better gird themselves for a fight.

Attorney and former Gunnison County Commissioner David Leinsdorf recognized in AMAX a rare example of a polished international corporation with the wherewithal to mine Mount Emmons. The suitors who have come in succession to prove their worth have fallen short. "My gut feeling," explained Leinsdorf, referring specifically to the "Lucky Jack" proposal, "is that these people today don't have the sophistication or capital to do the project."

Would any future proponent be as enlightened as AMAX sought to be? Would they have the requisite deep pockets? McMoRan is and does. But is it so far above the fray as to not turn around and place a value for Red Lady on its balance sheet? The promise of enriching corporate shareholders has furnished a steady lineup of potential players. Is it only a matter of time before the numbers crunch into a lucrative glory hole for Mt. Emmons, or will a permanent solution be realized? That's the billion-dollar question.

Stand on Elk Avenue and look west. You can't miss it. Just beyond town, where Coal Creek ripples and murmurs alongside the Kebler Pass Road, there stands Mt. Emmons. The shoulders of the mountain seem to shelter Crested Butte with their massive bulk. A mother lode of molybdenum lying beneath those shoulders attracts speculation, tantalizing the corporate mindset to scheme for capital investment, resource value, and the promise that perhaps one day they may reap enormous profits from extracting, processing and marketing the coveted gray sludge called molybdenum disulfide. Many equate such an act with an advance in civilization that is preordained.

"Mineral production is a primary industry providing the raw materials from which all value added goods derive," concluded Denis Hall in an "Earth Matters" column in 2009. "The industry of digging stuff out of the ground and making things from it is hardwired in our history and evolution; just ask your mountain bike. If you don't think the industrial extraction of a world-class molybdenum deposit can take place in our backyard, in our little slice of paradise, think again. If we believe the myth that a mine can never happen, we are doomed. Oh, we'll fight them, all right. We'll have to. That's hardwired, too."

Seven years later, Hall confessed something few mine opponents would—that over the forty years of going up against mining companies lusting over the rape of Red Lady, one develops an attachment to the role of combatant in a glorious and unremitting conflict. One becomes habituated to a mindset based on eternal vigilance: "Until Mount Emmons, its orebody, leases and private property, water treatment plant and all patented and unpatented mining claims are relinquished and congressionally withdrawn from mineral entry," Hall wrote, "some small part of me will remain in doubt. It is difficult to give up a lifetime of attachment to something as significant to our community and dear to me personally as Mt. Emmons and Red Lady Bowl. But I love a parade!"

"The mine won't happen unless we let it happen," summed up AMAX dragon slayer Don Bachman, laying the burden of defense squarely on the shoulders of future generations in Crested Butte who must oppose whatever plans and schemes align themselves for the mining of Mt. Emmons. The next battle will be inherited by a different set of strategists, a new generation of constituents, a younger group of activists.

According to a February 23, 2021 report from High Country Conservation Advocates, the town's fate will likely be determined by a Congressional withdrawal. This would mean a release of all claims and properties and ambitions—and the banishment of industrial mindsets from Mt Emmons—while allowing for more efficient management of on-site water treatment operations for historic acid mine drainage.

This current proposal includes a complex land exchange in conjunction with a federal withdrawal of mineral rights for the area where the Mt. Emmons mine and its operations had been previously proposed. In addition, the company would agree to a conservation easement that would forever prohibit mining on Mt. Emmons while preserving existing recreational opportunities.

"This is a big step towards a permanently mine-free Red Lady," said Julie Nania, HCCA Water Program Director. "However, we're still not to the finish line. There are significant practical details to work out."

Still, there is a glimmer of light at the end of a long tunnel. HCCA and the Town of Crested Butte have been working to remove the threat of a large-scale mine on Red Lady for 44 years. "This is a positive development for the future of our watershed and our community's way of life," reacted HCCA Executive Director, Brett Henderson. "We are cautiously hopeful that this is the pathway forward for permanent protection of Mt. Emmons that we have been fighting for along with thousands of members and supporters spanning generations."

Regardless of the outcome of the proposed withdrawal, the battle for the town's soul will be waged by those who care, by those willing and eager to fight, by those who say no, not here, not now, not ever. Mitchell's heartfelt plea from decades ago will with an irresistible call to arms: "No! Stop! We love our home!"

29
Saving the Lady— Forever

THEY CAME, one after another: AMAX...Phelps-Dodge..Cyprus-AMAX...Kobex...Thompson Creek Metals...and U.S. Energy. Then came another suitor whose seeming benevolence opened a door to a bright and shining future. This prince of good tidings bore the abbreviation—Freeport-McMoRan—and it completely changed the mining issue in Crested Butte.

It began when another acronym entered the Crested Butte lexicon: MEMC (Mt. Emmons Mining Company). This wholly owned subsidiary of Freeport-McMoRan took ownership of the mining rights of Red Lady in February 2015. Suddenly, the end of mining threats on Mt. Emmons became, not only credible, but likely.

Freeport-McMoRan is bigger than AMAX—way bigger. It swallowed AMAX whole in 2007, when it acquired Phelps Dodge and became the world's largest publicly traded producer of copper through what was then the largest mining acquisition in history. Freeport-McMoRan's aggregate holdings are staggeringly huge, as are its open pit mines.

The company was named from McMoRan Exploration, formed by Ken McWilliams ("Mc"), Jim Bob Moffett ("Mo") and Mack Rankin ("Ran"), an independent oil and gas exploration and production company based in South Louisiana.

The combined company—Freeport-McMoRan—was established in 1988, commensurate with the discovery of the Grasberg copper and gold deposit in Papua, Indonesia, the largest gold mine and the second-largest copper mine in the world. Following the acquisition of Phelps Dodge in 2007, FCX, as Freeport-McMoRan is known on Wall Street, "transformed into a dynamic industry leader and combined the assets and technical teams of two great companies," as stated on the corporate website. Freeport-McMoRan possesses, "A vast portfolio of mining assets acquired by several predecessor companies, including Freeport Minerals, Phelps Dodge, Cyprus Minerals, American Metal Company (AMAX), and Climax Molybdenum, among others. The many important milestones, which transpired over decades, make the company's portfolio of assets difficult to replicate today."

Freeport-McMoRan is one of the world's largest producers of copper, molybdenum and gold. It owns the Henderson and Climax molybdenum mines in Colorado, the former territory of AMAX. Other interests include oil and gas production and agricultural minerals, sulphur and phosphoric acid, with holdings in gold, copper, silver and uranium.

In 2021, Freeport-McMoRan touted Climax, a former AMAX property, as a 25,000 metric ton-per-day mill facility with the capacity to produce approximately 30 million pounds of molybdenum per year. Freeport-McMoRan claimed that mine operations generated almost $348 million in economic benefits for Colorado in 2018. "Combined, the Colorado mine operations employed 800, and the ripple effect of wages and taxes plus services we purchase created another 2,490 jobs."

The company's philosophy is underscored by a commitment to social awareness: "Many stakeholders share our view that we should serve a social purpose and make positive contributions to society for the long term. Our sustainable development programs facilitate our ability to deliver on this ambition."

In what might guide the company's budding relationship with Crested Butte, Freeport-McMoRan lays out a strategic corporate world view:

> While we seek to avoid causing adverse impacts, we acknowledge that they may occur despite our best efforts. By its nature, mining creates impacts on local communities. Working with local stakeholders, we implement mitigation measures for unavoidable adverse impacts and seek to maximize the delivery of positive, lasting social benefits. We engage with local stakeholders and their legitimate

representatives throughout project lifecycles to build relationships and the trust needed to create shared benefits. Our Community Policy mandates engagement and collaboration with local communities to minimize and mitigate unavoidable adverse impacts while maximizing opportunities to deliver value from our presence.

The company is up front about 226 community grievances recorded throughout its widespread global operations during 2018. In addition, "There were approximately 630 grievances related to dust events at our Sierrita operation in Arizona." (The Sierrita Mine is an open pit source of copper and molybdenum that has been in operation since 1959.) "Regardless of the type and credibility of the allegations, all cases reported are documented, reviewed and closed once a final decision is made and subsequent action is taken."

The company professes exemplary relations with communities:

> Open, transparent and regular engagement with a wide range of local stakeholders which builds our understanding of their interests and concerns, encourages communities to provide input into our operations and development projects and promotes understanding of our business. This helps reduce risks to our operations and our ability to deliver on our community development and engagement plans. Open communication and dialogue with local stakeholders and their representatives take a number of forms—formally through open house meetings linked to regulatory processes, informally through interactions with our community development specialists in the field, and via community partnership panels, community investment funds or foundations and targeted capacity-building efforts.

When Freeport-McMoRan acquired Phelps Dodge, it also acquired the largest open pit copper mine in the world at Morenci, Arizona. I drove through that property in the fall of 2020 and found no words to express my astonishment. My wife and I, peering out the windshield, were simply slack-jawed by the enormity of this historic mine, which dates to the 1860s. The Climax Mine, with its cavernous glory hole in what's left of Bartlett Mountain and its acres and acres of tailings ponds, dams and spillways, is dwarfed by the vastness and impossible scale of Morenci. Here, mega monster trucks are like Tonka toys against the immensity of tiered pits and gutted mountains spanning square miles in testament to the extraction of ore. Dystopian is the only word that truly conveys the extreme measure of blight and affront that has occurred in the century-plus that Morenci has been actively mined, including the historic city itself, all laid to waste as the pit enlarged to engulf everything in its path. Freeport-McMoRan inherited this mega-mine, and the company is working it today. If one is not shocked by the sight of it, then something has dulled in the senses and the soul.

Part of that acquisition was the Mt. Emmons property. Here was one of the largest known molybdenum orebodies in the world, but saddled with the liability of the Mt. Emmons Wastewate Treatment Plant, the albatross U.S. Energy had desperately wanted to be rid of. Forced by law to accept that costly liability, McMoRan expediently entered into a potentially magnanimous relationship with Crested Butte, whose notoriety in opposing mining overtures was no secret to the mining industry.

Along with the old Keystone Mine site came extensive holdings including patented and unpatented mining claims, fee simple properties, lode claims, mill site claims, placer claims, and tunnel site claims for underground holdings—a complex web of real estate that stretches from just outside Crested Butte, up and over Ohio Pass, and includes ranch property in Carbon Creek and Alkali Basin, to the west of Whetstone Mountain. All of this could return to the public trust if Freeport-McMoRan follows through with plans to forever remove mining from Mt. Emmons.

The Trust for Public Lands was consulted about preservation for some of the more prominent properties once they are released from Freeport-McMoRan's ownership. As for the orebody, the idea of an administrative or legislative mineral withdrawal came for the first time under serious consideration in late summer of 2016 when the *CB News* headlined: "Pact reached to keep Mt. Emmons mine-free." This would be a disappearing act done by legislatively withdrawing Mt. Emmons and Red Lady Bowl from industrial threats.

"The unique plan," explained the *CB News*, "relies on a heavyweight mining company asking the U.S. Congress to permanently withdraw mining claims from mining activity along with town voters passing a bond issue that won't raise taxes. The end result would be a mine-free Red Lady." The plan would exchange 9,000 acres of claims spread across the town's Coal Creek watershed in exchange for $2 million paid by the town. The acreage would go back into the federal land bank and never be allowed to be used for mining purposes.

Freeport-McMoRan has stated that it has no intention of mining Mt. Emmons, but instead wants an efficient way to treat the mine effluent for which it is now legally responsible. Taking a huge step toward making peace with Crested Butte, Freeport-McMoRan vowed to actively work toward a permanent solution to the decades-long prospect of mining Red Lady. In exchange for this assurance, Freeport-McMoRan said it would seek a local/state/federal partnership to take over the water treatment plant for the long term and erase the company's liability.

With these announcements, Crested Butte felt the weight of 300 million tons lift slightly from its shoulders. It all seemed too good to be true. Crested Butte town attorney John Belkin was cheered by the semblance of cooperative talks—the first truly substantive talks of this kind Crested Butte had taken on with a mining company eager for a final solution. "Everything at this time appears to be heading in the right direction," Belkin told the *CB News*.

In May 2016, Freeport-McMoRan terminated the ambitious Plan of Operations (POPs) U.S. Energy had speciously proposed in 2012. Freeport-McMoRan put up a reclamation bond to stabilize tailing dams and contain acid mine runoff. It offered two years of funding for the water treatment plant.

These acts of good faith lifted spirits in Crested Butte higher still, stated Alli Melton, High Country Conservation Advocates' Red Lady Program Director. (HCCA had by now changed its name in order to broaden its scope of environmental activism while not losing its familiar and trusted acronym.)

> These are significant, positive developments toward a long-term, sustainable, and permanent solution for Red Lady and our watershed. Off and on, for years, these PoOs have been hanging over our community like a black cloud. Now, the skies are clearing over Red Lady. The reclamation bond, in tandem with Freeport/MEMC prepaying Wastewater Treatment Plant operation for the next two years, is much needed assurance for what HCCA, other community groups,

and the Town and County have unwaveringly sought for years. This latest development continues us down the path to finding a permanent, mine-free solution for Red Lady and protection for our watershed. And, even though there's still much hard work to be done before this is achieved, we are ever closer to this end.

A November 2016 meeting in Denver convened Belkin, CB town planner Michael Yerman, the U.S. Forest Service, Freeport-McMoRan, and U.S. Senator Michael Bennett, a Democrat who had drafted a bill to provide Congressional withdrawal of the Mt. Emmons mineral rights. "We owe them a great deal of thanks," said Belkin of Freeport-McMoRan. "Ideally, the senator can get this through an act of Congress with the president [Obama] signing it into law. The vibe from his office has been super positive, and they are doing everything they can, but they are realistic. This requires an act of Congress, and that's never easy."

Then came the 2016 election of President Donald Trump and the start of a lame duck Congress. Suddenly, all bets were off, and the optimism that had boosted outlooks in Crested Butte fell to the grim realization that a mineral withdrawal could be at least four years in the offing. Talks stalled. Proposed legislation was sidelined. Uncertainty swept away hopes for a quick conclusion to this forty-year-long controversy.

National politics, however, had no ill effects on a growing collaborative effort to keep Coal Creek alive as a healthy riparian ecosystem. In April 2017, HCCA reported positive results with Freeport-McMoRan's commitment to clean water quality. "For the first time," wrote Alli Melton, "we are looking at concrete actions that are going to benefit water quality in Coal Creek."

At the same time, Red Lady Coalition, which had formed as an adjunct to HCCA, dissolved its 501c3 non-profit status and disbanded so that its members could actively lobby for the Mt. Emmons solution. Its newly stated goals were to protect Coal Creek and win a Congressional withdrawal of 6,000 acres of unpatented mining claims.

30
Disappearing Act on Mt. Emmons

THE OPTION FOR MINERAL WITHDRAWALS is stipulated by the Mining Law of 1872, the same law that staunchly mandates mining rights on federal lands. This vastly influential law was fathered by William Morris Stewart (1827–1909), a former mathematics teacher who gained national prominence as a lawyer, a politician and a mining advocate. Stewart was known in 1903 as the richest man in the US Senate, with a fortune of $25 million and ownership in silver mines.

According to Kalmiopsis Rivers, a conservation advocacy group in Oregon, the Mining Law of 1872 gives both Congress and the Secretary of the Interior the authority to establish mineral withdrawals; the former permanently through legislation; the latter through an extensive public process, and for no longer than 20 years. Withdrawals are made for the purpose of limiting mining activities in order to maintain greater public values or for reserving the land for a particular public purpose or program. These values and purposes may include protecting the quality of scientific, scenic, historical, ecological, environmental, air, water, or archaeological resources.

Precedent for mining withdrawals comes from the North Fork Watershed Protection Act of 2013, introduced in the US House of Representatives to withdraw 430,000 acres of federal lands in Montana from the potential development of geothermal and mineral resources. The affected lands lie adjacent to Glacier National Park, and the withdrawal resulted from an agreement between Canada and the United States on how to protect the trans-border area from the effects of mining.

The bill was introduced by Rep. Steve Daines, a Montana Republican, through the House Committee on Natural Resources. Daines stated his desire, "to rise above partisan politics, preserve the pristine landscape, and protect this critical watershed," which had support from conservationists and energy companies. The mayor of Whitefish, Montana, John Muhlfeld, stated that the bill would protect the town's water supply indefinitely and said the city fully supported the bill. The National Parks Conservation Association supported the bill, saying it "protects both our outdoor heritage and our economic future for generations to come." Supporters also argued that the bill would be good for tourism. The similarities to Crested Butte are obvious.

In another instance, then Secretary of Interior Ken Salazar had designated in 2012 a mineral withdrawal "to protect the iconic Grand Canyon and its vital watershed from the potential adverse effects of additional uranium and other hard rock mining on over 1 million acres of federal land for the next 20 years." This was to provide adequate time for monitoring that would inform future land use decisions. "A withdrawal is the right approach for this priceless American landscape," Salazar said at the time. "People from all over the country and around the world come to visit the Grand Canyon. Numerous American Indian tribes regard this magnificent icon as a sacred place, and millions of people in the Colorado River Basin depend on the river for drinking water, irrigation, industrial and environmental use. We have been entrusted to care for and protect our precious environmental and cultural resources, and we have chosen a responsible path that makes sense for this and future generations." Talking points for Crested Butte could not be more aligned.

Earlier still, on August 1, 2011, a Secretarial mineral withdrawal segregated 17 miles (5,610 acres) of the Wild and Scenic Chetco River. This 56-mile-long stream, located in southern Oregon within the Kalmiopsis Wilderness, flows through a rugged and isolated coastal region, dropping from 3,200 feet to sea level at the Pacific Ocean. The withdrawal was authorized by Congress through the 1872 Mining

The Morenci copper strip mine in Arizona staggers the imagination given the enormity of destruction that has taken place over more than a century of mining. Morenci is owned and operated by Freeport-McMoRan, the company that intends to end mining in Crested Butte. ARIZONA GEOLOGICAL SURVEY

Law, protecting the public's interest in high value conservation lands and rivers. This same language speaks to values in Crested Butte.

That withdrawal was made to counter proposals to mine almost half the river's length for ten years with dredges weighing up to one ton. According to the withdrawal findings: "The effect on the river's outstanding water quality and world class salmon and steelhead fishery would have been devastating. However, by closing the area to new mining claims and requiring existing claims to be valid, it was saved." The withdrawal also saved the public at least $350,000, the estimated cost of analyzing six of the proposed plans of operation on claims that were later forfeited. This withdrawal came under the Federal Land Policy and Act of 1976 (FLPMA).

HCCA has remained insistent that, until a withdrawal can be realized, Crested Butte's water quality must be protected by supporting sustainable solutions to mine wastewater. HCCA executive director Brett Henderson, in a December 2017 statement, extolled McMoRan's virtues as a trusted partner that shares this goal. "Last June was the first time we've ever entered a water quality hearing in agreement with the mining company in charge of the wastewater plant. Freeport appears to be forthcoming with information and willing to discuss options that would be agreeable to all parties."

Meanwhile, Freeport-McMoRan has been assessing whether target water quality improvements can be met through upgrading the existing water treatment plant, or whether the company will need to reconstruct the plant in its entirety. Long term compliance would ideally mean maintaining water quality in Coal Creek in perpetuity through a gravity-fed, passive system of natural filters, a pioneering approach that will need proving up.

Meanwhile, the old AMAX-era water treatment plant continues treating 320 gallons of water per minute every day of the year. The plant uses about as much electricity as the ski area and is the single largest customer of the Gunnison County landfill, where it deposits between 75 and 100 semi-truck loads of treated sludge annually.

Many in Crested Butte echo the hopeful sentiment of long-time activist Sue Navy, who said in spring 2020, "Now that we're closer to a permanent solution than ever before, we need to keep our vision focused on a successful outcome. We know the last pitch to the peak can be challenging, but with all our collaborative energy working toward resolution, I believe we will finally succeed."

Navy's optimism gained credibility when Trump was removed from office in January 2021, and Democrats Joe Biden and Kamala Harris took the executive roles that promise a return to ecological and environmental values in the White House. Whether that sea change ripples through Congress is another question. The outcome will directly influence the proposed mineral withdrawal necessary to securing Crested Butte's future, a future that requires leaving 300 million tons of molybdenum ore beneath Red Lady Bowl where geologic forces placed it millions of years ago.

As of the publication date of this book, The Town of Crested Butte, Gunnison County, and the Mount Emmons Mining Company (MEMC) had agreed to a Memorandum of Understanding (MOU) that plots the path forward to end the threat of mining on Red Lady.

A key component of the MOU is a contemplated federal legislative withdrawal from future mineral exploration, mining, and development of approximately 9,000 acres on and around Mount Emmons.

Because this requires an Act of Congress, HCCA and community partners have been in conversations with Senator Michael Bennet's office to add the Mount Emmons lands to withdrawal areas included in the Colorado Outdoor Recreation & Economy (CORE) Act. Adding the claims held by MEMC to this legislation could permanently withdraw them from future mining if the CORE Act becomes law.

In addition, MEMC has notified the U.S. Forest Service of its intent to pursue a land exchange to acquire approximately 450 acres of U.S. Forest Service land adjoining the 365 acres already owned by the company in order to allow for historic mine reclamation and to ensure the company can continue to operate its existing water treatment plant on the site. The land exchange proposal includes placing a conservation easement on all portions of the private property to restrict future mining and milling activities and allow for public recreational access and use.

But nothing has been set in stone. The MEMC proposal is purely theoretical. Anything can happen. And, judging from the history of this seemingly intractable issue, anything will.

As the final solution to mining promises hope for the future, Crested Butte faces its own reflection in a truth-telling mirror. The town is grappling with an irresistible and bounteous future based on recreation and a resort economy that is being laid at its doorstep in what seems like the best of all worlds.

But the law of unintended consequences has ruled against the town in ways no one could have imagined, leaving the town to grapple with a disintegration of the community it has for so long claimed as its moral, ethical and spiritual foundation.

Be careful what you wish for: Crested Butte's push for commercial success has resulted in big crowds, long lines and a reduced local ambiance under Vail's management. *PENNIE PHOTOGRAPHY*

PART IV
The Thrall of Tourism

*"A town, which is a community,
is a delicate organism.
Unlike an individual,
it cannot sue for invasion of privacy.
It cannot effectively determine
how many people can live in it.
It cannot even decide for itself
the number of visitors
with which it feels comfortable."*

—ORVILLE SCHELL

The Town that Fought to Save Itself

AUTHOR'S NOTE

AS I POURED OVER the news from Crested Butte, I realized that the mining threat had become overshadowed by the impacts of tourism. Crested Butte's dreamscape was attracting more and wealthier visitors, many of whom bought real estate and established the town's burgeoning second home community. This section traces the erosion of cherished social values as real estate prices soared, housing grew scarce, and much of the town's work force was forced out. This is a common dynamic in western communities today, which is sad to watch remotely, as I did with Crested Butte, and up close and personally, as I still do in Aspen.

The Company Store bench has for decades been a prime gathering place for townspeople who take the time to commune with their neighbors with an easy, informal manner that small towns provide.

CRESTED BUTTE CHRONICLE ARCHIVES

31
'Small is Beautiful'

"A TOWN IS PUBLIC PROPERTY," surmised Orville Schell, "not only for its residents, but for the world. In many ways, it is at the mercy of forces existing outside its boundaries, and of people whose names it does not know and whose faces its inhabitants will never see." Schell was writing about Bolinas, California, on the Pacific coast just north of San Francisco. His 1976 book, *The Town That Fought to Save Itself*, had helped inform HCCA during the early years of the AMAX fight. Long afterwards, Schell's warning bears even more gravitas.

The parallels between Bolinas and Crested Butte are many. Both towns are small, cozy, inviting, delicate and quaint by American standards. Both towns face pressures from the mainstream, outside world, from which most of their stewarding citizens once fled and against which many steadfastly stand guard. Both communities, one on the Pacific Rim, the other high in the Central Rockies, are subject to the immutable law of change. Both are vulnerable.

Like Crested Butte's trump card with AMAX, Bolinas identified water as the key to controlling and then stopping altogether rapid population growth. "We needed to find a way to stop, reevaluate and plan," wrote Schell. "A water hookup moratorium presented us with the only legal means available to stop runaway growth. In 1971, we became the first town in America that we know of to have a zero-growth control limitation."

Crested Butte, post-AMAX, had no intention of zero growth, though some would have cheered that as an ideal. It was assumed that since largescale industrial mining was not in the town's best interest, surely

A handful of bold women pioneered mountain biking in Crested Butte on vintage, rigid frame bikes in the late 1970s. (l. to r.) Cindy Petito, Kay Peterson, Emily Curray, Marla Holmes and LeAndra Gudowski.
CRESTED BUTTE CHRONICLE ARCHIVES

tourism could provide a comparatively clean and sustainable economy. It seemed logical that a thriving resort economy would be a reasonable rationale for opposing extractive industry. The growth impacts of tourism did not seem as potentially egregious as a boom town scenario based on mining.

Gradually, and somewhat unseen amid the tumult of mining battles, the Aspenization vilified for years in Crested Butte began to appear on Elk Avenue. It happened slowly, but grew incrementally into prominence and scale. T-shirt shops replaced commodity stores. Real estate offices crowded out inexpensive rental homes. Gentrification spread with an overlay of rising property values.

Wars are often followed by periods of economic vitality and development, and so it's been for Crested Butte. In the wake of hard fought campaigns against mining ventures, Crested Butte let down its guard, unlocked its chastity belt, and embraced the most persuasive of all suitors—prosperity.

This suitor is not a mining ogre, but a charming and embraceable swain. Rather than force itself on a community, prosperity knocks politely and is invited in. It brings with it monetary expectations from the outside world and creates an upwelling of aspirations from within. Wealth is a Trojan Horse willingly brought within the walls.

Crested Butte had kept its word from over forty years ago when it said "No" to AMAX and later to AMAX wannabes. Now the community faces the implications of saying yes to a far different kind of threat against which the town has few defenses and protectors. Ed Abbey's warning in *Desert Solitaire* proved right: "Industrial tourism is big business. It means money. . ." And money is a powerful inducement.

During the ongoing skirmishes with half a dozen mining companies since AMAX announced in 1977, the communities of the Gunnison Valley have wrestled with how to define success for the fledgling resort economy in which the entire Gunnison Valley has been invested. With AMAX gone, plotting the future without a looming adversary became a perplexing novelty that required identifying the interests, desires and directions of the broader community. Instead of vilifying an outside force, gazes turned inward with a Pogo-like realization: "We have met the enemy, and he is us."

Setting limits on the scope and scale of resort development became, for many who had fought the mine, a natural approach to controlling industrial tourism. Many rejected the excesses identified with Aspen and Vail; ironically, Vail was soon to become owner of the Crested Butte ski area. The idea was to have one's cake—tourism—and eat it, too with controlled and reasonable growth.

Controlling growth is in step with E. F. Schumacher's, *Small is Beautiful, Economics as if People Mattered*, which warns about carrying capacity: "An attitude to life which seeks fulfillment in the single-minded pursuit of wealth—in short, materialism—does not fit into this world, because it contains within itself no limiting principle, while the environment in which it is placed is strictly limited."

Today, given that Crested Butte has for decades denounced the excesses of industrial mining, one might assume there would be an equal sense of caution on becoming too successful as a resort. That made sense to some, but not to many who now hoped to capitalize on the town and surroundings. Crested Butte's battle with AMAX had saved it from becoming a boom town, but booms can derive from influences other than mining. Still, the prevailing belief has been that high-dollar tourism could provide guilt-free benefits in contrast to the anticipated depredations of mining. Given a choice of alternative economies, tourism seemed like a no-brainer.

"There was a very understandable concern about the future of the valley, and especially Crested Butte," reflected former AMAX executive Mike Rock in an interview in the 1990s. "I don't know if there would be agreement that Crested Butte today is what everybody back then had envisioned without the mine. There are probably mixed opinions on whether it's worse to have a miner drinking a beer in Kochevar's than having fur coats walking up and down the streets."

Terry Hamlin, former AMAX spokesman, provided a telling anecdote: While attending an "old-timer" birthday party in Crested Butte, years after AMAX had pulled up stakes, Hamlin noticed a change of mood, what he perceived as a communal sense of loss. "Some said that there was nothing real in Crested Butte anymore, that Elk Avenue looked like a movie set, that it was like Disneyland. People who came to Crested Butte in the '60s and '70s might not want to stay here today, and certainly couldn't afford to. Tourism will be a bigger impact than mining ever would have been. By now, a 25-year mine would have been revegetated and restored," he alleged. "There wouldn't be much trace of a mine today."

Where I lived on First Street, now known as the "Air Conditioned" house, was owned by my dear landlady, Frances "Granny" Yaklich. Rent: $175 per month. PAUL ANDERSEN COLLECTION

32
Pave It and They Will Come

MYLES RADEMAN, Crested Butte's original town planner, recalls how municipal improvements were essential to Crested Butte's viability at a time when the town's economic survival was at stake. An economic development grant in the 1970s allowed the town to improve streets and sidewalks, including landscaping a green strip between them. "The whole project," said Rademan in a June 2015 interview with the *CB News*, "turned into a battle cry that we were trying to Aspenize Crested Butte. People were opposed to change and said it was going to ruin our town."

Rademan described an ad hoc citizens group that formed under the name: "Save the Baby Potholes." Protesters held up signs at public meetings and were sincerely concerned that the loss of potholes would signal ultimate gentrification and a death knell for the town's humble appearance. Potholed streets, they believed, dissuaded investment and development and were emblematic of the town's rustic spirit.

Roy Smith, who had discovered Crested Butte as Brigadoon in 1969 and bought an original miner's house, recognized the ephemeral nature of the town. For Smith, irrevocable change came from paving the dirt streets and filling the potholes.

"Growth is an almost inevitable force," acknowledged Smith, "and its proponents usually win, and so it was with our town. To pave or not to pave was a social/cultural issue that divided the town. Paving represented encouraging growth. No paving represented closing the gate and keeping the town the way it was. Paving Elk Avenue is when the fortunes and future of the town became sealed. Next, it was the side streets, and then, as had been projected, they started to come and they kept on coming."

The paving argument won and perhaps paved the way to what Smith recognized in retrospect. "My 1200-square-foot house, bought for $12,000 in 1969, is now valued at around $1,200,000. I had unintentionally become part of the boom."

Using antics as a traditional form of expression in Crested Butte, in this case to advance the road improvement agenda, Rademan and town manager Bill Crank paraded down Elk Avenue in a 1970s July Fourth Parade having wrapped themselves in green toilet paper to anthropomorphize the proposed green strip.

Road paving has been a crucial increment of change in bubbles like Crested Butte and Aspen where resistance at times has been strident. Defiance to the onslaught of concrete and asphalt could be construed as a healthy sign of attachment to a place and a time, and such activism inevitably gets in the way of what others see as progress.

Fighting change can feel like a vainglorious effort to stop the clock of a fluid society and a world in flux. Emotional sentiment will always butt up against the rigid laws of economics, as Rademan philosophized almost fifty years after the paving project regarding the escalation of property values in Crested Butte:

> We create magical places that are oases, bubbles, unique, but they also function in an international and national economy, and our country was founded on individual rights to change. Nobody has figured out how to suspend the law of economics—if something is scarce, it's valuable. If something is valuable, it's expensive. And if it's expensive, only rich people can afford to buy it.

In her *CB News* column, "Earth Muffin Memos," Molly Murfee has become a community conscience who decries the encroaching homogenization of the town with appeals to self-awareness and restraint. Some columns preach non-conformity as a means of conforming to Crested Butte's non-conformist virtues. Can one be a non-conformist by conforming to non-conformity?

In a column titled, "We are not a tourist town," Murfee strove

Before the streets were paved: Crested Butte looking west toward Kebler Pass and Mt. Emmons when the town felt small, quiet, humble and blessedly intimate. CRESTED BUTTE CHRONICLE ARCHIVES

to throw off the stigma of the gentrified and commercialized resort Crested has become:

> Is being a tourist town a part of who we are? Sure. It is a part. But only a portion of one part—the economic part. An important part? Yes. But if we orient the sum total of our identity toward that one thing, we are not only being false to ourselves, but to those who come to visit as well. . . . We become just characters in the set, playing our superficial part, selling our souls for the almighty dollar.
>
> When we are just ourselves, we have the stupendous opportunity to attract just the right kind of person into our midst who is going to love our rough edges and our not quite so perfect anything. The person who can't wait to pedal their bike around town rather than complain about the lack of parking. The person who likes the fact that an icy sidewalk means you're really in the mountains, and that snowbanks are quaint and fantastic. They are going to embrace the unpolished rawness of it all. . . How much better for the whole when they just slide right in and join the party, and we're truly able to take care of our own. A natural fit. A forward-thinking utopia born right here in Paradise.

Those who have tasted the Crested Butte Cool-Aid will go to great lengths for a town fix. One letter writer, Cameron Wegemund, a diehard visitor from Australia, described the ordeal of travel required for getting to CB from his home in Pottsville, Northern NSW, Australia. While skiing is available closer by, Wegemund wrote, he endures travel trauma because of Crested Butte's magic, because of its soul.

> It's not the snow. It's not the resort facilities or the skiable terrain. . . It is walking to the town shuttle along quiet streets, passing winter cyclists with yoga mats or skate skiers with dogs heading to the Poop Loop. It is the excited smiles on the bus. It is seeing familiar faces and cars that stop for pedestrians. It is experiencing cars that stop in the streets while their drivers have a chat. It is the courtesy in the shops and at the restaurants. The person who chases you to return a glove you dropped. It is knowing that houses are left unlocked, cars have keys in the ignition, and that this is known but rarely abused.

Wegemund recalled the rustic beauty when town streets were unpaved and there existed an "isolationist frontier feeling about being at the end of the road." He praised people in town leading "meaningful lives in breathtaking surroundings." He wrote that today's international visitors can go anywhere with easy and rapid mobility, but that those who choose Crested Butte are different, and that the town treats them as specially invited guests who are integral to the town's expansive character.

But change was in the wind as was vehemently pointed out in an August 2018 letter from Trea Sciortino, who advised, "As Crested Butte changes. . .don't sit too high on your horse."

> Crested Butte seems to be getting a facelift, but not all face lifts look good. Cutting through our social fabric with a dull scalpel is a bit painful and leaves a nasty scar tissue. New people moving into our town with some strange attitudes. Pretentious, a bit greedy and narcissistic perhaps?
>
> I moved here from the Big Easy so transitioning to ski bum life in Crested Butte was seamless. I was addicted right away to the mountains here and the people who would make eye contact with you, smile and actually verbalize a 'hello.' I upheld a respect and a 'code of conduct' from those who had been here since the '60s and

'70s, battling the winters and financial hardships back then. Like me, they didn't move to Crested Butte to 'make a great investment' or get rich, for that matter.

Local newspapers are barometers of community mood, and letters-to-the-editor are representative of the culture. Take for example an edgy barb addressed to elites infiltrating town in which the tone reveals growing frustration and anger about an inexorable sea change in Crested Butte: "If you can't seem to remove the stick from your rear end while you're here, well then, Telluride and Aspen are only a few hours away, where everyone is a super important shining star, just like you."

A visit to the oft-disparaged Aspen by Mark Reaman brought on a reflection from hiking over 11,500 ft. West Maroon Pass. On top of the pass, Reaman counted thirty hikers, passing it off as, "a tad crowded, but not obnoxious." Then came his reaction to the city.

> Aspen was Aspen. Honestly, that valley is gorgeous with its red-tinted rock shimmering beneath blue skies where a certain manicured elegance was actually pleasant. Everything was tidy. Compared to Crested Butte, the houses are bigger and fancier, the celebrity second homeowners more well-known than most of those in Crested Butte (do we even have any?) and everything just feels cleaner.

People watching on the Aspen mall offered yet another vantage akin to the Company Store bench.

> The people, too, appeared more manicured than most of the people we see in Crested Butte. Coiffed and more made-up, with a bit more "work" than I'm used to seeing here. I could see why Arnold and Jack would enjoy spending summer days in Fat City. It was really pleasant and striking. The typical tourist in Aspen also sounded different from the typical Crested Butte tourist—more New York East Coast than Southern Texas and Oklahoma.

A stranger in a strange land, Reaman turned sociologist regarding his drive back home:

> Now my favorite part of the weekend visit to Fat City was coming back into Crested Butte. Driving down the dusty west

entrance to town after a beautiful dirt road journey over Kebler was sweet. The mountain looks huge from that perspective and the little houses are a comfortable welcome to a small town. . . But it was a lack of manicure that made me really happy. Some might say Crested Butte has a more, shall we say, unkempt, rugged feel for a mountain resort town—others might say it's more ghetto. And it is great. It is comfortable. It is real, and it is what keeps us different.

A community survey published in December 2018 found that, "Residents are largely outdoor enthusiasts who are open to accommodating responsible growth that preserves the town's unique historical character and developing a balanced economy with good-paying jobs and attainable housing."

A citizen comment within the study nailed it in two sentences: "Community is key. If we lose community, we become Disneyworld and just a façade."

**Crested Butte in the quiet years,
when the town slept under a mythic spell.**
PAUL ANDERSEN COLLECTION

33
The Budweiser Blues

RESORT DEVELOPMENT, not mining, has put home ownership in Crested Butte out of the reach of most local working people, many of whom have been forced to find affordable rents downvalley where they join growing ranks of commuters rushing back and forth on two-lane Highway 135. Currently, local businesses in the service industry are strapped to find employees to serve the growing numbers that throng to Crested Butte hoping to catch the magic of living the dream.

A walk through Crested Butte today reveals that community has been compromised by commodity, by making the physical accouterments of the town soulless objects to be bought and sold. As commercial values overrun the rustic, homespun humility of the past, luxury homes and deluxe condos have taken precedence over humble miner's cottages and voluntary simplicity. Gentrification is blotting out alley shacks, the Hobbit houses where real working people used to live. Short term rentals are gutting the vitality of the town's once vibrant core, and rising discontent is felt by those who identify with the Crested Butte vibe but cannot buy in on their service job wages.

When town council member Jackson Petito resigned his seat in May 2019, he and his family opted to follow the population pattern and migrate to Crested Butte South. Petito, son of long-time and much loved local, Lynda Jackson Petito, had garnered the highest number of votes in the council election. In his resignation letter, Petito issued a heartfelt message:

> Commoditization of a cool place is the basis of any tourism economy. People will pay top dollar to own a piece of a place like this, and that's why housing is so expensive... Money always has the last word, and big money is here. That's my warning: do what you can to fight money's influence on how this town operates... Giant houses sitting empty 50 weeks a year in the middle of a housing crisis is a sign of something wrong.

In the midst of a housing shortage, a full-page ad in the *CB News* in June 2019 announced in huge capital letters: CREATE YOUR DREAM LIFE. *Luxury* was another word emphasized by Sotheby's International Realty, where exclusivity is *de rigeur*. The accompanying photo showed an iconic mountain meadow bedecked with wildflowers. The peak of Crested Butte Mountain jutted in silhouette in the background.

Denis Hall, in his Earth Matters column, July 2019, identified big money as the heart of all evil, a truism Hall used to attack what he called "frenzied boosterism." By commercializing the town's charming character, local celebrations had become "tourist-oriented and no longer even a reflection of a 'local'. We put on a dog-and-pony show for the gapers...and we advertise it." Hall decried it all with an edge:

> The problem is, marketing worked. You done good, boys! You built it and they came. You wanted Front Range visitors to fill Crested Butte cash registers, and it worked! You wanted butts on every seat in every restaurant and heads on every pillow in the valley, and it worked. You wholesale marketed our precious backcountry, and the hordes arrived to drive through wildflowers and poop wherever the spirit moved them. Good work! The problem is our intense and indiscriminate marketing strategies will ultimately destroy the very 'product' we are marketing. Maybe it's time to stop.

As the Crested Butte resort economy has expanded, there has been a commensurate rush for real estate licenses. Property sales have doubled and tripled, eating up ranch land and open space while creating personal fortunes for those eager to profit on construction and land development. Opportunities abound for those with ready cash or a willingness to leverage debt. Making money has brought on a land rush energy that has redefined the direction of the town and driven wedges into the community.

The height of commercialization took place in 2007 with the Bud Light "Whatever, USA" promotion. Crested Butte became a parody of itself, generating the kind of mass appeal that defied and denied the simpler communal nature the community cherished in its fading age of innocence.

POWDER MAGAZINE

Not long after the AMAX fight, in the mid-1980s, beloved singer/songwriter Tracey Wickland married folk star Jesse Winchester, sold her adorable Crested Butte home and moved to Canada. Five years later, she returned to Crested Butte a disillusioned divorcee who was unable to buy back in. During the interim, the quaint log home she had hand built and sold for $100,000 was valued at $1 million. Recovering what she had lost was well beyond her reach. Since then, the value of her home has shot up again and again in a steep curve indicative of a changing value system where properties are seen, not as homes for celebrated locals, but as investments for outsiders.

A core of neo-old-timers has watched with chagrin as the town they fought to save from AMAX and the other mining companies has jumped on a fast track to profits. For many who had manned the barricades against mining, this is the saddest irony of all. The energies they had once given to fighting AMAX they now turn to the fight against gentrification.

The focal point of growth control at the start of the new millennium centered on opposition to Crested Butte Mountain

Resort plans to develop Snodgrass Mountain, which would be served by a new base area called North Village. As with the AMAX fight, Snodgrass coalesced a slow-growth faction vs. a pro-growth faction. Soon, divisive stereotypes were bandied about. "Trust funders" traded barbs with "dirt pimps" in a conflagration that threatened to divide the town and strain the bonds of community.

"A lot of people against the mine are against the ski area expansion, too," stated former Gunnison County Commissioner David Leinsdorf in a 2009 interview. "A lot of people in Crested Butte are more anti-capitalist than anti-mine. You can't be against both the mine and tourism, but there are a lot of people in this community who are against it all."

An opinion column in the *CB News*, by John Norton, "Norton's Notions," in February 2011, suggested that local resistance to tourist-related growth, both at the ski area and in ski communities, was serving mining interests by making a moly mine seem attractive. "People don't want this place to be trashed," acknowledged Norton. "But people are also tired of the anti-everythings winning all the arguments. People don't understand why a commercial building can't be built on commercial lots in town. People don't understand why the ski area can't expand the mountain on land zoned for skiing. The mine seems to be making some headway in part because elected officials and some others have strangled other economic opportunities."

Norton shared an email lament he had received from a despairing reader who complained of financial hardships in Crested Butte during a particularly slow winter. "In three nights of work at a popular local eating and drinking establishment, in the middle of the ski season, I have yet to make a hundred cumulative dollars. Tonight, I made $10. I used to say this town is dying. Well, now, I say, it's dead... We used to have three seasons here: winter, summer and off. Now we have two: summer and off. It doesn't' snow anymore, the airport and the airlines are killing us, the steeps don't open, we have no half pipe, and I really don't blame anyone for spending their winter vacation time elsewhere."

In May 2011, Crested Butte town council launched an effort to identify a community vision, which provoked head scratching and soul searching. "Does anyone really know what we want to be in the future?" asked a citizen participant. "What are we evolving toward?"

Three years later, beer giant Anheuser-Busch had an answer: "Whatever, USA."

> CRESTED BUTTE, Colo., Sept. 2014 — Workers have been busy in this bucolic, out-of-the-way ski town: The streets have been painted blue, as have the light poles. Blue props and fencing have been hauled in, rendering the place almost unrecognizable. And as final preparations take place for a three-day party, many residents are fuming, cursing the town for approving a clandestine deal to let a giant beer company turn it into a living advertisement in exchange for $500,000.

Now came the ultimate commercialization of Crested Butte, and the town bought in, or so described an article on the Internet: "The beer company flew in 1,000 young adults for a weekend of spring-break-style revelry, a stunt designed to publicize Bud Light. The town's main thoroughfare, Elk Avenue, has been adorned with outdoor hot tubs, a sand pit, concert lights and a stage. Restaurants and hotels have been stripped of many local markings and given beer-branded umbrellas and signs instead. When the filming starts, drinks will be unlimited, access to the main street will be restricted to people with company-issued bracelets, and beautiful, mountain-ringed Crested Butte will be rebranded as 'Whatever, U.S.A.'

"This is a mistake," commented a local of 20 years. "Frankly, it's vulgar and it's cheap."

Yet, the event took place, eroding Crested Butte's integrity by rebranding it as Whatever.... The Bud Light event was a symbolic death and rebirth into something unrecognizable from what the town had been.

"Just how long can a Bud Light hangover last?" asked a national newspaper headline as the blue color theme that had swept over town like a tsunami still defaced the community ten months later. "For the mountain town of Crested Butte, the after effects of a huge infusion of Bud Light are still being felt. That event involved literally painting the town's historic main thoroughfare of Elk Avenue Bud-Light blue and turning it into a giant fantasy-party stage for a weekend. Now, Elk Avenue is still a mess."

And so was town spirit. After standing off the largest mining companies in the world, Crested Butte had consorted shamelessly with Anheuser-Busch, the largest beer manufacturer in the world. Crested Butte had been willingly nuked, as an on-line journal reported following the event:

> The company did quickly whisk away 1,200 visiting beer drinkers along with a retinue of musicians, drag queens, minor celebrities and buskers. The hot tubs, the human-sized bowling and beer-pong games, the man-made sandy beaches, the giant blue King Kong and the petting-zoo animals were trucked away within days. But the three blocks of blue-painted street proved to be a lingering headache.
>
> First, a heavy rain started washing the paint off the roadway before it could be scraped up. Blue water running down town gutters and heading for local waterways did not make residents happy. Town public works officials decided to try to scrape up the paint. That was a noisy endeavor that created blue-paint dust clouds in downtown and left a bumpy street with blue patches. Bad weather thwarted plans to put a slurry coat of asphalt over the mess last fall.

A letter-to-the-editor in the *CB News* summarized the close of the event in cautious terms:

> Saturday night, as the zombie glow descended once again, citizens of 'Whatever. . .' got down to KC and the Sunshine Band under disco lights and a shower of blue confetti. Thankfully, organizers complemented the Bud Light supply with bottled water; I think I can speak for most of my fellow citizens when I say that by that time, stomaching another beer was physically impossible. 'Being allowed to drink vodka again after this weekend will be a privilege,' a partier remarked.
>
> Sunday morning, as blue feathers and confetti danced down our empty streets and the 48-hour hangover kicked in, I passed a dog whose face was still partially painted a bright shade of blue. I wondered if she was hurting from the weekend as much as the rest of us were. But Crested Butte had survived.
>
> Personally, I'm sticking with the theory that Bud Light chose

Crested Butte not only for its picturesque location, but also for its residents' ability to throw down. Give a Buttian an excuse to costume up and drink and you won't be disappointed, and this weekend was no exception. Whatever misgivings we might have felt about putting a half-million-dollar price tag on our town for the weekend, we did a fine job of cinching up our blue party pants and rising to the occasion. Maybe selling out isn't so bad after all.

Selling out? That's not what Crested Butte did with AMAX, or with Thompson Creek Metals, Phelps Dodge, Lucky Jack or U.S. Energy. Selling out would have been unconscionable, a violation of everything Crested Butte stood for. Selling out would have been a treasonous act, not only against the town, but against the collective integrity of the community.

Crested Butte's July Fourth parade packs Elk Avenue with throngs of spectators. "We've been July'ed" has made a verb out of the town's most popular, stressed-out month. TOWN OF CRESTED BUTTE.

34

'Love is Slipping Away'

I N JULY 2015, a *CB News* editorial was simply titled: "More." Editor Mark Reaman remarked on the madhouse of downtown Crested Butte as tourism seemed to reach an all-time high. One significant threshold was when it became evident that summer was busier than winter which, for most ski resorts, is something of a turning point that begs reflection. "Is more always better?" asked Reaman. "The answer is: No. But the alternative is rough, so it really depends."

One marker of busyness in the Butte is measured by toilet flushes. In that first week of July 2015, the CB Sanitation District reported an extra 12,000 toilet flushes per day. That's not the most appealing measure of success, but it's certainly telling. Toilet flushes are also a growth management metric that measures load capacities in water and sanitation systems. Raising tap fees required for new development ups the ante while ensuring a community does not exceed physical limits on basic municipal services.

Crested Butte's unprecedented growth caused Reaman to lapse into nostalgia as he recalled the easier mood of a decade or more before when the town was in a sweet spot. "Rents were cheap(er), jobs were plentiful and paid well, there was always one parking spot available on Elk at all times, and people had plenty of work and free time to enjoy the place. Businesses weren't stressed, and the town handled every visitor seamlessly."

Not in July 2015, when crowds pushed the town out of the sweet spot and into what Reaman assessed as a "servers nightmare of unceasing toil" with little time for personal pleasure. There was a commensurate run on housing—all of it expensive. In sum, service employees in the Butte faced a diminishing set of rewards for busting their butts. "There is just a general ding to morale for both locals and guests. Just having more without being able to handle the ramifications is not better."

Locals and visitors were warned against taking a dip in the "tainted" Slate River after an alarm was raised over e-coli contamination from too many campers discharging human waste—everywhere. Recreation, not mining, was the suspected source. The water quality on which Crested Butte had based recurring arguments against industrialization was now being compromised by pooping campers, not hard-hatted miners.

The *CB News* advised locals who could not handle swelling crowds to stay off Elk Avenue after 10 a.m., suggesting they walk the town's alleys instead of the streets. Off-piste camping trips away from the madding crowd were advised so that no one "lost it" amid Crested Butte's new pressure-cooker affluence. Even then, "the backcountry is getting pounded. . . Honestly," concluded Reaman, "I'm not sure we need to promote 'more' in July."

In September 2018, the CB town council discussed a moratorium against chain stores and franchises, which community leaders feared could homogenize Crested Butte's once homespun commercial core and jeopardize the viability of local businesses. This was especially salient given buy-in overtures by Vail Associates.

In October 2018, Vail officially took over operations at Crested Butte Mountain Resort where a lengthy transition began from family-owned to corporate. On the plus side were benefits for employees. On the downside was the corporate culture inserting itself on a non-corporate community.

There came dire warnings that Vail would lead Crested Butte into further homogenization, commercialization and a mass resort ideation for the upper East River Valley, an echo of the warning biologist Paul Ehrlich of the Rocky Mountain Biological Institute at Gothic had issued decades before during the AMAX fight:

> There are other values in the world than making a quick buck on your real estate, and the people of Gunnison County ought to think

very hard about whether they just want to make a quick buck, which I don't think they do. So many of the people who came out here to escape the Los Angeleses of the world are about to make a decision that will bring Los Angeles right here to Gunnison County."

In late 2018, Crested Butte town council reacted by imposing a rental tax as a disincentive to short-terming the community into empty streets and vacant homes. Chris Ladoulis, a council member, said: "No one wants to prohibit all short-term rentals. But no one wants to be the last house in the neighborhood that is surrounded by short-term rentals. I wouldn't want to live there."

"Monday's special Crested Butte council meeting on STRs had a primal scream element under the surface," editorialized Mark Reaman, reflecting on a disturbing sentiment that community was being lost to profits. This old song of lament was being sung by a growing choir in Crested Butte, with whom Reaman sympathized: "People who can't put their finger on exactly why, but feel a community they love is slipping away." Ultimately optimistic, he held to the faith. "As long as the community can come together to discuss controversial issues in an aura of respect, I think we haven't yet lost the unfettered spirit of Crested Butte."

Still, an undercurrent of commoditization was impossible to ignore if one paged through the *CB News Winter Guide*. Similar to promotional

What's not to love about a picture perfect townscape buried in deep pillows of snow? As one real estate company states in its ads: "We love it here, too!"

publications found in most resort towns, the Guide's focus has been on community, with reminiscences of early Crested Butte skiing, ever popular outdoor gear talk, a calendar of festive and colorful events, and an array of irresistible activities. Local color is now sandwiched between page-after-page of full-color real estate ads dominated by the recently formed and locally-based Blue Bird, along with ample representation from Coldwell Banker, Sotheby's and other national and international brokerages that have gained a solid foothold in Crested Butte.

There is a self-serving attitude visible among the upbeat mood of fetching words and imagery with which realtors exhibit the town. Beneath the magazine's gloss, the *Crested Butte Real Estate Report* incorporates, in prospectus form, the stair step charts of real estate values rising ever higher. The "Don't-Become-Another-Aspen" chant of yore is lost as real estate reaches all-time highs.

Such elite enclaves had defined Aspen decades before. Gated communities attract discriminating buyers who don't wish to mix with the riffraff and yet find the local vibe appealing, from a safe distance. "It's a long way home to Starwood in Aspen, to my sweet Rocky Mountain paradise. . ." sang John Denver. The reference was to Star Mesa where Denver and other notables like Rupert Murdoch and Saudi Prince Bandar bin Sultan owned residential properties. Later came Wildcat, a gated subdivision fronted by actor Michael Douglas that covers an enormous area of exclusivity spread over thousands of acres of rambling hills highlighted by a private lake.

The *CB News* filled more and more of its pages with glossy ads for high-tone properties, the descriptions for which sound a lot like Aspen, Vail and Telluride. In the newspaper business, real estate ads are a lucrative source of income so, in Crested Butte, the rising tide is floating some prominent boats.

"Say Goodbye to Cutthroat Competition,' punned Coldwell Banker Bighorn Realty for the Reserve on the East River, with a scenic fly fisherman-in-the-river photo. The ad cooed about "approximately two miles of private access to the crystal clear East River. Full-time property management and equestrian services. A lodge for socializing. An opportunity to build a lifetime of memories. Unspoiled. Unforgettable."

And for most of the residents of Crested Butte—unaffordable.

35

The Vail-ization of Crested Butte

IN A JUNE 2018 letter-to-the-editor titled, "The death of another Colorado community," Peter Richmond of Holualoa, Hawai'i warned Crested Butte of Vail's corporate reputation: "The Gunnison Valley should start preparing for poverty wages, unregulated tourism, abuse of workers' rights, environmental degradation, condo fortresses, and a complete change in the valley. I grew up in Blue River and Frisco, Colorado where I witnessed first-hand what Vail Resorts' economic vision does to our world."

Richmond and others forecast that, because Vail Resorts is a real estate company that develops the land around ski mountains, its focus is on profits for shareholders. The values of the Crested Butte lifestyle would therefore take a backseat to land development. "They have no interest in the quality of skiing, being a steward for the environment, or human rights," charged Richmond.

"Go ski Breck on a powder day and then tell me Vail Resorts cares about skiing quality; it's overpopulated and unregulated anarchy on the slopes. I know many of you in Crested Butte think Breck is lame. Well, it didn't used to be. It used to be very similar to Crested Butte. . . You have to make corporate vampires like Vail Resorts perform justly or they will take advantage in every way possible."

John Norton, who had been a vice president at CBMR and later served a similar executive position with the Aspen Skiing Company, differed pointedly in his *CB News* column, "Norton's Notions—Another Voice." Norton, who had left Crested Butte in the 1980s for Aspen, then returned in the 1990s, fired off a counterpoint from his rural residence up Cement Creek:

> Some people have voiced concern that with the purchase of CBMR, Crested Butte will lose its vibe. This notion is absurd. The Crested Butte vibe is not nearly that fragile and easy to eradicate. But if people are concerned, the most effective strategy we can pursue to ensure that the vibe stays strong and predominant is to make the valley sustainable so the guardians of the vibe, those of us who have affirmatively chosen Crested Butte over other places to live, are able to continue with the inevitable changes that the purchase of the resort will bring. If we don't want a bunch of people living in CB who are not signed on to our irreverent and iconoclastic gestalt, then we should make sure that the people who are signed on can continue to afford to live here and can continue to find good, rewarding jobs, and we should celebrate our recent successes and adopt a more positive and cooperative attitude among ourselves and a more proactive and considered approach toward the coming changes.

Meanwhile, the town's economy was purring along on an uphill trend as town government felt flush thanks to sales tax, property tax, building permits, use tax and real estate transfer tax—the lucre of commerce and land development. But it is in the housing market that Crested Butte faces existential angst, unable to provide homes for working people who give the town its vitality. Instead, short term tourist rentals have caused community disintegration in the downtown residential core.

Crested Butte and Gunnison County brought on a clash with a rising cadre of second homeowners during the advent of COVID in March 2020, when the pandemic raged into Gunnison County along with an influx of tourists and second homeowners seeking remote quarantine. The *High Country News* reported in January 2021 that a cabal of second homeowners in Crested Butte and Mt. Crested Butte, mostly from Texas, created a donor PAC to contest a county commissioner election with the intent of ousting incumbents who had supported a "go home" order to non-residents. That order was issued to protect health care capacity in Gunnison County from overwhelm by virus-stricken visitors.

Led by second homeowner Jim Moran, who owns a 7,000-plus-square-foot residence in Mt. Crested Butte, the movement failed. However, the effort clearly pitted second homeowners against what some consider obdurate locals. The second homeowners' Facebook page posted descriptions of Crested Butte locals as "irresponsible, non-tax-paying bored children" and "entitled takers" who slap the hands that feed them. Meanwhile, real estate prices under COVID spiked to unprecedented heights, putting housing yet further beyond the range of local workers.

Tracking Crested Butte's sobering transformation, writer Dawne Belloise laid it out with a straightforward, frank and courageous analysis in a two-part series in November 2019. "Poor Little Rich Town" described what was becoming of the "little town that could," stating that, "The trends are overwhelmingly evident: Crested Butte is in a vortex of upheaval and change."

Belloise interviewed local shop owners who had, or were about to, close up their businesses because of high rents, unaffordable overhead, and a lack of workers. The latter tied into the lack of employee housing due to prohibitively high rents. Belloise described Chris Sullivan, owner of Mountain Oven. After nine years operating in Crested Butte, the Oven closed and the baking company moved to more affordable Paonia. "Crested Butte is a really special place, and the exceptional community of long-term residents is trying to protect this place," confided Sullivan. "But I see the people who are moving here, buying property here, and they're not my people."

The town felt a huge loss when the long-standing and ever-popular Donita's Cantina closed for the same reasons other business have given up on the town—exorbitant rents. "Donita's closing," wrote Belloise, "left little doubt of how Crested Butte is changing. . .its community of wildness seems to be transforming into a more gentrified, wealthy culture."

In a tone of sad acceptance, Donita's co-owner, Heli Mae Peterson, acknowledged an undeniable shift in the town's population. "These people are moving to Crested Butte and love it. And, you know, I came here from somewhere else. I can't shut the door on it, but I can hang onto community. You've got to have tourism when your rent is $10,000

Deep snow, cold weather and an iconic mountain peak set Crested Butte in a class of its own, especially when complemented by an historic town with a vibrant community nestled in the valley below.
GUNNISON-CRESTED BUTTE TOURISM ASSOCIATION

a month and going up 50 percent. I believe that we're all hanging onto community."

In a second installment, under the subhead, "It Ain't Easy (being rich and pretty)," Belloise concluded that Crested Butte is being deserted by "a migration of residents to more affordable towns where home ownership is realistically attainable. Many feel it's not the locals who are going to have a say in this town's future and development—it's the big money." Belloise ended the series with a note of optimism and hope that community bonds will endure despite a gradual erosion of local housing and business opportunities.

A glance over the hill at Aspen lends a different and sobering vantage, where high rents displaced most of the local retail flavor with big name franchise stores. These trendy boutiques are the only businesses that can write off ever-escalating rents in exchange for high-end visibility and the Aspen imprint on promotional branding materials. On the housing front, Aspen has been a leader in underwriting affordable rents and employee property buy-ins for a segment of its workforce in an effort to maintain a mixed population to perpetuate what Aspen planning guidelines refer to as "messy vitality." Maintaining a local community has been crucial to Aspen's sense of place, but given the larger scale of the Roaring Fork Valley and far easier tourist access than in Crested Butte, those local values and the community of people that still honor them have been diluted by huge influxes of seasonal visitors and second homeowners. Under COVID, this imbalance became even more acute.

Crested Butte town council tried to legislate a solution by prohibiting a franchise overrun on Elk Avenue, but there is no legislation that can turn down the volume of wealthy elites who have set their sights on assimilating small town values while unknowingly undermining the town's fragile soul with expectations for upscale appurtenances, services and conformity to conservative political correctness.

A "kerfuffle" over the pagan festival Vinotok came to a head after the election of Donald Trump in 2016 when the traditional burning of the Grump became the burning of the Trump—in effigy. Many visitors and second homeowners were offended, and they wrote letters of scold to the *CB News* and also to Vail Associates, which was erroneously assumed to have influence over Crested Butte. Many in Crested Butte have come to realize that the town's brand of irreverence is not for everybody. A glaring dichotomy is revealed by outrageous acts like the immolation of a likeness of the President of the United States or the cheeky displays on the infamous "moon bus," while the town depends on economic viability from insulted visitors who finance the community.

Saying no to monolithic mining companies is one thing, but saying no to big money flooding into your community is another. Adapting behaviors that suit a town's persona without alienating cash flow is a serious challenge in Crested Butte, where irreverence and non-conformity are marks of creativity, pride, spirit and identity. Ironically, these very traits attract wealthy outsiders who are envious of the unfettered lifestyles in which they may eventually find fatal flaws.

Today, Crested Butte wrestles with resort development and culture clashes while the threat of mining still lingers. A multiplicity of challenges has left much of the town divided and embittered by resentments that have no easy solutions and elicit sorrow from those who knew the town when. . .

EPILOGUE

The Soul of "The Little Town that Could"

WHAT SAVED CRESTED BUTTE from mining, and what may save Crested Butte from commoditization, is what Webster's Dictionary describes as soul: "The spiritual or immaterial part of a human being; the essence of something intangible."

Soul is what Sandra Cortner invoked with her 2015 book: *Crested Butte: Love at First Sight.* Soul is what Flauschink celebrates, and Vinotok, the Red Lady Salvation Ball, the Townie Takeover, the Chainless Race, the Zombie Prom, the Alley Loop, and dozens of celebrations. Collectively, these community fetes exude mirthful exuberance and cast the warm glow of joy on the town stage and its improvisational actors. The soul of Crested Butte is a zeitgeist that's playful, compassionate, heartening—and highly contagious.

The soul of a town is a unique measure of community, a collective way of being. It was the soul of Crested Butte that won international esteem in December 2013, when Crested Butte was awarded the title of "Best Ski Town in North America" by *Powder Magazine.* The recognition didn't merely weigh the physical amenities of the overall resort. The award recognized something special about Crested Butte. The town's soul gave Crested Butte an edge over the more homogenous resorts. "It was a community push," said then CBMR marketing director Erica Mueller. "Everyone should be proud." A letter writer to the *CB News* wrote: "This has gotten us a ton of publicity lately and hopefully lots more to come. We are 'the little town that could,' and now it is known. Be proud to call this home; I know I am."

The designation of Crested Butte as a "Creative District" in 2016 assigned an official mandate "to develop cultural patronage so creatives and creative business could thrive by nurturing a vibrant creative culture in downtown Crested Butte with support for local artists, collaborations between art groups and increased visibility of the arts and creativity." The Creative District not only gave license for pageants, costumes, street theater and errant behaviors, but became a directive to pursue these displays as forms of expression that are contingent on being a Crested Butte citizen and a contributor to the town's collective soul.

Many of the AMAX front liners shared pride in Crested Butte when the soul of the town was different than it is today, formed as it was under different conditions and a funkier, less glossy essence. Soul became a bond for a cohort of today's neo old-timers who cultivated a deep sense of belonging that held the community together as a force to reckon with during the all-out fight against AMAX and subsequent mining threats.

Mark Reaman, in August 2019, reflected about a unique celebration, the 40-year town reunion. Here was a celebration of soul if there ever was one. Reaman's editorial was titled: "Don't give up on the love."

> I was on the edge of that group of early Crested Butte residents who came to the end of the road, found dirt streets, old miners and not a whole lot else. It was cheap, easy, good living by all accounts. These were not 20-year-olds on Tinder. These were old friends. No offense. It sounds like more than a thousand people converged to reminisce with like-minded souls. And from what I have been told, the weekend was full of love: love of the place; love of the people; love of what they experienced and what Crested Butte left in their soul. There is nothing wrong with love.
>
> There is a lot to love here at the end of the road and it seems more than a few people are forgetting that as they focus on bad drivers, worse parkers and the difficult ability to buy a place and actually live here. Those are not inconsequential things, but there are things to love here. . .

Reaman then latched onto a strangely beloved landmark and a link to the mining era—Gronk—the concrete superstructure that served as a coal tipple at the Peanut Mine and Mill north of town in the Slate River Valley. "I love that there is a weird concrete structure named the Gronk and most everyone knows what it is. Gronk. I love that the family that owns the Gronk property loves the Gronk."

To consider Gronk as part of Crested Butte's soul reflects a strange and almost incomprehensible attachment to the weird. Gronk is a monument to something beyond mountain biking, skiing, hiking, costumed craziness and all the accoutrements of the town. Gronk is a Stonehenge-like monolith harking to a mythic Druidic spirit that attracts a seemingly endless procession of devotees.

Reaman suggested the town's soul includes "cool mornings and evenings, and a bear totaling a vehicle for cookies. . ." But, he emphasized, "The scale is still small town. The values are still compassionate. The vibe is still mountain town. Do not lose sight that there is a lot to love. . . and there is nothing wrong with love."

Honoring the town's 40th anniversary with an unprecedented reunion in summer 2019, long-time local Kathleen Mary offered a free verse insight where nicknames are a sign of community intimacy, the polar opposite of anonymity. She identified neo old-timers for their col-

Crested Butte backcountry skiers took part in a protest ski tour over Pearl Pass to Aspen in 1981 to call for united action against industrial mining on both sides of the Elk Range. CRESTED BUTTE CHRONICLE ARCHIVES

EPILOGUE • 241

lective eccentricity, and appropriately titled it: "The Witness Protection Program of Crested Butte."

> Who else hides here? Well there's Glo, Flo, Tree, Max, Waz, Dirdge, Strat, Rat, Peel, Derf...who's going to believe a Koo, Zoo and Roo. Can anyone find Du, Bugs, Pi and Cap? No because the whole damn family is on the lam. Frogs and Dildos, Pelts and Wheels. Gerbils, Pinballs, Pappy and Danno, Vito, Bird, Ronco, Corky, Rollo and Churches...we got lots of Churches...and Flying Petitos, which every town needs.

When Reaman cautioned in an editorial in August 2016 that "the old days" of Crested Butte, while sweet and soulful, did not exist "without a lot of hardship," Joe Grabowski, a voice from those old days, offered a telling and savory history, along with a lesson in values derived from those of us fortunate enough to qualify as 40-plus year alumni:

> Hardship? Being able to work part-time, live in town, and spend the majority of your days hiking, fishing, skiing, hanging with your friends in the bars. Hardship? Cutting, splitting wood on a crisp autumn day and watching with satisfaction as your winter wood stash grew day by day. Hardship? Knowing everyone (and their dogs) on a first-name basis, and catching up on their latest adventures at the post office at noon. Hardship? Having your pick of wonderful places to eat and drink at a reasonable price with no wait. Hardship? Purchasing season passes for everyone in the family without taking out a loan, and the mountain experience of short lift lines, skiing with half the town on a powder day, followed by cocktails on the Artichoke deck at a base area that didn't resemble a small city.

"The 'old days' were as good as advertised," emphasized Grabowski, "and it is an indication of the gentrification of Crested Butte that what you now consider hardships were merely part of a hearty, unrestrained, joyful lifestyle."

The Crested Butte lifestyle to which Joe refers could not be scripted or choreographed. It was spontaneous and serendipitous and unique, a once-in-forever-flower-power-love-in-organic-planetary-alignment. There was no tutorial on how to be a local, and there was no recreating it, because the coveted lifestyle had grown naturally and was nurtured with spirit. It flowered and then went to seed.

Comparisons of epochs spent in the ethereal glow of Crested Butte's vibe are difficult because there is no objectivity in deeply personal emotional connections with this place. Is the past always better than the present or the future? Reaman offered some reasons to cheer and reasons to lament a changing Crested Butte in a September 2018 editorial simply titled, "Then and Now."

"Used to be $11/hour was a pretty good wage in the valley. These days, $11/hour is a decent wage for a middle-school kid, but not for an adult trying to live here. Used to be that a house selling for $190,000 was pretty expensive. These days, a house selling for $190,000 is cheap (okay, almost impossible) and will be sold within minutes. Used to be you could rent a house in town for a couple hundred bucks a month, and it was easy to find a place. These days it costs an arm and a leg to rent most places in town, and there aren't many affordable places for workers. Used to be a lot of lights on at night in houses in CB, and a few hardy souls chose to live in CB South. These days there are still lights on in the local neighborhood but there are more lights in CB South. Used to be the Lower Loop had one of the best views in the country. These days, the Lower Loop has one of the best views in the country."

Among things to love, Reaman wrote, is "End of July and the busyness of business." In a letter-to-the-editor, "We've been Julyed!" Mary Picciano amplified the point. "The heat has let up and the crowds are thinning and maybe our patience and tolerance will improve. . . Perhaps these huge changes such as Vail and the increase of population can be expected, and maybe we can start at the roots of our tribe and build from there a place of true community with positive attitudes instead of fueling the negative. Yes, I miss the good old days and will dread next July, yet it has happened and I can't think of anywhere else I would rather be. So, thank you, July, I judged you wrong as insane, intense and overrun as I felt you brought free music, new friends and some savings for the off-season ahead as I'm sure it did for all of you. Be chill and much love."

"Don't forget that this place is about the soul," reminded a letter-to-the-editor from Deborah Tutnauer. "The 40th Reunion was wonderful! It was a beautiful reminder of why we made Crested Butte our home—whether 20, 30, 40 or more years ago. The soul of this town was

Community spirit arouses the primal in biologists with the Rocky Mountain Biological Laboratory of Gothic during a July Fourth parade in the '80s.
CRESTED BUTTE CHRONICLE ARCHIVES

in that tent last night—dancing up a storm, hugging and reconnecting with a community that nurtures its own and truly loves this valley for what it is, not for what they can make it become. It was a much-needed gathering particularly for those suffering from the 'July Sacrifice.'"

Another reader credited the neo old-timers at the 40-year reunion with contributing heart and soul and shaping the Crested Butte of the present. "Crested Butte exists as it is today because of the people in that tent last night. Let's make decisions moving forward that allow their children, grandchildren and all future generations to share the values of community, caring, stewardship of nature and all the things that make Crested Butte unique. Rock On!"

Sandy Fails, a Texas transplant, who in 1984 took the helm of the *Crested Butte Chronicle* as my successor, shared a soulful sense of place in an opening chapter of her 1989 book, *Crested Butte: The Edge of Paradise.* Her words complemented picture perfect images by former *Chronicle* photographer Nathan Bilow in a coffee table book published by Jeff Newman, a former Aspenite who owned Crested Butte Printing through the 1980s and shares, as I do, affection for both sides of the Elk Range. "Crested Butte has cleared my head, toughened my skin and touched my heart," wrote Fails. "I've been infatuated with her, fed up by her, cramped and charmed by her. I've made the mud season escape to catch some big city bright lights. And I've always returned to the mountains with the deep, welcome sense of coming home."

Letters-to-the-editor register a community pulse, like the one titled, "Our community has a big heart," written by Judi Theis, acknowledging the passing of her husband, Dave.

> The whole time we were fighting Dave's illnesses, our community stepped in where we could not. Not just once, but over and over again, we received financial help, meals, housekeeping, drives to the doctors, visits, lots of cards and well-wishing phone calls. The financial help allowed me to advocate and care for Dave at home. Our community, close and far, including friends and family, have such wonderful hearts. Regardless of all the changes going in our world and our community, we always pull together, share and care. I am forever grateful to everyone for caring. I couldn't have done it without this community. You all made his great care possible.

This is the love over which Reaman and others exult. Love of neighbors, unconditionally, is a palpable part of Crested Butte's soul. But some began to recognize changes that were disconcerting—of newcomers who were not schooled in CB lore and love, of the gentrification of the town's charming alley shacks that were both humble and homey, of the advent of slick commercial promotions from real estate developers.

Many of those alley "shacks" are labeled ADUs, or accessory dwelling units. Columnist Molly Murfee, in January 2019, identified herself as the "dweller of an ADU in the pulsing heart of downtown Crested Butte." She painted the picture of a giving and dedicated local. "I work for non-profits, codirect one of the most iconic grassroots festivals of the community, go to local fundraisers, buy local goods. I ride my townie, rarely drive my truck. I love this land, its creatures, its plants and its people as much as I love anything else on this earth. . ."

Having shared a cup of tea with Molly in winter 2020, I know that her feelings are authentic, that her love is real. Her soul is linked with Crested Butte because she, like many before her, chose "the road not taken." She credits personal fulfillment with that choice. "We are the ones who chose a different path, and that path didn't involve making butt-loads of cash. . .We didn't exactly sign up to be investment bankers and acquisition specialists."

Murfee underscores the soul of Crested Butte by championing the value of the town's 15 mph speed limit. She encourages a vocal local to shout at you for driving too fast and then politely explain why a slower speed is a good fit with the town. Her message is particularly salient given at least one tragic death by traffic in recent memory.

> The speed limit in Crested Butte is 15 miles per hour, as any good bench-sitting local will yell at you. Yes, it is slow. Intentionally so. Luxuriously, wonderfully, decadently so. . . Life is different here. There exists a different pace, a different orientation. Roll down your window. Stick your elbow out. Smile and wave. You're on parade. You coast so slowly, you can wave to your friends on the sidewalk, check out who's catching a late afternoon beer on the deck, have a moving conversation with the biker next to you.
>
> No one comes to Crested Butte to be normal. Even if you're here to visit, chances are high you came because here is different. . .Don't busy yourself replicating the very rat race you flee from. This is a ripe opportunity. Step out of the norm of life. . . Experience another framework, an alternative approach to the world, more conscious and creative ways to interact with it. . . Let the unhurried approach seep into your marrow. Feel the sunshine on your elbow, the wind on your cheek and just coast at 15 mph. Or, for a more advanced immersion, get out of your tin can of entrapment, and saunter.

"Hugs are important, pass them along. . ." reminded Mark Reaman in a September 2018 editorial as he reflected on travels abroad and of seeing Crested Butte through a new lens. "This is as beautiful a place in the world as one can find. Gathering Sunday to celebrate the life of a young man who graduated from high school with my son again demonstrated the power of real community. In good times and sad, this place gathers to celebrate and mourn. We hold one another up and share energy through hugs and stories. . . This community is made up of real stories shared by real people. Even in sad times the goodness of this community shines. We will all eventually pass through this dimension of life so we might as well do it together and in real life—not just virtually on the computer. This community is good at that. Thank God."

Crested Butte's soul shines in the collective and individual lives of those who have been touched by it. Honoring, celebrating and nurturing soul is a constant commitment. Those who feel the town's soul

A sunrise, mountaintop bivouac on Mt. Emmons describes a spiritual connection to a place. Here is seen the contrast of intense solitude coupled with the warm communal bond that Crested Butte offers to those sensitive enough to appreciate and live it. XAVI FANE

know that Crested Butte must do everything it can to retain its heartfelt integrity despite the threats of mining, commercial development and homogenization, despite its ever-changing character.

On July 23, 2012, almost 30 years after leaving Crested Butte, I wrote in my weekly *Aspen Times* column about the need for conservation of Thompson Divide, a wilderness-quality landscape near Carbondale. I could have written the same about Crested Butte: "People who have the good fortune and good sense to live in communities adjacent to wild and beautiful places are left with the responsibility not only to enjoy them but to protect them. Such is a community's lifelong mission when stewarding national treasures that are valued as a heritage from the past and an inheritance for the future."

Paul Hitchcock, a neo-old-timer, CB expat, took it deeper still in an "Overheard" from March 2016 in the *CB News*. Paul described to a visitor what it means to be a local: "It's not how long you've lived here, it's how much you're here in spirit."

A BRIEF HISTORY OF THE **Mt. Emmons/Red Lady Mining Issue**

- **1872** The **Mining Law of 1872** guarantees the right-to-mine.
- **1880** **Crested Butte** is incorporated
- **1916** American Metals Company (**AMCO**) opens the Climax Mine on Bartlett Mountain near Leadville
- **1952** Crested Butte's **last operating coal mine, shuts down**
- **1954** The D&RGW Railroad **pulls up its tracks**
- **1950s** American Smelting and Refinery Corporation (**ASARCO**) **extracts heavy metals** from the Keystone Mine on Mt. Emmons/Red Lady
- **1957** AMCO merges with Climax Molybdenum to form American Metals at Climax (**AMAX**)
- **1960s** **U.S. Energy** buys Keystone Mine on Mt. Emmons from **ASARCO**
- **1973** AMAX buys the Keystone Mine from **U.S. Energy** and begins **drilling** on Mt. Emmons/Red Lady
- **1977** AMAX announces **plans to mine** Mt. Emmons at a Crested Butte town meeting
  - **High Country Citizens' Alliance (HCCA)** is founded
  - **Mitchell is elected mayor** of Crested Butte
- **1978** **Colorado Joint Review Process (CJRP)** launches Environmental Assessment
- **1979** A **forest fire** breaks out at AMAX's Mt. Emmons Mine
- **1980** AMAX offers a plan to **clean up** poluted Coal Creek with a wastewater treatment plant
  - AMAX maps the Mt. Emmons orebody at 300 million tons of low-grade molybdenum ore
  - Crested Butte sends out a **fund-raising request** to support its fight against AMAX
  - Crested Butte passes the **Crested Butte Watershed Ordinance**
  - AMAX's "Boomtown Tour" visits coal mining sites in Wyoming
- **1981** Quaker "Meetings" are held in Alkali Basin
  - The price of **molybdenum plummets** on the International Metals Market
  - AMAX announces it has **postponed** plans to mine Mt. Emmons/Red Lady
- **1984** The price of **molybdenum bottoms out** at $2.50/pound
  - AMAX announces that the Mt. Emmons Mine *is* **no longer viable**
  - Crested Butte holds the **"AMAX Going Away Party"**
- **1988** **Freeport-McMoRan** is established. (Ranked 215th largest corporation in the U.S. in 2021)
- **1991** AMAX proposes a **"small mine"** option, then almost immediately abandons it
- **1993** AMAX becomes **Cyprus-AMAX** when it joins with Cyprus Mineral Company
- **1999** Cyprus-AMAX is acquired by **Phelps-Dodge** in a hostile takeover
- **2006** Phelps-Dodge wins a lawsuit to return the Mt. Emmons/Red Lady Mine to **U.S. Energy**
  - **U.S. Energy** announces a new partnership with Kobex Resources, Ltd., of Vancouver, Canada, and renames the Mt. Emmons/Red Lady Mine **"Lucky Jack"**
- **2007** **Freeport-McMoRan** gobbles up **Phelps-Dodge** in largest mining acquisition in history
- **2008** Mt. Emmons/Red Lady Mine **"Lucky Jack" strikes out** and Thompson Creek Metals Company USA comes in as a mining partner with **U.S. Energy**
- **2012** "Lucky Jack" **dies** and **U.S. Energy** tries to go it alone with another threat of a big mine on Mt. Emmons/Red Lady
- **2014** Burdened by mine effluent **water treatment costs** of Coal Creek, **U.S. Energy** holds a conciliatory meeting with **HCCA**, **Red Lady Coalition** and **Crested Butte**
- **2016** A legal finding forces **Freeport-McMoRan** to take over the Mt. Emmons/Red Lady Mine from **U.S. Energy** and open negotiations to **end mining forever** on Mt. Emmons/Red Lady
- **2018-22** Plans for a **sustainable water treatment system** at the Mt. Emmons Mine are advanced toward a lasting solution to toxic mine effluent in Coal Creek
- **2019-22** Multi-party negotiations lead toward a **mineral withdrawal of mining claims** on Mt. Emmons/Red Lady by **Freeport-McMoRan** and a **permanent cessation of mining** threats to Crested Butte

ADDENDUM

Song Medley

FROM THE RED LADY SALVATION BALL

Written and performed in Crested Butte by
Tracey Wickland and Paul Andersen

Moly Moly Hallelujah
(to *Glory, Glory Hallelujah*)

Mine eyes have seen the glory of the mining of the ore.
It has trampled down the mountains it has filled the valley floor.
It has made a mighty industry where nothing stood before.
As AMAX marches on.

Moly Moly Hallelujah
Moly Moly what's it to yuh?
Moly Moly's gonna screw yuh
As AMAX marches on.

Seventy-Six Drill Rigs
(to *Seventy Six Trombones*)

Seventy-six drill rigs caught the morning sun
With a hundred and ten dump trucks right in line
They were followed by rows and rows of the finest front-end
    loaders,
The cream of every famous mine

Seventy-six drill rigs caught the morning sun
With a hundred and ten dump trucks right behind
There was more than a million bucks in machinery and trucks
There were tools of every shape and size.

There was dynamite to light the night with big KA-BOOMS
Thundering, thundering all along the way
Seismic shocks that split the rocks and noxious fumes
Every fume taking your breath away.

Exploratory demolitions underground
Thundering, thundering louder than before
Blasting caps of every kind, so many it would blow your mind
And three hundred million tons of ore.

Seventy-six drill rigs led the big parade
With a hundred and ten dump trucks on the way
Everybody said "Drill! Drill! Drill! Tailings ponds we soon will fill."
And they're mining still, right today!

I Want a Mine Just like the Mine . . .
(to *I Want a Girl*)

I want a mine, just like the mine, that buried dear old dad.
He fell in a drift on the graveyard shift and mommy is so sad
A good old-fashioned mine is all I wish
Daddy loved it until he went squish (yuk!)
I want a mine, just like the mine that buried dear old Dad.

Subside by Subside
(to *Side-by-Side*)

Oh, we just got a barrel of moly
That's why we're happy and jolly
Just to tunnel along
'Til the mountains are gone
Subside by subside.

Oh, we don't know what we'll find tomorrow
But we'll leave a permanent scar-o
As we tunnel along
'Til the mountains are gone
Subside by subside

Through our mighty efforts
What if the mountains fall?
As long as we make profits
It doesn't matter at all.

When we've ruined your town and departed
We'll find a new place to start it
As we tunnel along
'Til the mountains are gone
Subside by subside
Yes, we'll tunnel along
'Til all the mountains are gone
Subside by subside.

Over Hill Over Dale
(to *As the Caissons Go Rolling Along*)

Over hill over dale AMAX lays another rail
As the ore trains come rolling along
You can yell, you can shout, but you'll never drive us out
As the ore trains come rolling along.

And it's hi, hi, hee, bring the TNT
Set off those charges loud and strong
And they'll thank us yet back in old Connecticut
When those ore trains come rolling along.

Old Mayor Mitchell
(to *Old Man River*)

Old Mayor Mitchell
That bold Mayor Mitchell
He don't fear nothin'

And he must know somethin'
That old Mayor Mitchell
He just keeps rollin' along

You and me
We sweat and toil
Bodies all achin'
And racked with pain

Lift that chair
Gotta tote that mayor
Gotta get him up
Another stair.

He's so filled with
Love and affection
It must be time for
A new election

That old Mayor Mitchell
He just keeps rollin'
He just keeps rollin' along

Oh, Mister Rademan
(to *Mister Sandman*)

Oh, Mister Rademan
Bring us a dream
Make it the best place we've ever seen
Fill it with golf courses, green strips and clover
And tell us that the mining days are over

Rademan
Plan us a town
Make it the best place we've ever found
We only want peaches and cream
Mister Rademan, bring us a dream

Mister Rademan
Give us a plan
Heaven on earth is all we demand
We don't want an overflowing cornucopia
Just your basic everyday utopia

Rademan
Make us a plan
Heaven on earth is all we demand
So smile on us your magic beam
Mister Rademan, bring us a dream

Big Don
(to *Big John*)

He stood six-foot-six, he weighed 125
And everybody knew you didn't give no jive
To Big Don

He came out here with Sam, his dog.
At Tony's Tavern sold 3.2 grog.
Kinda narrow at the shoulder,
Kinda narrow at the hip
But you can hear it thunder when he shoots from the lip
Big Don

And then one day old AMAX came
To stake a giant mining claim.
They said they'd build a big boom town,
And most of us thought things was looking down
Except Don

His voice rang out like a mighty blow
And he told AMAX, "It's time you go!"
By the time his vocal chords went slack
They was halfway back to Hackensack.

Now there's only one boom in this here land
And it's the big, big voice of a big, big man,
Big Don. . .Big Don. . .Big Don

Attorney Wesley Light
(to *Strangers in the Night*)

Attorney Wesley Light
Renowned esquire
Guarding human rights
His one desire
Studied hard at school
And Light came shining through.

Move to Crested Butte
As town attorney
Scorning all the loot
He could be earning
Not what you'd expect
A CU grad to do

Now he studies law
Concerning water
He's the fastest moving jaw
You really oughta

Hear him pleading to the bench
Enough to make you wrench
The water shed is in his head
The mining laws his only cause

Now Wes may not succeed
Like F. Lee Bailey
But at the JRP
He'll cause a melee
And though he's always right
To us he's still Les Bright

Susan Cottingham
(to *Harrigan, That's Me!*)

C-O-double-T-I N-G-ham
That's Cottingham
Her head displays the latest fashion hairdo
To help her fight for wilderness and RARE II

No, Red Lady need not fear
Cottingham is here
No one will be abusin'
The land long as Susan
Cottingham is here
(She's the Cottingham what am.)

Chuck Malick
(to *Up On the Housetop*)

Up on Red Lady, here they come
AMAX wants molybdenum
HCCA is coming, quick, quick, quick
Taking the lead is Chuck Malick.

Ho, ho, ho—they've gotta go
Blow by blow—wouldn't you know
They're down off Mt. Emmons, real quick
They had not a chance with Chuck Malick

Bye-Bye AMAX
(to *Bye-Bye, Baby, Bye-Bye*)

Now the time has come for us to sigh
Good-bye, oh me oh my
Amax says it must be checking out
The time is here to shed a tear
And sing and dance and shout—and tell them
Bye-bye Amax, bye-bye
Bye-bye Amax don't cry
All we can say is golly
We're sorry but the bottom just dropped out of moly
Bye-bye drill rigs—aw shucks
Bye-bye to all those trucks
We wish we could say We'd like you to stay
But all we know is that we're glad you're going away—and so it's
Bye-bye Amax, bye-bye
Bye-bye Amax bye-bye

INDEX

10th Mountain Huts 144, 265
40-year town reunion 240

A

Abbey, Edward 141, 142, 186
Aboriginal natives 115
A Day in the Life 6
Africa 30, 186
Alkali Basin 72, 102, 202
Alpineer Building 83
Alumax Pacific Corporation 114
AMAX Going Away Party 151
AMAX War Against Humanity 114
American Dream 63
American Metals at Climax (AMAX) vi, viii, ix, x, 28-32, 34-49, 52- 54, 56, 57, 59, 60-74, 76-102, 104-128, 130-135, 137-144, 145-152, 154-173, 176-182, 185-188, 190, 191, 193, 194, 196, 198-200, 208, 213, 215, 216, 224-226, 229, 231, 240, 241, 248, 250, 252, 254, 255
American Metal Company (AMCO) 29, 30
American Smelting and Refinery Corporation (ASARCO) 30, 31
America's backyard 74, 75, 80
Anderson, Perry 182, 183
Andrus, Cecil 98
Anheuser-Busch 227, 228
anthracite coal 16
Arapaho National Forest 108
Arkansas River 46
Ashcroft, Colorado 14, 78
Aspen i, ii, 13, 35, 54, 63, 81, 134, 136, 144, 152, 164, 168, 171, 173, 176, 185, 196, 212, 215, 218, 221, 233-235, 237, 247
Aspen Institute 144, 185, 265
Aspenization 63, 214
Aspenize 168, 217
Aspen Skiing Company 234
Aspen Times 176, 247, 265
Astoria, Oregon 115

Augsburger, Herschel 159
Australia 115, 158, 220
Avalauncher 34

B

Baby Boom 18
Bachman, Don 9, 42, 43, 71, 103, 157, 160, 171, 198
Bandar bin Sultan 233
Barnett, Ralph 37, 40, 42, 83, 84, 85, 86, 101
Bartlett Mountain 29, 122, 191
Bauer, Carol "Bowzer" 11
Baumgartner, Bruce 55
Baumgartner, Kuziak, Rademan (BKR) 55
Beatles 6
Belkin, John 203
Belloise, Dawne 236
Bennett, Michael 204
Bernholtz, Alan 181
best mine in the world 106
Best Ski Town in North America 239
Biddle, Art 37, 40, 68, 83, 84, 85, 93, 94, 101, 109, 121, 149, 158, 172
Bighorn Realty 233
Big Mine 16, 67
Bilow, Nathan ix, 244
Blackwell, Bruce 154
Blue Bird 233
Blue Mesa Reservoir 4
Bock, Jennifer 188, 190
Bolinas, California 75, 213
Boom Town Tour 118, 120, 121
Boundary Waters Wilderness Area 37, 109
Bratton, Dick 101
Breeze, Joe 11
Brower, David 144
Bud Light 225, 227, 228
Burford, Gail 11
Burns, Mike 33
Bye-Bye, AMAX, Bye-Bye 155

C

Cahn, Robert 107
Callaway, Howard "Bo" 25, 127
Camp Hale 191

Carbon Creek 189, 202
Carbondale, Colorado 247
Carter, President Jimmy 53
Castle Creek 13
Catlin, Illinois 113
CB News Winter Guide 232
Cement Creek 235
Centennial State 14
Chetco River 206
Chief Seattle 129
Child, Bob 134
Cinnamon Rainbow Leather 78
Civil War 14, 98
Clean Air Act Amendment 113
Climax Mine 116, 191, 201
Coal Creek 15, 46, 69, 70, 75, 76, 88-96, 112, 139, 179, 181, 183, 188-192, 197, 202-204, 208
Coldwell Banker 233
Collegiate Peaks Wilderness Area 139
Colorado Department of Natural Resources 99
Colorado Department of Public Health and Environment 69, 192
Colorado Energy Coordinating Advisory Committee 79
Colorado Fuel & Iron (CF&I) 16, 17
Colorado Joint Review Process (CJRP) 93, 99, 100, 101
Colorado Mineral Belt 35, 36, 43
Colorado Open Space Council 107
Colorado Outdoor Recreation & Economy (CORE) Act 209
Colorado Supreme Court 96, 178
Colorado Trail 191
Colorado Water Conservation Board 192
Commons 61
Concerned Citizens, The 124
Congressional withdrawal 198, 204
Conundrum Hot Springs 12
Cook, Don and Steve 11
Copper Lake 135
Copper Mountain 191
Cortner, Sandra 130, 135, 239
Cottingham, Susan 75, 92, 158, 159, 170, 171, 254

Cousteau, Jacques-Yves 115
Cox, Thom 168
Craig, Colorado 118
Crank, Bill 218
Crested Butte Chronicle vi, ix, xi, xiv, 12, 20, 22, 34, 37, 43, 47, 50, 53, 56, 71, 78, 81, 91, 101-104, 119, 123, 125, 126, 136, 141-143, 145, 146, 153, 159, 161, 169, 212, 214, 241, 244
Crested Butte Corporation 31, 179
Crested Butte Hot Shots 57
Crested Butte: Love at First Sight 130, 135, 239
Crested Butte Mining Law Conference 98
Crested Butte Mountain 3, 12, 13, 22, 24, 25, 26, 154, 195, 224, 225, 231
Crested Butte Mountain Resort 26, 195, 225, 231
Crested Butte News 56, 172, 175, 176, 181, 183, 186, 187
Crested Butte Pilot ix, 127, 172
Crested Butte Real Estate Report 233
Crested Butte Ski Patrol 33
Crested Butte South 223
Crested Butte Watershed Ordinance 89
Croatian Hall 17
Crystal, Colorado 14
Cumberland Plateau 113
Cunningham, Charlie 11
Cunningham, Glo 159
Curran, Mike 91, 94
Curray, Emily 214
Curray, Steve 11
Cyprus-AMAX 178, 199
Cyprus Mineral Company 178

D

Daines, Steve 206
Dawson, Pat 77
Delta Strip Mine 113
Dempsey, Stan 35, 40, 70, 83, 86, 94, 107, 111, 116, 117, 158
Denver, John 3, 145, 156, 233
Denver & Rio Grande Western Railroad 15
Department of the Interior 92, 98, 106, 196

Department of Tobacco and Firearms 83
Desert Solitaire 141, 215
Disneyland 216
Disneyworld 222
Dolan, Terry 113
Donita's Cantina 33, 236
Dorchester, Colorado 14
Douglas, Michael 233
Dowell, Marcia 159
Durango, Colorado 96
Dyson, Greg 189, 191

E

Earth Muffin Memos 218
East Maroon Pass 135
East River Valley 3, 15, 26, 47, 104, 183, 231
Eflin, Dick 24
Ehrlich, Dr. Paul 140, 141
Elk Avenue 8, 23, 130, 135, 154, 186, 195, 197, 214, 216, 218, 227, 228, 229, 231, 238
Elk Creek 189
Elk Mountain Lodge 103
Elk Range 3, 13, 14, 45, 57, 63, 77, 134, 139, 152, 176, 185, 244
Emerson, Ralph Waldo 63
Emmons, Samuel Franklin 14
Environmental Assessment (EA) 100
Environmental Impact Statement (EIS) 92, 100, 104, 158
Ervin, Jane and Lee 127
Evans, Arnold 118
Evans, George S. 143
Experiment in Ecology 107, 108, 111, 116
explosives 71, 250

F

Fails, Sandy ix, 244
Farris Creek 11
Fat City 221, 222
FBI 83
Federal Land Policy and Act (FLPMA) 207

Ferraro, Geraldine 54
Fisher, Gary 11
Flauschink 20, 135, 239
Footprints on the Planet 107, 122
Frank & Gal's 17
Freedom of Information Act 188
Freeport-McMoRan 176, 196, 199, 200-204, 207, 208
Fremont Pass 46

G

Gaia 144
Gelwix, Max 37, 40
geologists 14, 28, 31, 34, 62, 71, 72
Ghost Bikers in the Sky 11
Gibson's Ridge 9, 19
Gillette, Wyoming 118
Glacier National Park 205
Glitter Gulch 62
glory hole 44, 46, 73, 122, 155, 197, 201
Goff, Jack 36
Gothic, Colorado 12, 13, 14, 36, 79, 102, 135, 140, 145, 231, 244
Gothic Peak 13
Gousseland, Pierre 36
Grabowski, Joe 242
Grasberg copper and gold deposit 199
Greenwich, Connecticut 27, 35, 80, 118, 158
Gronk 45, 241
Grubstake Saloon 38, 57, 58, 59, 130, 169
Gudowski, LeAndra 214
Gunnison ix, xi, 2-6, 12, 15, 20, 22, 24, 33, 35, 39, 42, 43, 45, 48, 51, 56, 69, 70-72, 74, 80, 82, 85, 91, 95, 99, 101-104, 110, 116-118, 120-123, 125, 131, 138, 139, 158-161, 163-165, 178, 181-184, 189, 192, 196, 208, 215, 226, 231-235
Gunnison Country Times ix, xi, 39, 42, 45, 118, 164
Gunnison County 56, 69, 70-72, 74, 80, 82, 85, 95, 99, 103, 116-118, 120-123, 138, 158-161, 163, 178, 181, 182, 184, 189, 196, 208, 226, 231, 232, 235
Gunsight Pass 151

260 • THE TOWN THAT SAID 'HELL NO!'

H

Hall, Denis 172, 174, 180, 197, 224
Hamlin, Becky 34
Hamlin, Terry 32, 34, 35, 37, 70, 81, 84, 121, 167, 172, 216
Hansen, Roger 107, 108
Hart, Gary 54
Harvard University 61, 98, 101
Haskell, Floyd 54, 101
Hayden, Ferdinand Vandeveer 13
Head Start 55
Hearn, Casey 33
Henderson, Brett 198, 207
Henderson Mine 34, 36, 38, 46, 106, 107, 115, 116
Hersch, Gil ix, 125, 164
Hersch, Marion ix, 125
Heutchy, Lynn 39
High Country Citizens' Alliance (HCCA) 75-79, 105, 132, 157-161, 171, 172, 177, 178, 183, 185, 186-194, 198, 203, 204, 207, 209, 213, 254
High Country Conservation Advocates 155, 203
High Country News 77, 235
Highway 135 22, 62, 76, 102, 223
hippie 2, 6, 7, 8, 9, 33, 40, 56, 117
Hitchcock, Paul 247
Hoffman, Mitch 11
Holmes House 7
Holmes, Marla 214
Homestake Mining Company 131
Homestead Act 97
Horse Ranch Park 77, 101
hotbox 9
House Committee on Natural Resources 206
Howitt, Richard 115
Hunker, Terry 121
Huts for Vets 265

I

Illuminations 169
Independence, Colorado 14, 67
industrial imperialism 114, 115
Iron Range 110

J

Johnson, Dorothy 101
Joint Review Process (JRP) 110, 111, 253

K

Kalmiopsis Rivers 205
Kalmiopsis Wilderness 206
Kebler Pass 30, 32, 77, 89, 90, 91, 189, 197, 219
Kelly, Charlie 11
Keystone Mine 28, 30, 31, 69, 71, 90, 91, 95, 157, 189, 202
Kinsley, Michael 81, 134
klunkers 41
Kobex Resources, Ltd. 182, 183, 199
Kokomo Pass 191

L

Ladoulis, Chris 232
Lake Irwin 89
Lamm, Richard "Dick" 80, 134, 135
Landeck, Ron 149
Larsen, Keith 180, 186
Larsen, Mark 179
Law Science Academy 7
Leadville, Colorado 29, 35, 122, 140
Leftwich, Marilyn 132
Leinsdorf, David 70, 95, 100, 158, 161, 178, 196, 226
Leinsdorf, Erich 100
Light, Wes 54, 66, 71, 89-91, 93, 96, 97, 102, 149, 157, 160, 164, 171
Lindsey, Dave 11
lobbyists 95
Loughrey, Kevin 184
Louisiana Pacific 172
Lucky Jack viii, 182, 196, 229
Lypps, Roxie 11

M

Mace, Stuart 78, 152
Machiavellian 62
MacVittie, Cece 75
Malensek Ranch 24
Malick, Chuck 71, 75, 78, 156, 157, 159, 169, 171, 254

Malick, Jacque 75
Marble Base Camp 23
Maroon Bells-Snowmass Wilderness Area 139
Maroon Creek 135
Marshall Pass 131
Marston, Ed 77
Mary, Kathleen 241
McDermott, Wendy 177, 182
Means, George 95
Melton, Alli 203, 204
Mt. Emmons Mining Company (MEMC) 199
Memorandum of Understanding (MOU) 208
Mihelich, Tony 10
military-industrial complex 61
Mill Creek 189
Mined Land Reclamation Board 106
mining claims 71, 92, 93, 139, 149, 179, 180, 183, 187, 197, 202, 203, 204, 207
Mining Law of 1872 87, 97, 179, 205
MinnAmax Project 37, 83, 109
Mitchell, W vi, vii, 48-54, 60, 66, 73, 79, 81, 90-93, 120, 124, 128, 134, 142, 144, 146, 147, 150, 152, 153, 155, 156, 163, 166, 168, 169, 171, 198, 250, 251
mitigation plan 110
moly 86, 133, 156, 248, 249, 254, 255
molybdenum xiv, 29-31, 35, 36, 40-42, 44, 46, 68, 72, 74, 81, 86-88, 99, 100, 106, 108, 112, 113, 118, 122, 138, 141, 144, 148, 150, 151, 153, 156, 160, 161, 174, 177-186, 191, 193, 195, 196, 197, 200-202, 208, 226, 249, 254, 255
molybdenum disulfide (MoS2) 72
Moly News, The 81
Monkeywrencher 142
Monkey Wrench Gang, The 141
Moore, Patrick Albert 182
Moran, Jim 236
Morenci, Arizona 201
Morgan, Chris 181
Mountain Bike Hall of Fame 11
mountain bikes 11, 151
Mountain Oven 236

Mountain Song, The 129, 145
Mountain Utes 13
Mount Emmons Mining Company (MEMC) 208
Mt. Crested Butte, Colorado 24, 26, 35, 63, 181, 182, 183, 195, 235, 236
Mt. Emmons vi, viii, xiv, 14, 28, 31, 32, 34-42, 44, 46, 61, 62, 65, 69, 71-74, 76, 77, 80, 81, 85, 87, 88, 89, 92, 95, 97-100, 102, 106, 107, 109, 110-113, 117, 120, 122-124, 131, 135, 138, 139, 140, 141, 148, 149, 151, 152, 155, 156, 158, 160, 165, 167, 174, 176, 177-179, 180-185, 187, 188, 193, 194, 197-199, 202-205, 219, 241, 247, 254
Mt. Emmons Project 32, 35-39, 44, 61, 65, 69, 72, 76, 77, 81, 85, 87, 88, 95, 97, 98-100, 102, 106, 107, 109-111, 113, 117, 120, 124, 139, 140, 148, 149, 158, 160, 165, 167, 177, 178, 182, 183, 185
Mt. Hayden 13
Muhlfeld, John 206
Muirhead, Mary 75
multinational corporation 114
Murdoch, Rupert 233
Murfee, Molly 218, 245
Murray, Ceil 75
Murray, Honeydew 143
Nania, Julie 198

N

Nash, Dr. Roderick Frazier 143
National Avalanche School 34, 51
National Forest Organic Act 102
National Historic designation 124
National Parks Conservation Association 206
National Resources Defense Council 98
Navy, Sue x, 155, 159, 208
Newman, Jeff 244
Noonkanbah 115
North Fork Times 77
North Fork Watershed Protection Act 205

North Village 226
Norton, John 226, 234

O
Oh-Be-Joyful 92, 134, 139, 192
Ohio Creek 103, 189
old rock schoolhouse 15
old-timers 10, 18, 19, 21, 26, 38, 42, 64, 82, 124, 162, 163, 166, 225, 240, 242, 244
Olick, Karen 33
O'Neil, Tip 53
Orazem, Frank 10, 28
orebody 31, 35-37, 42, 44, 71-73, 98, 99, 138, 149, 150, 178, 179, 180, 181, 196, 197, 202
Oregon Environmental Quality Commission 115
Outward Bound 23, 134

P
Panek, Jack 25
Panian, Pauly 9
Paonia, Colorado 77, 102
Paradise Divide 3
People's Grand Jury, The 114
Peanut Lake 45
Peanut Mine 241
Pearl Pass 11, 134, 136
Penelope's 39
Perko, Annie 9
Peterson, Heli Mae 236
Peterson, Kay 11, 214
Petito, Cindy 214
Petito, Jackson 223
Petito, Lynda Jackson 223
Phelan, Jacque "Alice B. Toeclips" 11
Phelps-Dodge viii, 177-181, 190, 199
Picciano, Mary 243
Pieplant, Colorado 14
Pinchot, Gifford 87
Pitts, John Paul 164
Platonic ideal 62
polka 23, 24
Poor Little Rich Town 236
Population Bomb, The 140

Poverty Gulch 46
Powder Magazine 225, 239
Princess Theater 9
prospectors 14, 98
Puerto Rico 114

Q
Quaker Meeting 102
Quality of life 66, 67

R
Rademan, Myles 55, 56, 59, 60, 76, 92, 95, 125, 130, 143, 158, 168, 217
Raggeds Wilderness Area 139
Railroad Act 97
Reaman, Mark 175, 176, 181, 190, 192, 195, 221, 230, 232, 240, 246
reclamation 73, 106, 112, 203, 204, 209
Red Lady vi, viii, x, xiv, 28, 36, 42, 44, 46, 59, 73, 132, 135, 137, 142, 151, 152, 153, 155, 164, 177, 179, 180, 187, 189-192, 193, 197-199, 202-204, 208, 239, 248, 254
Red Lady Bowl vi, x, xiv, 28, 44, 59, 135, 137, 151, 152, 179, 180, 197, 202, 208
Red Lady Coalition 187, 189, 191, 192, 204
Red Lady Salvation Ball 132, 239
Redwell Basin 34, 42
refugees 19, 21, 64
Reid, Will 103
resource colonialism 186
Rethinking Resource Management: Justice, Sustainability and Indigenous Peoples 115
Rice, Fred 24
Richards, Claudia 53, 105
Richmond, Peter 234
Rights of Nature, The 143
right-to-mine 87, 96-99, 160, 196
Ritchie, Linette 33
Ritchie, Tom 11
Robert J. 154
Rock, Mike 84, 101, 149, 150, 172, 196, 216
Rock Schoolhouse 17

Rock Springs, Wyoming 118
Rocky Mountain Biological Laboratory (RMBL) 79, 93, 102, 135, 140, 141
Rocky Mountains 30, 53, 193
Roemer, Eric 39
Ronai, Bill 189
Ruby, Colorado 14
Rust, Mike 11

S

sacrifice zone 65, 74, 120, 186
Salazar, Ken 206
Saline County, Illinois 113
Salter, Bob 183
Sams, Perkins 164
Save Our Cumberland Mountains (SOCM) 113
Save the Baby Potholes 217
Save the Lady vii, 81, 124, 134, 136
Save the Lady ski tours 134, 136
Schell, Orville 75, 211, 213
Schofield, Colorado 14
Schofield Pass 11, 23
Schumacher, E. F. 215
Sciortino, Trea 220
Securities and Exchange Commission 181
seismic echoes 72
seismic testing 71, 139
Serbo-Croatian 19
Shangri-La 26
Sherman, Harris 99
Shifty Freewheel (a.k.a. Paul Andersen) 11
Sibley, George 20, 127
Sierra Club 98, 107, 110, 144
Silverton 190
Simon and Garfunkel 64
Simon, Paul 54
Sixties 2, 22, 24, 26, 127, 128
Slate River 10, 15, 16, 23, 89, 92, 189, 192, 231, 241
Small is Beautiful, Economics as if People Mattered viii, 66, 213, 215
small mine alternative 101
Smith, Dr. Hubert W. 7

Smith, Roy 23, 134, 159, 217
Sneller, Tommy 9
Snodgrass Mountain 160, 225
socio-economic impacts 88, 109, 110, 120, 189
Somrak, Johnny and Frances 10
Sotheby's 224, 233
Spann, Lee 103
Spann Ranches 102
Splains Gulch 189
Sporcich, Gary 53
Spritzer, Botsie 19
Squished Upon the Road 11
Stan Dempsey 35, 40, 70, 83, 86, 94, 107, 111, 116, 117, 158
Stanford University i, 140
Starr, Annie 159
Starr, Jim 191
Stefanic's Grocery 17, 162, 163
Stefanic, Tony and Eleanor 10, 162
Steinitz, Dr. Carl 102
Stewart, William Morris 205
St. Jude's thrift store 77
Strang, Mike 54
Subside by Subside 133, 249
subsidence 44, 122, 133
Sullivan, Chris 236
Sunshine's Paradise Bathhouse 12, 47, 63
Swarthmore College 102
Sweitzer, Dick 33
Swift Lectro-Clear 69

T

tailings 31, 44, 66, 69, 71-73, 90, 98, 102, 108, 122, 132, 138, 191, 201
Tailings bar 135
telemark turn 10, 11
Teocalli Mountain 3, 13
Tezak, Teeny 10
Theis, Judi 245
The Town that Fought to Save Itself 75, 211
The Who 5
Thompson Creek Metals Company 183
Thompson Divide 247
Thoreau, Henry David 63, 64, 144

Timber Act 97
Tony's Conoco 10, 17
Tony's Tavern 8, 9, 17, 42, 43, 252
townies 41
Triangle Pass 12
Trust for Public Lands 202
Tsumeb copper mine 114
Tutnauer, Deborah 243

U
Union Army 14
University of Colorado 89, 253
University of Wisconsin 89
U.S. Congress 203
U.S. Energy 31, 175, 176, 179-193, 202, 203, 229
U.S. Forest Service 87, 88, 90-94, 97-99, 102, 106, 127, 139, 149, 150, 158, 160, 188-190, 204, 209

V
Vermont Castings 49, 51, 128
Verzuh, Tony 9
Vietnam War 2, 50, 52, 125, 130
Vincente, Victor 11
Vinotok 238, 239
Volk, George 103
Voluntary Clean-Up Plan (VCUP) 190, 192, 193

W
Walden 64
Walton, Ralph 25
Warren, Rocky 101
Watershed Ordinance 89, 90, 96, 139
Way Station 17, 33, 127
Wegemund, Cameron 220
Western Colorado University 2, 20, 265
Western Slope 30, 84, 85, 108, 178
Western Slope Environmental Resource Council 178
Western State College 2, 25, 33, 82
West Maroon Pass 11, 173, 221
Whatever, U.S.A. 227
Wheatland, Wyoming 118, 121
Wheeler, Freeman "Trip" 57
Whitefish, Montana 206
Wickland, Tracey 12, 80, 126, 129, 130, 133, 145, 154, 155, 156, 225, 248
Wilderness and the American Mind i, 143
Wilderness Seminar, The 144
Williams, Joanne ix, 48
Wingerson, Dick 75, 101, 161
Winter of Un, The 90
Wirth, Tim 54
W Mountain 5, 117
Wooden Nickel 38, 136
World Trade Organization 128
Wright City, Wyoming 118
Wright, Jim 54

Y
Yaklich, Frances "Granny" 9
Yelenick, Mary and Frank 10
Yerman, Michael 204
Youngs Bay Estuary 115

ABOUT THE AUTHOR

Paul Andersen has been a writer for 45 years. He has written fifteen books and hundreds of feature articles for regional magazines. He has been a reporter, editor, regular columnist and contributing writer with the *Aspen Times* for 36 years.

Paul's writing career has earned him credits as a television scriptwriter for ESPN and screenwriter for an IMAX film. He has authored a dozen books on regional history and a collection of fiction short stories, *Moonlight Over Pearl*. In 2015, his book, *High Road to Aspen* (2014) won the Colorado Book Award's Gold Medal.

In 2005, Andersen co-created Nature & Society, an executive seminar for the Aspen Institute that immerses participants in wilderness while exploring philosophical, literary and historical perspectives on man and nature.

In 2013, Paul founded Huts For Vets, a non-profit designed to offer veterans healing opportunities in the wilderness at the 10th Mountain Huts of Aspen. With a context of philosophical readings, veterans find solace from psycho-emotional trauma, post-traumatic stress, traumatic brain injury and military sexual trauma.

Paul leads wilderness hikes, culture tours, and moderates the Great Books seminar series for the Aspen Institute. He enjoys reading philosophy and literature, writing poetry and playing guitar, piano and drums. He hikes, skis and bikes the mountains and deserts of the American West and beyond. Self-supported bicycle tours have led him across Europe, Eurasia and the Middle East.

Andersen was born in Chicago in 1951. He grew up in suburban Glenview, graduated New Trier High School in 1969, and earned a BA degree from Western Colorado University. Paul lives at Seven Castles in the Frying Pan Valley, 25 miles from Aspen, with his psychotherapist wife, Lu Krueger-Andersen. Their son, Tait, and his wife, Sarah, live nearby in Basalt.

www.ingramcontent.com/pod-product-compliance
Lightning Source LLC
Chambersburg PA
CBHW030903080526
44589CB00010B/124